Mr Evil

Graeme McLagan
& Nick Lowles

JOHN BLAKE

Published by John Blake Publishing, 2000

Published by John Blake Publishing Ltd,
3 Bramber Court, 2 Bramber Road,
London W14 9PB, England

ISBN 1-85782-416-4

British Library Cataloguing-in-Publication Data:
A catalogue record for this book is available from
the British Library.

Typeset by Jon Davies

Printed in England by CPD (Wales), Ebbw Vale, Gwent

1 3 5 7 9 10 8 6 4 2

Papers used by John Blake Publishing Limited are natural, recyclable
products made from wood grown in sustainable forests.
The manufacturing processes conform to the environmental
regulations of the country of origin.

Contents

Many people, including individual
police officers, have contributed to this telling
of what motivated David Copeland to carry
out these dreadful acts.

We are very grateful to them all,
especially Arthur and Charles, for their
particular insights.

Introduction

VERONICA SANDE STOOD OVER THE SPORTS BAG, deeply worried. The hold-all lay on the floor, with no obvious owner. The young man who had just walked out of the pub may have left it behind, said one customer. Another customer thought the young man had been wearing a baseball cap. Veronica's thoughts raced to the TV footage she had seen the previous day and then skipped to the photos that had appeared on almost every newspaper front page — CCTV footage, released by the police, of the main suspect for the bombs that had wreaked havoc in London over the previous two weekends. The police were looking for a young man, wearing a baseball cap. In both instances, the bomb was delivered in a sports hold-all. Glancing back down at the bag, Veronica called her boss and asked him to ring 999.

Directly across the road from the Admiral Duncan pub on Old Compton Street, the heart of London's gay community, Pete Searle was watching the TV news in his small flat. The windows were open, allowing a cool breeze to ventilate his room. In the bar below him Simon Edwards was drinking with friends. It was a warm and pleasant Friday evening, the beginning of the May Bank Holiday weekend, and always a busy time in Soho. The streets were already filling up. Around the corner, in Dean Street, Jean-Pierre Trevor, a film-maker, was finishing off some work at Image Makers. He, too, was keen to join the party. Andy Sellins was just finishing work, strolling along Old Compton Street, in anticipation of the long weekend. For Suzi Godson, a graphic designer, the weekend had already begun. She was drinking with friends in the Minty bar, two doors down from the Admiral Duncan.

Until the moment when Veronica raised the alarm Mark Taylor, the manager of the Admiral Duncan, had been having a good day. A quick makeover that afternoon had put him in the right mood for the evening ahead and the usual after-work drinking crowd at the pub was being joined by pre-theatre goers and revellers, all keen to exploit the long weekend. Mark hesitated, unsure what to do. 'Are you sure it doesn't belong to anyone?' he asked. At that moment one of his regular customers ran out into the street, trying to find the young man who had been standing at the bar moments before. Mark mentioned to one of his staff that the bag did, indeed, look very suspicious.

Mark went over to take a closer look. As he stood over the bag, he shouted: 'Shit! It is a bomb!' The words had hardly left his mouth when a huge explosion ripped through the bar, a ball of flame lighting up the pub, followed almost instantly by a cloud of thick black smoke.

Some of those in the pub at that moment recollect a blue flash rising up from the centre of the room, while others recall the terrifying bang that tore through their eardrums. One person, who was in a nearby bar at the time of the explosion, thought it was a thunderclap, but many others knew it for what it was. And then life stood still. It was as though time had stopped momentarily, a milli-second lull before the effects of the nail-bomb blast were seen or felt. An eerie silence descended on the scene. Shock, panic and fear descended on everyone as minds struggled to comprehend what had just happened. And then came a different noise, as the deafening blast of the explosion was replaced by the shrieks and cries of those caught in its wake, and the shouts of horror from those outside who had witnessed this appalling incident.

For Pete Searle, the noise of the explosion was followed seconds later by the noise of his own windows crumbling under the force of the blast. Simon Edwards looked on in disbelief as the entire front of the Admiral Duncan blew out, followed almost immediately by wood, glass and even people. Despite being a street away from the explosion, Jean-Pierre Trevor was blown across the room, ending in a heap on the floor with several of his colleagues. Suzi Godson gazed in disbelief as glass and debris flew past the window of the Minty bar. Andy Sellins looked on in horror as a man, presumed to have been walking past the front of the pub at the time of the blast, was thrown a full thirty feet across the street, with parts of curtain and window frame wrapped around him.

Inside the pub the bomb had blasted Mark Taylor up into the air, landing him in a heap on top of the bag. Unconscious for several seconds, he started to come round, but thought he was dead. Everything was dark, and there was a horrible choking smell. He heard terrible screams and could make out silhouettes. Everything moved in slow motion. Mark got to his feet and staggered to where he thought the doorway was, but he went the wrong way and collapsed again at the back of the pub. He felt like going to sleep, but a rescuer warned him that he was losing it, that he should stay awake. 'Part of my face was falling off, and one of the staff tried to hold it in place as I was carried outside,' he said. 'My legs had been hit. My trousers were in tatters, like Robinson Crusoe's, and I had seventy-five per cent burns.'

Veronica struggled against the black smoke that had descended on the pub like a terrifying fog. She looked around for her boss, but could not see him. Fearing the worst she made for the door, or where the door had been moments before. She stumbled over bodies but there was little she could do, her mind focused on escaping the carnage around her. Screaming, she finally stepped out into the road and paused to catch her breath, as injured bodies lay all around her.

Across the street a man lay in obvious agony, his leg in tatters. Around him were four men, sitting on white plastic seats and covered in blood. No one spoke, there was just stunned silence. People streamed out into the street, most with cuts and bruises, some with serious flash burns and others with skin literally peeling off their bodies. The nails from the bomb that were not stuck in people littered the street around the pub.

The street began to fill up as bystanders whose initial reaction had been to flee the blast returned out of curiosity and a desire to help. A traffic warden, who had been checking cars a few yards from the pub, was one of the first to run towards the pub. He was joined by dozens of others, all keen to pitch in where they could. Some leapt over the debris and got into the pub, hoping to help in the rescue operation, but were soon forced out by the sulphurous smoke consuming their lungs. Simon Edwards was slightly more successful. He had leapt up from his seat in the bar opposite and dragged a man whose leg had been blown off out of the Admiral Duncan. Within four minutes the first paramedic arrived at the scene. He was soon followed by a fleet of twenty-one ambulances, an air ambulance and other emergency service vehicles. As police battled to clear the area, worried that there might be another explosive device nearby, more and more people streamed into the area, their tense faces reflecting the horror of the scene.

Mr Evil

No one who was present in Old Compton Street on that spring evening could escape the tragedy that was unfolding around them. A black policeman ran to the pub, tears streaming down his face as he shouted at people to get out of the area. One man sat huddled up, sobbing for his girlfriend who was still missing. A priest gave the last rites to one victim and then rushed around the immediate area trying to comfort survivors.

Almost ten minutes after the blast, the first body was lifted on to a trolley and taken away. People looked on in horror as the stretcher was raised into a waiting ambulance, their own injuries and panic momentarily forgotten. Three people died as a result of the nail-bomb, over one hundred more were injured, some seriously. One of the victims was pregnant. The Soho nail-bomb was the third and most horrific of the three bombings that terrified Londoners during April 1999.

*   *   *

The call to the Flying Squad office in North Finchley came that same Friday evening, a few hours after the deadly Soho bomb. Eight officers had been waiting in the empty office building, deserted for the Bank Holiday weekend, biding their time until the call came through. Some had been playing cards when the phone rang, while others had taken the opportunity to catch up on paperwork. The call from Scotland Yard was brief but to the point. They were instructed to make their way to Farnborough in Hampshire where they were to check on a suspect identified from the CCTV footage of the Brixton bombing, two weekends previously. The CCTV pictures had been broadcast widely and the TV appeal had brought in over 500 calls, but only a few were considered real possibilities.

Detective Sergeant Basnett and his men left their North Finchley base, taking the Westbound North Circular until they hit the A3 and then the M3. Across London, other Flying Squad officers were also on standby, ninety-six officers working over a twenty-four-hour period demonstrated the political imperative in finding the London nailbomber. Elsewhere across the capital, specialist surveillance units of the Anti-Terrorist Squad, Special Branch and the Security Service were moving into position to monitor the movements of suspects in what was to be the largest police intelligence operation of its kind in the capital. Markets, railway stations, bus terminals and shopping centres were all watched by uniformed and plain clothes officers in the hope of catching the bomber.

Some time after midnight, Basnett and his team reached Cove, a suburb of Farnborough. They had felt no great sense of urgency in the call from Scotland Yard. It was, to all intents and purposes, one of several missions being carried out by Flying Squad officers to eliminate suspects from the police investigation. Earlier that day, another police team had been dispatched only to find the suspect looking nothing like the CCTV footage from Brixton. Turning into Sunnybank Road, the two cars pulled over, both vehicles in eyeshot of number 25. Their movements so late at night alerted a neighbour who, for one moment, contemplated ringing the local police. The element of surprise could have been blown.

From the downstairs front window of the otherwise nondescript semi-detached house, a glimmer of light shone through a chink in the curtain. 'Someone is up,' one of the men remarked.

After a few more minutes contemplating the options, Basnett decided to make his move. The officers exited their cars and strode towards the front door. Basnett looked around to check his men were ready, took a deep breath and rang the bell. After a short wait, a young woman wearing a dressing gown peered from around the door. 'Yes?' she whispered, her voice showing signs of unease.

'Sorry to bother you at this time, but we're police officers,' said Basnett in his most apologetic voice, as he showed the woman his identification. 'Does a David Copeland live here?'

'Hmmm. I'm not sure. There's a David who lives upstairs but I don't know his surname,' she replied.

'Do you mind if we come in?' said Basnett, already feeling awkward about waking a household in the early hours of the morning. The woman moved aside, allowing the four men to move past her. 'It's the bedroom next to the bathroom,' she added. The staircase was narrow, as was the corridor leading to Copeland's door. So narrow, in fact, that there was room only for Basnett and one colleague, the others had to line up on the stairs.

Basnett knocked on the door and a reply of 'Who's there?' came from inside.

'It's the police,' the officer replied, his head moving towards the door as though engaging in an illicit conversation. 'Please open up.' A moment's silence was broken with what was obviously movement towards the door. Basnett and his colleague, not knowing what to expect, adjusted themselves slightly, taking a step back to give themselves more space. The lock turned and the door opened.

Basnett gazed ahead. In front of him was a short, bare-chested, fit-looking young man, dressed only in tracksuit trousers. In the room behind him a Nazi flag was pinned prominently to the wall. Basnett's eyes flicked from the man in front of him to the small photo in his hand, a picture of the bomb suspect given to him by base. He jerked his head back in shock. 'It's him,' he exclaimed. 'It's him, the bomber.'

His shock was shared by the officer standing next to him. Rather than immediately moving forward to apprehend the suspect, he turned to the other men on the stairs. 'It's him. We've got him.'

Copeland himself was slightly surprised at the

astonishment on the faces of the two officers in front of him. 'Yeah, they're all down to me. I did them all.' At the bottom of the cupboard in the room behind him were explosives and fireworks. By his bed was a loaded crossbow, ready to fire.

*   *   *

The relief was obvious on the faces of the police officers sitting at the table at a hastily convened press conference the following day. The world's media had been invited to hear that after a two-week bombing campaign a man had been arrested and was due to be charged the following day.

'It is with deep regret that lives have been lost,' said David Veness, Assistant Commissioner of the Metropolitan Police and the man responsible for the specialist police squads that had led the investigation. 'Our thoughts and sympathies are with the victims, their families and their friends. In the past few weeks three people have died and over a hundred more have been injured as a result of bombings in London. Fifteen people remain in hospital from Friday's bombing, eight of whom are in a critical condition. Three people are still in hospital following the bomb in Brixton.'

Camera flashes lit up the room as journalists scribbled down Veness' words. In what would normally have been a quiet press day, with the simple regurgitating and slight expansion on the news from the Sunday papers, Monday's editions were going to carry breaking news. Smiling contentedly at the gathered media, there was no doubt in Veness' mind that the police had got their man. David Copeland, a 22-year-old engineer from Cove, Hampshire, had been arrested in the early hours of the previous day, he continued. Coming so soon after the release of the McPherson Report into the death of the black teenager Stephen Lawrence, in which the Metropolitan Police had been accused of institutionalised racism, the swift conclusion to the bombing campaign was all the more timely.

Although he knew there were strict legal restrictions on what could and could not be said, Veness was keen to prove that they had the man responsible for all three bombings. Various items, including explosive material, had been found in a search of his room. They were, he added, looking for no one else.

'There is no suggestion at this stage that the arrest is linked in any way to the extreme right-wing groups that have claimed responsibility for these attacks on innocent people,' Veness continued. 'There appears to be no trigger event or specific date that has sparked these attacks, which were clearly the responsibility of the same person. The man is not a member of any group that made claims of responsibility for the bombings, nor did he make any of the claims using their names. It is understood he was working alone for his own motives.'

The murmer of excitement that filled the hall grew louder as newspaper journalists and TV and radio reporters clamoured to get their questions heard, but the Assistant Commissioner was unwilling to divulge further details. Copeland would, said Veness, winding up the conference, appear in court the following day and be charged with three counts of causing explosions to endanger life and three counts of murder. The bombing case had, it seemed, been settled.

*   *   *

Despite Veness' reassuring words, that was not quite the end of the story. While the Assistant Commissioner had selected his words carefully, later allowing him to claim his comments had been misreported, the vast majority of journalists accepted the message he was keen to put out. Copeland was a loner, with no link to right-wing organisations, and his motives remained a mystery. The newspapers duly reprinted Veness' assertions, effectively drawing a line under the entire episode.

Now, at last, in *Mr Evil*, the truth of the bombings has emerged. While David Copeland may have indeed planted the three bombs on his own, he was not quite alone in the forming of his racist views. A young man with a troubled childhood and a fixation with chaos and destruction, his mind had been filled with racist literature, much of which had emanated from the USA. He joined the far-right British National Party (BNP) in 1997, a decision that launched him on a right-wing odyssey. He flirted in and out of right-wing groups, all the time becoming more extreme and discontent. When he left his home on the morning of 17 April 1999 with the sole aim of planting a bomb in the predominantly black area of Brixton, his mind was all-consumed with racist hatred. By this time he had also incorporated religion into his politics. Like many of the perpetrators of the worst acts of right-wing terrorism in the USA, he saw himself as one of God's soldiers, enacting a battle prophesied in the Old Testament. A follower of Christian Identity, a right-wing religion, which depicts the white race as God's chosen people and black people as 'mud people', Copeland was even to claim that he was a prophet.

Mr Evil tells the inside story of what motivated this very disturbed young man. Drawing on his police confession, which ran to almost three hundred pages, psychiatric reports, interviews with his family and workmates and our own correspondence with him while in prison and at Broadmoor, we have pieced together the elements and motivations that comprise this complex character. Only semi-literate, Copeland could build powerful bombs, but could not handle some simple, everyday tasks. He killed without remorse, but was also capable of tenderness. Small in height and of low self-esteem, he craved fame and notoriety and aimed to achieve it with the horrific nailbombings that killed, maimed and spread panic.

This book details how, despite major handicaps, the police hunted him down. Lacking key intelligence on

the extreme right wing, Scotland Yard was wrongfooted
by Copeland who, but for one fatal mistake, could have
carried out many more bombings before being caught. We
hear from the man who tipped off detectives and describe
how the 1.00 am arrest of the nailbomber came close to
disaster.

Captivated by US white supremacist tales of race war,
Copeland set out on those three days of nail-bombs to light a
spark. Hoping to ignite a violent reaction from Britain's black
communities, he thought that white and black would be
drawn together in conflict, the end result being racial
separation and a BNP government.

In an increasingly diminishing world, where modern
technology and communications are breaking down national
borders, Copeland's actions placed him on an international
list of right-wing terrorists. While not directly connected,
each act of barbarism — be it the Oklahoma City bombing in
1995 or the Centennial Park bombing at the 1996 Atlanta
Olympics — acted as a spur to like-minded groups and
individuals around the world. With material and
propaganda so easily available, Copeland was able to pick
and choose from different groups in order to justify his quest
for violence.

However uncomfortable it might make us feel, there is
nothing in Copeland that is not present in thousands of other
people in our society. While they might not resort to the level
of violence perpetrated by him, in their own ways they are
just as dangerous. Copeland is part of a growing breed of
young white men all too ready to use extreme violence to
reach a political goal. Increasingly alienated and detached
from mainstream society, these far-right groups are becoming
a community of the dispossessed and the unstable. And this
community is no longer confined within national borders,
but is backed by rising right-wing nationalism throughout
Europe and North America and supported by the increasing
availability of the Internet — within seconds of an event

occurring in one country people across the globe are able to access the images. While Copeland may have been the first, he will not be the last.

Mr Evil is the book the authorities did not want written. Far better to condemn the actions of Copeland as those of a crazed, mentally disturbed young man rather than analyse what motivated and encouraged him. How convenient to dismiss his work as that of a loner rather than admit the system failed and that he was caught only because of a lucky break. *Mr Evil* poses the difficult questions that few would have the courage to answer. Why would a young man become so consumed with hatred that he looked to terrorism? Why was it so easy for him to build powerful bombs without any prior training? How could the police know nothing of his right-wing links despite his membership of several fascist organisations? How can this be stopped in the future? More worryingly, how many other David Copelands are out there?

Mr Evil is the story of David Copeland and the racist bomb campaign that shook London to its very foundations.

1

Mr Angry

'My family fucked me up.'

David Copeland

DAVID COPELAND'S BOMBING CAMPAIGN was not simply a strike against a society he despised. True, he wanted to ignite a race war, pitching black against white, with the eventual outcome a National Socialist state, but considerably more than this motivated the young man during those thirteen days in April 1999. It was an act of revenge against all the people he believed had caused him such pain, misery and anger over the years. By unleashing a bombing campaign on the capital, he was exorcising demons from his past, a past of bullying, low self-esteem, unhappiness and a sexual inferiority complex. By his mayhem, he was setting himself free.

Copeland blames his parents for what he was to tell

police had been 'a horrible, bad childhood'. 'They fucked me up,' he said of his parents to a workmate prior to the bombings. But while his parents may have unwittingly contributed to the hatred that festered in their son, they did all they could to help him overcome another problem that was to play an important part in shaping his life and attitudes — his physique. A very late developer, he was always small for his age and was both physically and mentally immature. With hindsight, there were hints throughout his youth that pointed to an increasing disaffection with society. He had an inferiority complex and compensated for this in his teens by acting tough, developing a unhealthy taste for violence. What began as a fascination with human suffering, gradually turned into a psychopathic urge to cause pain and suffering himself.

David Copeland was born in 1976 to Stephen and Caroline Copeland. Even at birth he was different, and there was medical concern about the size of his testicles. He remained very small for his age and, when fifteen years old and still failing to grow, he was sent to a special clinic. The memory of that, particularly a detailed examination of his genitalia, was to haunt him in later life. Even in adulthood he remains only 5ft 6in, although he is taller than both his parents. He is the middle child of three boys, Jon being two years older and Paul three years younger. However, he was to be the smallest of the trio and shared few facial resemblances.

His parents came from comfortable lower middle-class homes in the Twickenham/Hampton suburbs of west London and married in 1973. Their first home together was in nearby Hanworth, a time David remembers fondly, recalling that he had two good friends at his local primary school. One of these boys may have been the source of his first major conflict with his parents — according to Copeland many years later, they disapproved of his friendship with one of the boys, who lived on a nearby council estate. It was when he was eight years old that he showed the first sign of racism. One of his friends, Daniel, who had darker skin than David Copeland, went home crying on one occasion, complaining that David had refused to go swimming with him because he was black. Daniel's mother raised this with Mrs Copeland who insisted that David apologise. He did so and the friendship continued. Where such early views came from is unclear, but Mrs Copeland was to recall later that when the three boys were small, her husband spent nine months working in Trinidad, and on his return complained that the people there had been lazy, had carried machetes, and had called him 'a white honky'. When David was nine, his parents decided to move to a bigger house so each of the boys could have their own bedroom. Although Mr Copeland was earning good money as an engineer, buying a four-bedroomed house in the same area was beyond the means of the couple and, besides, they wanted to get away from the hustle and filth of London. So they decided to move thirty or so miles south-west to Yateley, a small town in north Hampshire.

Yateley has a village atmosphere. Located in a traditional military area, close to the RAF base at Farnborough and the military garrisons at Sandhurst, Aldershot and Camberley, it is a conservative, almost completely white area, with few black or Asian faces to be seen. The local MP is the right-wing Conservative Gerald Howarth. In Yateley, the Copelands bought a four-bedroom detached house at the corner of a road in an estate of mostly semi-detached houses. Although each of the boys now had their own room, the move from a lively place liked by David to somewhere strange where he knew no one, had been a big upheaval and he took time to settle. Ironically it was during this period of his childhood that his medical notes record his desire to be a policeman later in life. His favourite TV programme was *The Bill*.

At St Peter's, his new primary school in Yateley, he eventually became friendly with another boy, Lee.

Unfortunately for David this was to prove short-lived as Lee's family moved to Wales. David struggled academically, and was put in a remedial reading group, but he was quite good at art, music and maths. When they were at primary school, the three brothers were always taken there and met at the schoolgate at the end of the day by their mother, Caroline. They told her they did not want her there, that they could easily manage the short walk there and back on their own, but their objections fell on deaf ears. This routine only stopped when David moved to the local comprehensive, Yateley School, at the age of eleven. With more than a thousand pupils, Yateley School has a reputation for producing high achievers, a status the young Copeland was never to achieve. His problems were compounded when he was bullied, a consequence of his being small and under developed. His elder brother, Jon, known for toughness, came to his aid, and from then on, David was left alone. Not being able to defend himself must have only contributed to his inferiority complex and his reliance on his brother.

The two boys did not tell their mother about the trouble as, by that age, they resented her interference. For her part, she obviously took the view that the school would contact her if there was any problem. Despite regularly attending parents' evenings, she never learned of the bullying. Perhaps unsurprisingly, Yateley School is now very defensive about any role it may have had in creating the man Copeland was to become. Claiming its records do not stretch back that far and that staff do not remember anything about him, the school contends that he must have been an average pupil. However, Copeland was one of a growing group of children that education experts label as 'invisible pupils'. No one really notices them and they are left largely to themselves, with only bright children or those causing a lot of trouble being remembered. His family say his school reports were of the 'could do better' variety.

Looking back on those early years, Mrs Copeland remembers David as someone special. 'You love children in different ways. He was so sweet, gentle and kind, with a pretty face. He wasn't naughty at all.' She says her two other sons were more clever, like their father Steve, while she and David were not at all academically inclined. She recognises that the middle children in families can have special problems. They can never be like the eldest, although they probably want to, and when the third child comes along, they are no longer the baby. To compensate, she tried to give more love and attention to David, though now in hindsight she believes she was probably overly protective. Several years later Copeland told his mother exactly that, believing that she had hidden from him the realities of the outside world.

At school, he had a few friends, his closest being Lawrence and Tim. He formed a band with other friends after he had been given a guitar. His favourite music was heavy metal, of a particularly bleak variety, as played by groups like Metallica, Anthrax and his special favourite, Slayer. He grew his hair long and began to dress the part, wearing black clothes and adopting what seemed to be an almost permanent frown. His increasingly dour image earned him the nickname 'Mr Angry', though quite what he was angry about was unclear. 'We let him get on with it,' recalls one young man who knew him during this period. 'We weren't interested in him or why he was angry.'

With few friends, Copeland was also finding life with his younger brother Paul difficult. The two disliked each other intensely, Paul dating the start of their bad relationship to when David was fourteen or fifteen and jealous of his younger brother, who although then only 10 or 11 years old, was as tall as David. David was still suffering from being small and desperately wanted to increase his stature. 'I suppose I started disliking him, because he disliked me,' said

Paul. 'At the end we hated the sight of each other and tried to avoid one another.'

The relationship between the three boys and their father was also becoming strained. He had spent a lot of time with his children when they were younger, but as they passed into adolescence it was Mrs Copeland who dealt largely with the associated problems. The boys, for example, liked to play their music loud. Their mother did not mind but it angered Mr Copeland and to avoid rows between them, she was constantly telling the boys to turn the sound down because 'their dad was about to come home from work'.

Copeland started to get into trouble, often as a consequence of hanging around with other disaffected youths. He is remembered by one family friend as someone who was always trying to make an impression. 'They'd dare one another, for instance, to throw a stone at a window, and it would be David who'd do it. If they played chicken, running across the road in front of a car, forcing it to brake hard, it would be David who'd win.' One incident while still at school is remembered proudly, even now, by Copeland. Someone had managed to get hold of a 'snuff movie', a video showing someone being tortured, apparently to death. Ten boys started watching it, but with scenes including the breaking of human parts and bones, they gradually dropped out, unable to stomach any more of the horrific violence. Copeland boasts that he was one of only two boys who sat through to the end.

In 1992, at sixteen, he passed eight GCSEs but with low grades. The majority of children at Yateley School stay on into the Sixth Form for Advanced Level GCEs, but Copeland was keen to leave. His parents were very disappointed and wanted him to re-sit some of the exams to improve his job prospects, but he preferred to hang out with other youths, some of whom were living in a squat and causing trouble for the local police.

Copeland's first conviction was in September 1993, when

he appeared at Aldershot Magistrates Court charged with causing criminal damage to some property. He pleaded guilty, was given a conditional discharge and ordered to pay £94 compensation. The circumstances are vividly remembered by Copeland's mother. She describes him at sixteen, as having become more laddish. She recalls that the family had got through the 1992 Christmas and New Year celebrations without any problems, but a few days later David had persuaded her to give him £5 so he could go out with his friends. That night the police telephoned to say he was in custody with his friends, having 'smashed up part of Sandhurst'. She drove to Bracknell Police Station and saw a new side to her son. He was aggressive, towards her and towards the police, who told her they did not know whether he had taken drink or drugs or a combination of both. 'He was in such a state,' she says, 'that I didn't dare take him home because his dad would have gone mad.' Instead, the pair sat in the car for several hours, waiting for him to recover.

Copeland's next conviction, again at Aldershot, was a year later on 4 November 1994, this time for assault. Once again Mrs Copeland was involved, but on this occasion far more directly. Returning home after a night's drinking David and his brother Jon began arguing loudly outside their house in the early hours of the morning, waking several neighbours. Lying in bed, Mrs Copeland heard them, too, despite Jon's efforts to quieten David in case they woke their parents. Mrs Copeland put on her dressing gown and went out into the street to try to separate her two sons, who were by that stage exchanging blows. One of the neighbours then came out to remonstrate, telling them he was going to call the police. Mrs Copeland says she, Jon and David all apologised and, led by her, started to cross the road towards the man, urging him not to contact the police. Mrs Copeland says a stone was thrown at the advancing group, just missing her head. Outraged, the two Copeland brothers forgot their differences and turned on the neighbour. David Copeland was convicted of common assault, ordered to pay £50 compensation to the neighbour and given a community service order. He was getting out of control.

Time and again it was his mother who was called upon to sort out his problems, turning up at the police station and the courts. But even at that stage, if she had been told that one of her sons was a potential bomber, David would have been the last she would have chosen. She remembers him at a big family get-together, with grandparents, uncles and aunts and cousins. The adults were all together enjoying themselves, ignoring or forgetting that the young children there needed attention. David, by then in his late teens, was the only older person looking after them for much of the time, reading stories and joining in their play.

But against that picture of contentment, Copeland was becoming more disturbed, with particular anger being directed at those casting doubts on his sexuality. His was, and is, a male world. He seems to have had only one short-lived relationship with a girl and that ended, he was to confide later, in his humiliation. The size of his sex organs worried him and he describes himself as 'not being very talented down there'. Paranoid that any public toilet was a haunt for gay men, he would always go into a cubicle to urinate rather than standing with others at the urinal. He says his lack of girlfriends was a constant theme in family discussion. He was regarded as gay, he claims, and was told that if he had stronger feelings for boys or men, then he should not worry or feel abnormal. He remembers teasing, too. One episode, whether real or imaginary, has stuck in his mind. Returning home one day, he says his family were singing the Flintstone song, the introduction to the TV cartoon series: 'Flintstones, we're the Flintstones, we're the modern stone age family ... we'll have a zoo time, a yabadoo time, we'll have a *gay* old time ...' Copeland took the reference to 'gay' as being aimed at him. He was to say later that this constant reference to his possible 'problem', started to drive him mad and contributed to his subsequent homophobia. As he was to say later: 'I've got a thing about homosexuals, 'cos I had strange parents. It was just mental torture as a child … I just don't like talking about it.' He said he had not been physically assaulted as a child, but he continued: 'I was tortured mentally by my parents, you know. I don't know if it was malicious or nothing. It probably wasn't. It was just stupidity on their part.'

His parents recall no conversations about homosexuality, at least not at that stage, although they admit the family did like watching *The Flintstones* and would sometimes sing along to the signature tune, but never with David in mind. Mrs Copeland, however, does remember the boys winding each other up with verbal insults and David, in particular, calling his younger brother 'gay-boy'.

There was also resentment about money. The boys had each been left £2,000, but the money was not to be given to them until they were 21 years old. However, Jon had been allowed to draw on his money to buy a car and, when he turned seventeen, David asked to do the same. He had a particular car in mind, a bargain, he said, but he was refused the money and told he would have to learn to drive first. He failed his first test, but after a few more lessons, he succeeded at the second attempt. After yet more arguments, his parents eventually gave in and gave him the money for a car and insurance cover. As a young, first-time driver with criminal convictions, the insurance premiums were very high, so he could only afford an old van. Within a few weeks it had broken down and although more money was spent on trying to make it roadworthy, it was beyond repair. Copeland lost all his money and blamed his parents, contending that if they had given him the money for the car in the first place, there would have been no problem.

Copeland had kept his racist thoughts from his liberal-minded mother since being criticised years before for upsetting his childhood friend Daniel because he had a darker skin. But in 1994, when eighteen years old, there was another incident. Mrs Copeland had taken her son to buy a pair of trainers in Camberley. She had insisted on accompanying him to make sure that David spent the money in the shoe shop and not on drink. While in the shop, Mrs Copeland asked for help from a woman assistant who then helped them to choose a pair of trainers. On leaving the shop, Copeland complained to his mother: 'Why did you call her? She's Indian!'

At this time Caroline Copeland was herself wrestling with a major family problem, as relations with her husband were breaking down. Those who know the couple describe them as being as different as chalk and cheese. While Mrs Copeland had stayed at home looking after the three boys during their early childhood, she took a part-time job helping in a home for mentally handicapped young people when they got older. She was sociable, liked meeting people and going out with them in the evenings. She is a caring person, regarded by some as being too lenient with her children. Her husband Stephen, on the other hand, was stricter and more of a traditionalist. He worked hard as a self-employed engineer and when he came home at the end of a day, preferred to stay in, either watching television or busying himself around the house. The distance between them grew greater, especially after Mr Copeland had a serious motorbike accident in 1993 and was off work for many months and constantly around the house. He, too, has been described as a loner. He does not drink or smoke, never had sexual relationships outside his marriage and saw himself as a good father and provider. But he wanted a daughter and was disappointed each time his wife gave birth to a boy.

Trouble was never far from Copeland's life and on 20 March 1995 he received his third conviction, once again at Aldershot Magistrates Court — this time for evading paying for something he had taken. He was fined £30 and ordered to pay £12 compensation.

Two months later, Mrs Copeland walked out on her family. She had had enough. She wanted her own life, her freedom. After an argument with her husband on the sixteenth birthday of their son Paul, she left, devastating her husband who says it had been totally unexpected. She left in a hurry, taking only her clothes and later asked for what she described as her most precious possession, family photograph albums that she had carefully put together over the years. She says her husband told her he had burned them, along with their wedding photographs and mementoes she had kept of their sons when they were babies. The couple were later divorced and Mrs Copeland reverted to her maiden name. (To avoid confusion, in this book we have continued to refer to her by her married name.)

Even now, Mr Copeland does not understand why she ended their life together, especially after she made it clear that no other man was involved. He wanted her back, but the split was terminal as far as she was concerned. Jon Copeland says her leaving did not affect him or David very much as they had seen their parents growing apart. But Mr Copeland disagrees, claiming that David in particular took it badly, going on heavy drinking bouts and returning home very drunk. Mr Copeland says he telephoned his wife when she was staying with her parents, blaming her for what was happening to David. Even now he asserts that none of his son's later problems, including the bombings, would have occurred if his wife had stayed. She disagrees, saying that David has told her that the separation had no effect on him. It is worth noting that his previous criminal convictions all pre-date his mother's departure.

By late 1995 David Copeland was, by his own account, out of control. He was drinking heavily, particularly vodka, and taking a variety of drugs, including cannabis, Ecstasy and LSD, sometimes all together as a potentially lethal cocktail. There was also cocaine, crack and heroin. He had started getting high as a fifteen-year-old when he sniffed glue and used aerosols. That phase lasted until he was seventeen, when he moved on to cannabis, smoking it every day. He first used amphetamines and tried LSD when he was sixteen and used it daily until he was seventeen. His 'trips' varied. He recalls how he would 'laugh and see stuff' in the good ones, but he would get 'like a panic attack' in the bad ones. Ecstasy gave him 'a buzz' for a couple of years, when he took it mainly at weekends. As for Class A drugs, he says he used cocaine on five or six occasions and crack cocaine twice. He also smoked heroin 'a few times'. For a year, to fund his habits and give him ready money, he used to steal cash and valuables from houses. He has boasted that he was a good cat burglar, taking the LSD to keep awake and also because it improved his sense of hearing. 'I'd only take things that I could put in my pockets,' he says. 'I never got caught. I was good at what I did.'

At this time, Copeland was doing only occasional, casual work. Several months after leaving school, he had started going to Farnborough Technical College for one day a week, doing a year-long foundation course in electrical engineering. It is unclear whether he even went once a week because the college says its detailed attendance records have been destroyed. However, while most people in his position followed this introductory course with full-time study in order to obtain a proper qualification, Copeland did not, preferring to go on the dole and occasionally working as a roofer or carpet layer. He worked for a few weeks at Fleet Services on the M3 and lasted only a month at an electrical company in Farnborough. He is remembered there because he was so hopeless, showing no interest in the work, which is perhaps unsurprising given that he was forced to take the job by the benefits agency.

By 1996, Copeland had developed strong racist views. Some of these stemmed from his inability to secure a decent job — he blamed immigrants for being given the best jobs, particularly by local authorities who he saw as favouring ethnic minorities in their pursuit of equal employment opportunities. In an area where ethnic minorities comprised such a small proportion of the local population, it seemed an illogical position to hold. In the mid-1980s, it is understood that there was only one black pupil out of about 1,500 children at Copeland's community comprehensive school and, even now, there are only a handful, mostly children of Asian origin. His lack of work had, in reality, more to do with his own unwillingness to graft. However, racial prejudice itself is illogical, with the most racist areas of the country often having the least direct contact with ethnic minorities. Copeland would have been in daily contact with people who fell into this category, people who would regularly use terms such as 'nigger' and 'Paki' without thinking that anyone could find that offensive. When an individual close to Copeland was shown, following his arrest, some of the racist literature that he had received, he reacted by saying that it was not a crime to belong to a party like the British National Party. When shown a crude leaflet with photos attempting to demonstrate the similarities between black people and apes, he commented: 'Well, you have to agree, there is something in it.'

In 1996, Copeland was also stirred by events surrounding the build-up to the European Football Championships. He told his father that he wanted to show his patriotism and support for the England team by getting a tattoo. Sibling rivalry was probably involved too, with Copeland wanting to show that he could be tougher than his elder brother. Jon had talked about wanting a tattoo, but had never got round to it. He had also discussed having an ear pierced for an earring but had not done it. Copeland was determined to have both. His father says he tried to talk his son out of it, without success. Copeland got an earring and a large tattoo featuring a bulldog, the Union Flag, and 'England' spelled out underneath. The almost nightly TV pictures of xenophobic English football hooligans on the rampage in central London excited him, in much the same way that he had been enthralled by the violence that ended England's match against Ireland the previous year. He bought a Euro '96 T-shirt. Three years later, he was to wear that very same T-shirt on his bombing missions.

Other graphic TV pictures that summer also had a big effect on him. They came from the Olympic Games in Atlanta. On the ninth day of the Games, thousands of people were celebrating at a rock concert in Centennial Park when a bomb went off near the main stage, killing a woman and injuring more than one hundred others. All the horror and the terror on people's faces and the awful, widespread injuries were caught on cameras covering the concert. The hunt was soon on for the lone bomber believed responsible. Copeland was excited by the chaos and suffering, and the fact that one man had been responsible for it all. After his arrest, he told police that the Atlanta incident had given him the first idea for doing a bombing himself. He had wondered what effect a bomb like that would have on the crowds of people at the largely West Indian Notting Hill Carnival in London, telling police: 'I just thought in my head, why can't someone blow that place up? That'll be a good 'un, you know. That will piss everyone off.'

That incident, coupled with the strange pleasure he experienced, may have provided him with a calling, something to aim for, a direction in what until then had been an unhappy, unstable life. At about the same time Copeland, then 20, underwent a major change in his lifestyle. Quite suddenly, he gave up drugs and drinking binges, explaining that he was fed up going to the pub every night. He now thought it boring, pointless and a waste of money. 'Boring' was a word he was to use with increasing frequency. Giving up drinking also meant, he was to say later, giving up all his friends. Instead, he started to spend time trying to build

himself up by going to a local fitness centre, the regular
work-outs transforming him into a muscular young man,
though quite what lasting damage the binges of drugs and
drink did to him mentally is impossible to quantify.

Meanwhile his father, working as an engineer on the
Jubilee Line extension to the London Underground system,
offered to help his son get a job as his assistant. David
agreed, but not before he experienced some exotic adventure
in Thailand. He turned for financial help to his mother, then
living with her parents in Twickenham in West London,
having never returned to the family home in Yateley since
she walked out. She says she would not telephone there in
case her husband answered and she believed her boys would
contact her. After obtaining money from his mother and
others, Copeland reckoned that he had enough to stay in
Thailand for at least three months, after which he would
return to work with his father. But the trip — Copeland's first
abroad — ended abruptly in failure after only a few weeks.
He ran out of cash, claiming it had been stolen. He made
transfer charge phone calls to his mother appealing for more
money, which she sent. A short time later he wanted more,
this time for a flight home. Eventually, he flew back to
Heathrow where he was met by his mother's father, who had
agreed to take him back to Yateley. Her parents, the
Woolards, had always taken a great interest in their
grandsons, giving them weekly pocket money and
particularly spoiling them at Christmas. However, on this
occasion, Mr Woolard was hurt when told by his grandson
that he could not enter the house because of his father's
hostility towards the Woolards since the marriage break-up.
When Mrs Copeland asked her son if he had met any 'nice
girls' in Thailand, he replied that he had spent almost the
entire holiday with a receptionist at the Diana Inn in Pattaya.
He would not answer his mother's further questions as to
whether he might see the girl again.

Stephen Copeland is a very single-minded, determined

man. After several weeks in hospital following his motorbike accident, he was warned that his right leg had been so badly broken that he would probably never be able to walk properly again. For months, he went on long daily walks, exercising his leg. Eventually, far from being a semi-cripple, he ran in the London marathon.

Back home, David Copeland found his father obsessed with a feeling of persecution, which was to embroil David, too. Mr Copeland, never particularly sociable, was known in the area as someone who kept himself to himself, a recluse, especially since his wife had walked out on him. There had been disputes with neighbours over parking in the fairly narrow street. Living opposite was the manager of a transport company who often had vans parked outside, reducing the space available to others in the street. The manager's car was vandalised, but the culprit was never found. Then Mr Copeland started to suffer. His front garden was targeted. There were two large ornamental stone balls resting on the walls on either side of the short path leading to the front door. Someone kept knocking them off in the middle of the night, sometimes damaging flowers and other plants. Mr Copeland decided to act.

Anyone visiting the house in Hall Farm Crescent is confronted with a video camera above the front door and signs saying no callers allowed without prior notice. With the Copeland's telephone number being ex-directory, it is clear that casual visitors are unwelcome. But stranger still, there are sheets of paper across the glass panels beside the front door. There is also paper on the windows covering the space between the bottom of the net curtains and the window sills of the downstairs room. This effectively prevents anyone from seeing inside the house. Journalists who went there after the bomber's arrest at first thought the paper had been hastily put up to prevent photographers from seeing inside. But this was not the case. The paper had been up for some years and had a dual function — it allowed Mr Copeland to look out, without being seen by anyone outside and he could lie in wait for the people who were persecuting him. The video camera had been installed for the same reason. With a monitor in the family room, he could see anyone approaching the front of the house. The precautions worked, but what happened next was to add to Mr Copeland's frustrations.

One night in February 1996, at about one o'clock in the morning, Mr Copeland saw one of two youths knock one of the balls off the wall. He dashed out through the garage door and grabbed hold of the youth, who was a year younger than his son David and known to him. He was the son of a policeman who lived about a hundred yards up the street. Mr Copeland marched him back to the house, intending to call the police. But the garage door had slammed shut behind him and he did not have any keys, so he rang the bell and shouted for David in the room above the front door to come and let him in. Eventually his sleepy son opened the door and Mr Copeland pushed the offending youth inside, telling David to hold on to him while he went to look for the other miscreant. He found the second youth, took him back to the house and called the police. The pair, who had been drinking, were taken to Aldershot Police Station where they were put in cells until later in the morning.

Mr Copeland was proud of what he had done, boasting to the local newspaper, the *Farnborough Star*, of his citizen's arrest: 'I'm only 5ft 4in tall, but I was so angry nothing was going to stop me catching this pair. It was the second time in a week that the balls had been knocked off the wall. In fact, they've been kicked off several times, and I'm fed up with it.'

Mr Copeland was furious when both boys escaped prosecution. Neither had been in trouble before and police thought a night in the cells to sober up and an official caution was sufficient punishment. Mr Copeland, however, disagreed, believing that the first youth was given favourable treatment because his father was a policeman. While the episode still rankles with Mr Copeland, the way he had single-handedly dealt with the problem by taking the law into his own hands impressed his son. Two years later, David Copeland was to do what he saw as the same thing, only this time dealing with a perceived threat from blacks, Asians and gays.

2

Joining the BNP

'Dave Copeland just wanted to get rid of blacks and Asians. His racism was overt but at the same time he didn't seem very different from other young men in society. His language was nothing out of the ordinary — nigger, Paki, stuff like that.'

BNP member

'I WILL PROMISE ONLY THIS. There will eventually come a day of judgement, a real day when the people who have betrayed the British race and nation for so long will themselves be put in the dock.' The speaker shouted as he reached the climax of his presentation, his wispy hair fluttering against a background of Union Jack flags.

Thumping the table, his face reddening, he continued. 'This is what this party is dedicated to bringing about. And there is something from which we will never budge. We will never do what some councillors do, to get a few votes, get a few extra members here and there, to make ourselves nicer and more respectable we should dilute our programme for the obligatory, if necessary obligatory, repatriation of the ethnic minorities in this country. We are pledged never to abandon that policy. Never, never, never. We are resolved that one day, no matter how long it takes, we are going to take back this country and hand it back to the English.'

As the audience rose, giving John Tyndall, the leader of the racist BNP, a standing ovation, so did David Copeland. He had watched the party's 1997 annual rally from the back of the hall, where he had been seated with the other party stewards. With an armband on the upper part of his right arm, Copeland was a card-carrying member of Britain's most extreme racist political organisation.

Copeland had joined the BNP in late Spring 1997. Perhaps he had received one of its General Election leaflets through the door, or maybe he had seen the five-minute party political broadcast with its emphasis on how the East End of London was changing for the worse. Either way, it was during the election campaign that he first made contact with the BNP, and it was to be the beginning of his journey through Britain's violent far right.

Membership of the BNP followed shortly after Copeland had moved to London. In March 1997 he took a job working on the Jubilee Line for the contractors Drake and Scull. His father had told the company that his son had some technical experience, and he was taken on as a commissioning engineer's assistant. Although sounding rather grand and important, it was a job that required no qualifications. While Copeland was little more than a labourer, it was regular work and the money was good. However, it was not long before the travelling took its toll. While his father made his way to work each day on his motorbike, his son was keen to assert his independence, but it was at a price. Every day, Copeland would cycle to nearby Fleet railway station in

Hampshire and then, with his bike, take a train to London, changing for yet another train to Barking, where he was working at the tube station only to repeat the operation at the end of each day. This daily ritual became too much, being both time-consuming and costly. Deciding to move closer to work, Copeland rented a room above a shop in Station Parade, Newham, close to Barking railway station.

There could not have been a greater contrast between his new surroundings and that of Yateley. He had swapped a comfortable detached house for a dingy bedsit; a relatively affluent commuter town for a deprived London borough; and, possibly more importantly for Copeland, a virtually all-white area for a more multiracial community. All his long-held prejudices must have come to the surface in a very short space of time. Views that he had grown up with, particularly about race, must have been vindicated in these new, strange surroundings. Copeland moved into a first floor room in the parade. In another room on the same floor lived Alistair, who had moved in a few weeks before. The pair of young men met in the house's TV lounge and went for a drink together at the nearby pub The Barking Dog. Copeland's racism emerged. 'I remember him talking about the National Front. He was either a member, or trying to become a member,' Alistair recalled. 'I told him I was a member of the Orange Order and that I did not believe in the views held by the NF. My politics revolved around one day of the year, July the 12th. We did not really hit it off together and did not talk any more about the National Front. I found him quite strange over the months that he lived in the house. He was very much a bit of a loner. I cannot remember him having any friends or any associates who came to visit. He spent a lot of his time inside his room playing music, and I recall asking him on one occasion to turn it down as it was so loud.'

Copeland expressed racist and anti-gay sentiments to another tenant, Fiona. 'I was around when he watched TV. He struck me as being homophobic. I remember one incident watching EastEnders when the gay man was beaten up and David said, "He deserved that." He called the girl downstairs, who was black, "a darkie" all the time. I can't recall him having any visitors whilst I was there.'

So it was perhaps of no surprise that, when he came across the BNP election material in late April, Copeland quickly latched on to their ideas. For a man who found London lonely and alienating, the BNP provided him with a personal and political home.

Back home in Yateley, his father was fairly pleased to see him go. While recovering from his motorbike accident, and unable to exercise fully, Stephen Copeland had developed an interest in shooting, particularly clay-pigeon shooting, on a nearby range. He had applied for his own shotgun licence in 1996, but the application had been turned down by Hampshire Police because of his son's criminal convictions. With Copeland moving to London, his father was finally able to get his licence.

* * *

The BNP was formed in 1982 by John Tyndall, one of Britain's foremost postwar Nazis whose political career spanned almost 45 years. Tyndall began his political life in the late 1950s and has since moved through a succession of Nazi organisations. By 1960 he was a leading member of the earlier version of the BNP before leaving to set up the National Socialist Movement in 1962. In the same year Tyndall received the first of several convictions after being found guilty of organising a paramilitary group, called Spearhead, the name he was to later give his monthly magazine. In 1964 Tyndall formed and headed the Greater Britain Movement (GBM). Within two years he was in trouble again — he was found, with several others, in possession of offensive weapons, including 30 wooden coshes and an assortment of metal bars and saws. Later that year, he received a six-month sentence for possessing a loaded gun.

Tyndall was not a founding member of the National Front (NF) when it was formed in 1967, but this did not prevent him from securing its leadership within one year of joining. Surrounding himself with former GBM activists, he led the NF during its peak period in 1974 when it had 17,500 members. However, his Nazi past was never far away and as NF fortunes dipped, more liberal forces worked to oust him. Recriminations and splits followed the election of Thatcher in 1979 and the NF was never to recover. The following year Tyndall left the party after its executive committee blocked his attempts for greater centralised power and formed the New National Front. It was to be a short-lived project, as within eighteen months he was forming the BNP.

The BNP secured dominance over the NF in 1989. More hardline than its rival, the BNP attracted some of the most dangerous racists in the country through a confrontational approach in the early 1990s, specifically targeting inner city white communities in east and south-east London and West Yorkshire and holding provocative marches and rallies in densely multicultural areas. In 1989 a demonstration in Dewsbury, West Yorkshire, ended with 300 local white youths going on the rampage through the town, attacking Asian people wherever they were encountered. In Bermondsey, south-east London, the BNP worked up a 1,000-strong crowd and attacked an anti-racist march in the area. Local Asian shops were looted and black drivers were pulled out of cars and assaulted.

The violence was not confined to the street thugs at the fringe of a political party. In September 1993 the BNP's National Organiser, Richard Edmonds, was arrested with three other members for attacking a black man and a white woman in a pub in east London. All four were sent to prison. Two years earlier, the BNP newspaper *British Nationalist* gloated after several BNP supporters stabbed an African immigrant at London Bridge station. The victim had his 'kidney surgically removed', the paper boasted.

Yet amidst this violence the BNP hit the headlines in September 1993 when it secured its first election victory in the Tower Hamlets ward of Millwall. Exploiting local anger at the Docklands redevelopment project and a shortage of affordable housing and other local amenities, Derek Beakon, the BNP candidate, beat off Labour to take the seat in a council by-election. While his reign was to be short-lived (he lost his seat in the London elections the following May), the BNP saw not only its vote increase in Millwall, but significant advances across East London, particularly in Newham where it remains a political force to this day.

Uncompromising in its political beliefs, the BNP that Copeland joined was in favour of the total repatriation of all non-white people living in Britain, regardless of whether they were born here or not, making homosexuality illegal and capital punishment. It believed that the Holocaust did not occur but was simply a trick by the Jews to gain worldwide sympathy and so obscure their domination of the world. In 1997, during the time Copeland was a member, the BNP produced *Mindbenders*, purporting to illustrate Jewish control over the British media by listing every person of Jewish decent working in the media. At a BNP annual rally, held in east London in 1991, Richard Edmonds greeted one member, Matthew Collins, with the words: 'Welcome to Nuremberg, Bethnal Green-style.' Three years later, some supporters greeted John Tyndall with chants of 'Führer' and 'Sieg Heil', as the leader addressed the 1994 annual rally.

It was during this period of street violence and political confrontations that the BNP spawned Combat 18, a group that took its name from the first and eighth letter of the alphabet, A and H — the initials of Adolf Hitler. This group later attempted a letter-bombing campaign and was initially suspected by the press as being responsible for the three bombs in London. Throughout 1992, C18, whose support came largely from the football hooligan firms of Chelsea, West Ham and Charlton, provided security for BNP meetings and rallies across the country. When C18 went out to attack its political opponents, its ranks included many leading BNP members. While the BNP was eventually forced to distance itself from C18, even prohibiting dual membership, it was at a cost. Virtually all the party's activists under 30 years of age left, leaving behind an ageing and physically weak organisation in the capital.

That said, it remained the sort of party within which Copeland would have felt remarkably comfortable, with his patriotism, racism and homophobia fitting in perfectly with those around him. Writing off for more information, Copeland would have received a standard BNP pack — a *Where We Stand* statement of core beliefs and goals, the latest copies of the party's publications, *Spearhead* and *British Nationalist*, the 1997 BNP election manifesto and an assortment of recent leaflets. A cursory glance through this material would obviously have excited the 20-year-old Copeland. Turning to page 4 of his free copy of *British Nationalist*, Copeland would have seen the lead headline: 'Multi-racialism is evil'. The article, which blamed multi-racialism for all Britain's problems, concluded: 'The multi-racial experiment has proved a disaster. It is not an enlightened policy. It is evil. The evil of multi-racialism destroys all races, all cultures in an effort to erase racial and cultural differences and so leads to needless social strife. The BNP wishes to end that strife. And the way to do it is through repatriation — for the good of all.'

Quite right, Copeland must have thought, his own racism being compounded by his move to the ethnically diverse area of Newham. Other articles in that and subsequent issues would have only reinforced this notion of a nation under siege, one that could only be saved by the BNP. In the August issue, Copeland would have learnt that the Tories had invited five million Chinese into Britain, in addition to the 2.6 million the BNP claimed had been admitted from elsewhere in the world. By November, he was being told that 700,000 gypsies were poised to enter Britain from eastern Europe. Having lived so close to several military garrisons, Copeland must have agreed wholeheartedly with the front page of the July issue which read: 'Intern the Terrorists', and contained a vicious attack on the Northern Ireland peace process.

Slightly less vitriolic, but no less uncompromising was John Tyndall's own magazine, *Spearhead*, which would also have been to the new recruit's liking. 'Dark warning' ran the November cover, with a quote from the Indonesian Prime Minister urging that 'masses of Asians and Africans should inundate Europe and America'. Inside, he would have read a stinging attack on the main political parties for courting homosexuals. Homophobia was a regular theme of the magazine, an issue about which Copeland felt strongly. In June he would have read Frank-Kimbal Johnson's view of AIDS. Pandering to Copeland's every prejudice, the author wrote: 'Far from being a real menace to humanity, the AIDS virus should be seen as an entirely benevolent and eugenic agent of the evolutionary process, serving to eliminate degenerates. It is therefore our duty to expose and isolate AIDS carriers. Lists of known homosexuals and members of other high-risk groups, should be compiled and circulated to homes, hospitals, schools, restaurants, pubs, food shops and insurance companies. In short, the demise of AIDS carriers (except where innocently infected) is a positive benefit to mankind.'

Buoyed up with such crude propaganda, Copeland was soon increasing his involvement in the BNP. Within a few weeks of enquiring, he was a party member and before long he was attending local meetings and activities.

One of his first public activities was a BNP leafleting session in Uxbridge, west London on 26 July 1997. The BNP was challenging a parliamentary by-election called after the sudden death of Sir Michael Shersby, who had held the seat for the Conservatives by a slim majority. While the BNP knew their vote was going to be marginal, it poured resources into the contest to beat off competition from rival right-wing groups, the NF and the National Democrats, which had split from the NF in 1995. While the BNP was unquestionably the largest right-wing extremist group in Britain it was, and is still today, unable to compete with the major political parties and is resigned to the hollow victory of dominance over the far right.

The thirty BNP members who turned up for the leafleting session met at West Drayton railway station at 10.30 am, before splitting into two groups and heading into Uxbridge. A convoy of cars and a minibus were supposed to ferry the members about, but when party leader John Tyndall got lost and Richard Edmonds, its National Organiser, failed to turn up, the day turned into farce with little leafleting done. As is usual for BNP activities, much of the day was taken up in the pub, with discussions about football, other far-right groups, the forthcoming trial of Nick Griffin and Croydon organiser Paul Ballard for incitement to racial hatred, and a skinhead gig planned for that evening in Leicestershire. Copeland was obviously a new member. He kept himself to himself, talking only occasionally with other members. He admitted to the others present that he knew little about the far right and its political opponents, but he had heard of C18 through the press.

The BNP is a predominantly male club, centred on pub culture, football hooliganism and racist violence. With the majority of London activists in their thirties and forties, it had become an exclusive social club into which new members, especially people of Copeland's age, often found it hard to enter.

'He was the youngest person there,' says Arthur, a London BNP member who got to know Copeland during his time in the party. 'He seemed pretty quiet, but I think that was largely due to the fact that he was new to the party. He was surrounded by people who had seen a lot of life.'

Unbeknown to both Copeland and the BNP generally, Arthur was passing information over to the anti-fascist magazine *Searchlight*. He had joined the BNP with the sole purpose of exposing its racism and undermining its activities.

Copeland was, however, keen. Over the next few months he was to become an integral member of east London BNP, one of the two main regional branches in London, the other being south London, centred around Croydon. East London was itself sub-divided into several BNP units, though not all could be considered properly functioning outfits. Newham, to which Copeland was attached, was the largest branch, with as many as two hundred members, sympathisers, recently lapsed members and more loosely affiliated contacts on the local list. Meetings, however, rarely attracted more than thirty people and some of those would be from outside the area. Other than Newham, the London boroughs of Tower Hamlets, Dagenham, Ilford, Hackney and Waltham Forest also had BNP units.

Meetings tended to follow a similar pattern. They were almost invariably held in pubs, sometimes with the landlords' consent, while on other occasions, when the landlord or brewery would not be so sympathetic, falsely booked in the name of a book club, history society or motor enthusiasts. They would also invariably start late, with those attending often strolling into the room long after the allotted time agreed or preferring to stay in the bar for one more drink. The meeting itself would be conducted from a top table, with the local branch or regional organiser opening the proceedings, followed by a national officer as the guest speaker. Future activities would be discussed, and the meeting would always end with a collection or raffle to help pay for the room and local bulletins. At one meeting in Newham a football card was circulated, with each person paying £1 to select a team with the winner getting a bottle of wine. Copeland chose Southampton.

Copeland attended meetings in his local Newham branch, the first of which was a week after the Uxbridge leafleting session. Ken Francis, who had only recently been installed as the Newham BNP organiser, met Copeland for the first time at Uxbridge, informing him of the forthcoming meeting. The meeting itself was held on Tuesday, 5 August and was addressed by Barry Osborne, a veteran BNP activist from Tower Hamlets and the party's Director of Publicity, Nick Griffin, who had turned up straight from Harrow Crown Court where he had been attending a preliminary hearing for incitement to racial hatred for his magazine *The Rune*. As is the case with most BNP meetings, Copeland was initially given only a redirection point, rather than the actual venue. Paranoia is rampant throughout the far right, with even longstanding members not being trusted with details and venues of meetings in case they turn out to be anti-fascist informers and the meeting is stopped. For his first Newham meeting, Copeland was told to go to Plaistow Broadway, opposite the Coach and Horses pub for 7.30 pm. Only then was he directed to the actual venue.

Nick Griffin, the meeting's main speaker, was a former leader of the National Front. He became the new leader of the BNP in September 1999, replacing Tyndall in a forced election contest. Griffin had earned an unenviable reputation for his strange political views and friendships during the 1980s. In 1986, as Vice-Chairman of the NF, Griffin visited Libya in the hope of securing money from Colonel Ghadafi. During the same period, the NF was calling for an anti-Zionist (a right-wing euphemism for anti-Semitism) and anti-capitalist crusade with Ghadafi, the Iranian spiritual leader Ayatollah Khomeini and the American black nationalist, Louis Farrakhan.

Griffin left the NF in 1989, forming a new fascist party, the International Third Position (ITP) along with an

Italian, Roberto Fiore. Heavily influenced by Catholic fundamentalism and the Italian fascist theorist Julius Evola, the ITP married traditional right-wing anti-communism with a strong anti-capitalist stance, in particular opposition to the USA, which it depicted as Zionist (Jewish) controlled. In this fascist war against capitalism, Griffin busied himself in Shrewsbury distributing 'Death to the Cities', 'Buy Organic Products' and 'Boycott Coca-Cola' stickers. It was during his time in the ITP that Griffin had an accident with a shotgun, resulting in him losing one eye. Griffin was not to remain on the lunatic fringe for long, leaving the ITP in 1991 and entering BNP circles in 1993. Four years later he was not only its Director of Publicity, but editor of its monthly magazine, *Spearhead*.

Fortunately Copeland knew nothing of Griffin's bizarre political past when he attended the Newham meeting. One can only assume that if he had known of Griffin's links to Arab dictators and black nationalists he would undoubtedly have been appalled.

Though a member of the Newham branch, Copeland was also quite prepared to travel further afield to other party events. One such meeting was held on 11 August 1997 in Redbridge, on the outskirts of east London. Again Griffin was the speaker. As at his Newham meeting, Griffin spoke of his forthcoming trial for incitement to racial hatred, at which he was later found guilty, telling the audience that the suffering and anguish this would cause his family was nothing to what his and other members' children would face as a result of the multiracial society. 'What future for your princess in streets ruled by Taliban fundamentalists, who already have the support of 20 per cent of Britain's Muslims?' he told the crowd. 'What future for your prince in a society where the media presents 250,000 perverts in Clapham Common as a wonderful example of tolerance and diversity, and tell youngsters that they've made a "valid lifestyle choice"?' The reference to the Gay Rights Pride march in late

June particularly pleased Copeland. He dipped into his pocket and made a telling contribution towards the £136 raised at the end of the meeting.

Like most new recruits to the BNP, Copeland's political awareness was negligible. 'He just wanted to get rid of blacks and Asians,' remembers Arthur. 'His racism was overt but at the same time he didn't seem very different from other young men in society. His language was nothing out of the ordinary — nigger, Paki, stuff like that. But at the same time he was perhaps softer than other people. He didn't say anything about Zionism. I remember once or twice people bringing that up, but he didn't make any contribution at all. He didn't indicate that he agreed or disagreed. I think it was something new to him. Maybe I'm wrong, but any anti-Zionism he had, he picked up later.'

Copeland was never heard to express his hatred of homosexuals. While that may seem strange considering his strong personal views on the subject, Arthur was not surprised. 'I would be pretty surprised if he did mention gays because no one did,' he recollects. 'But again, generally, young working class men aren't particularly keen on homosexuals whether they are in the BNP or not.'

One incident that did surprise Arthur was Copeland's attitude towards the death of Princess Diana. While the vast majority of the BNP membership held her, along with the majority of the Royal Family, in contempt, Copeland was totally devastated by her death. 'He was very cut up about the Princess of Wales dying,' Arthur adds. 'He was just really upset. There was a lot of anger around at the time directed at various quarters but particularly at the paparazzi, and I suppose the only inkling I could get that he was capable of doing what he later did was he said that the paparazzi should be hung and I could see that he meant it.'

And this was despite Copeland saying that she was 'shagging an Arab'.

Keeping himself to himself, Copeland rarely socialised

with the other members. He would enjoy a drink or two after political events, but was never seen to get drunk. 'He seemed pretty working class,' recollects Arthur. 'Fairly softly spoken. He definitely wasn't a loud person.'

In fact, Copeland would not say much about anything, least of all his family. 'He only talked about his job. He was really keen about the job he was doing,' adds Arthur. 'He was on good money putting wiring through carriages on the Jubilee Line.'

When younger, Copeland had been interested in football and, like his elder brother Jon, had supported Tottenham Hotspur. There is a family photograph of him wearing a Spurs shirt at the age of seven or eight. After moving to east London and joining the BNP, however, Copeland's interest switched to supporting the two London teams most associated with racist football hooliganism, Millwall and Chelsea. Despite not registering any obvious interest in football or overt violence, Arthur remembers a sparkle in Copeland's eyes when talking about football hooliganism. 'He mentioned the riots they [C18] did in Dublin and grinned. He didn't say very much, but I think he was very positive about it.' That, and bemoaning the lack of BNP activity were the only signs Arthur saw that this was a man who wanted to do more. With a few exceptions, Copeland came across as the perfect BNP recruit. 'He didn't show any indication that putting leaflets out was a waste of time or that we should burn down synagogues or anything like that,' recalls Arthur. 'I think from the point of view of John Tyndall he would have seemed the ideal member because he was an ordinary bloke, he appeared to be keen on taking the legal way and he wasn't covered in swastikas.' That would all change, but when Copeland first joined the BNP there was nothing untoward.

That Redbridge meeting in 1997 would have also introduced Copeland to another leading BNP member. Tony Lecomber was the party's East London regional organiser, with added responsibility for the Redbridge and Dagenham branches. Unlike party leader John Tyndall, Copeland would have found Lecomber far more approachable, almost one of the lads. While in the BNP leadership, Lecomber had earned respect from ordinary members as a Nazi hardman, politically and physically. Lecomber began his political life as a teenager in the National Front in the late 1970s, but in 1982 he followed John Tyndall out of the party and formed the BNP. From its inception, Lecomber was an integral part of its East London organisation. Fearing that his name sounded too foreign, Lecomber changed his surname to Wells, and then later to East. It was as Tony Wells that he first attracted public attention when, in 1985, he began producing the *Young Nationalist*, a youth bulletin produced by East London BNP in an attempt to emulate the relative success of a similar NF publication, *Bulldog*. It was a hardline racist and anti-semitic paper — the Holocaust was dismissed as a lie, Hitler was praised as a hero, black people were caricatured as monkeys and race war was promised.

While this racism may have been shocking to many, it was nothing compared to the act that really catapulted Lecomber into the national spotlight. In late 1985 he was arrested after trying to blow up the headquarters of the left-wing Workers' Revolutionary Party. Unfortunately for Lecomber, his home-made bomb short-circuited in its biscuit tin container and exploded in his car while he sat there eating Kentucky Fried Chicken. Lecomber escaped with only minor injuries. When police later searched his home they found bomb-making equipment and home-made hand grenades. Sentenced to three years in prison, he was released only to find himself heading swiftly back when he attacked a Jewish school teacher for peeling off a BNP sticker on the London Underground. Within weeks of coming out of prison for that attack, he was in trouble again, though this time he was on the receiving end of a beating from a leading C18 thug, Will Browning. This fight ended with Lecomber lodged down a manhole.

It is doubtful whether Lecomber would have divulged his violent past to Copeland, but it seems inconceivable that the young BNP member would not have quickly learnt of it. With Lecomber regularly being dubbed 'the mad bomber' by political opponents, his notoriety preceded him. Several months after meeting Lecomber, in what was obviously a coincidence, Copeland, in much the same way as his BNP regional organiser had done before him, obtained Do-It-Yourself bomb designs with the intention of bombing his political opponents.

Copeland rarely missed a BNP meeting in the second half of 1997. However, despite his and the party's best efforts, meetings did not always go according to plan. One such meeting was the party's 15th Anniversary Rally, originally billed for the beginning of September. A combination of poor organising and the death of Princess Diana conspired to postpone what was supposed to be a celebratory rally. It was rearranged for the 20th September, with the party's top brass all due to speak. The intended venue was The Swan pub in Stratford, a regular meeting point for the local BNP. However, word got out and as the BNP members began to gather so, too, did anti-fascists and local people determined to prevent the racists from celebrating their anniversary. Scuffles broke out outside the pub, with most of the BNP members taking refuge inside or fleeing the area immediately. Not so lucky was BNP leader John Tyndall who was caught outside the pub by a number of people. His bloodied face was testament to the anger his politics aroused in those opposed to him.

Copeland arrived on the scene with Tony Lecomber and a few other East London activists, only to flee the area at the first sign of trouble. When he returned, police were swarming all over the area. However, for Tyndall, it was too late. Pulling himself off the ground, he bitterly remonstrated with the police to take swift action against his assailants. Copeland, dressed in a blue Adidas baseball cap, Harrington jacket, blue jeans and chequered shirt, drifted past the watching crowd to what he presumed was the safety of a group around Tyndall. In what was later to prove a fateful moment for the BNP, he was photographed by *Searchlight*, the anti-fascist magazine, standing next to his party leader. Copeland was pictured remonstrating with an Asian policeman, urging him to stop more photographs being taken by the anti-fascist demonstrators. One of the three photographers there remembers Copeland quite clearly and how he was younger than the other BNP members. 'He shouted at me to stop taking pictures. I refused and told him he'd understand more when he grew up. Saying that made him really angry. I wondered at the time when he would surface again.' When the *Daily Mirror* ran the *Searchlight* picture across its front page two weeks after Copeland's arrest, it was to blow the BNP denials of association out of the water.

BNP activists were furious with the disruption to their rally. Though they regrouped in nearby Bow, any thoughts of continuing with the rally were long gone. Drinking heavily in a local pub, an increasingly bitter group of London activists, Copeland included, sought revenge. A short journey along the District Line brought a group of four BNP activists to Artillery Row, a small side street off Victoria Street, near St James's Park tube. After a final drink in the pub opposite, they headed across the road and into Politico's bookshop. Glasses and beer bottles in hand, Copeland and the others stormed the shop. 'Communist Jews,' shouted one of the attacking group. Copies of *Searchlight* were pulled off the shelf and ripped up. It was shortly before closing and the shop was empty, bar the one member of staff behind the counter. 'A couple of them began abusing my staff member, but another pointed out that he was only staff and should be left alone,' the manager told *Searchlight* a couple of days later. He was quite annoyed about the whole affair, as he was, after all, a libertarian

Conservative. The police were called, but Copeland and his friends had already left the area.

The aborted Anniversary Rally was a serious blow for the BNP. Despite Tyndall's assurances that the party would continue its political campaigning uninterrupted, both he and the local East London activists thought twice about such open activism for some time. Recriminations flew in the party, with Lecomber and chief steward Ian Dell, who was also injured on the day, furious at the East London organisers, Ken Francis and Dave Hill, for what they perceived as a lack of security and inadequate protection for Tyndall. More damagingly, a hunt for the source of the leaked information began. Everyone came under suspicion.

The effect on the party's East London operation was debilitating. Meetings became less frequent until they eventually stopped completely. The Tower Hamlets branch, for so long the party's stronghold and scene of its only political election victory in 1993, collapsed as Dave Hill was sacked from his job as organiser, eventually switching his allegiances to the NF. Copeland hung on in the BNP, but there was little to do. Possibly the last meeting that he attended was the party's Annual Rally, held on 22 November 1997 at Thame Football Club. This annual event provides the BNP with an opportunity to bring its activists and supporters together, to act as a rallying cry for future activities and, perhaps more importantly, to raise funds.

The November rally attracted just over 250 people, slightly down on previous years and disappointing considering the 29,000 votes and 3,500 enquiries the party claimed it attracted as a result of its General Election effort. Speaking at the event was BNP leader John Tyndall, Director of Publicity Nick Griffin, and National Organiser Richard Edmonds. Because of past disruption by anti-fascist opponents and rival racist groups, to say nothing of the continuing paranoia caused by the Stratford incident, the BNP chief steward was taking no chances. He pulled together a group of BNP toughs, largely drawn from the London area. Among them was David Copeland, sporting a BNP steward armband.

'In the BNP you have the permanent stewards, the senior stewards that is,' recalls Arthur, 'and then you have those who are roped in for the day. Senior stewards would wear blue armbands with the BNP logo, while the temporary stewards would wear red ones with the BNP logo. Copeland was part of the latter group.'

The meeting opened with regional organisers reporting on the party activity in their areas. First up was Keith Axon, who spoke for the West Midlands, followed by John Peacock representing the East Midlands. Andrew Wearden from the North West told those gathered why it was important for activists to improve their speaking schools, while the Scottish Organiser, Scott McLean, reported that having the three Scottish BNP candidates in the 1997 election was their best effort to date. Yorkshire organiser Tony McDowell brought cheers from the audience when he recounted how 'anti-British communist organisations' had been run out of Bradford. Ending this session was Tony Lecomber, reporting on activities in the capital.

Copeland knew all of the main speakers. Nick Griffin, who had addressed two meetings that Copeland had attended, spoke about the precarious state of the international economy. Pointing to the recent economic collapse in the Far East, Griffin believed that the BNP provided the nationalist alternative that was needed to rescue Britain: 'Inculcating people with the need for disciplined, responsible political action, for professionalism and to have the positive attitudes that make people realise that, in the BNP, we have a movement that can win!' Next up was National Organiser Richard Edmonds. Applauding the work done by the membership, he spoke approvingly of the party's election campaign. 'Our man,' he said, referring to leader John Tyndall, 'spoke to the great British people for five uninterrupted minutes.' He continued by looking to the future, with the next test for the party being the 1999 European elections.

Ending the meeting was Tyndall himself. As a speaker, he was far superior to the others, although in other circumstances his rather pompous style drew its fair share of criticism from the rank and file. Tyndall said that British nationalism had been held up by Conservatives for far too long, but with its abysmal showing in the 1997 elections, it was now too discredited to be an alternative to Labour. This, he added, provided the BNP with its best opportunity to progress. He ended his speech in typically uncompromising style. While the mainstream political parties were endlessly changing their policies to suit the latest opinion polls, the BNP stayed true to its beliefs. And there was no other issue that marked the BNP as different than its willingness to repatriate all non-white people from Britain. 'We will never, never, never change our policy on repatriation.'

While the day passed off uneventfully for Copeland and the other stewards, it was to be his last meeting. A combination of changing personal circumstances and political development drew Copeland away from the BNP, for a while at least. His desire to travel led him to tell some people that he was heading for Russia, a lifelong dream, while his fascination with violence and chaos was drawing him further to the right. Meetings were all well and good, but now he wanted more.

When news of his arrest broke eighteen months later, a veil of amnesia seemed to descend on the BNP. Tony Lecomber boldly stated that the David Copeland who joined the BNP had moved to Russia, while others who had met him on party activities seemed to forget about his existence altogether. This was the initial view of the BNP nationally. Seizing on the Metropolitan Police's statement that Copeland was a loner not attached to any of the organisations that claimed the bombings, the party immediately issued a statement deriding the press for trying to establish a connection between the bombs and the BNP.

It was a lie that was eventually exposed when the *Mirror*,

using a photograph supplied by *Searchlight*, ran a front-page story titled 'The Link'. Across the front page was a colour picture of Copeland standing alongside a bloodied John Tyndall at the aborted 15th Anniversary Rally. 'HE is the nail bomb suspect ... and HE is the leader of the BNP', ran the accompanying photo caption. The photo proved beyond any doubt that Copeland was connected to the BNP.

Faced with undeniable evidence, the BNP began shifting its story. Eventually Copeland's membership details for 1997 were found, but the party leadership insisted that he had only been a member for a few months before writing a letter asking to be taken off its list. Despite repeated requests, the party was unable to produce a copy of the letter. Now admitting that Copeland had in fact been involved in the party, the BNP stressed the brevity of his connection. 'We knew nothing about him,' said John Tyndall. 'I think he was in the Newham branch and he went to one or two meetings, but I don't know which meetings or where that information came from or who would know more.'

Writing in the June 1999 issue of *Spearhead*, Griffin admitted Copeland's involvement in the BNP. 'A David Copeland was briefly involved with the party in East London in 1997. He made no particular impression on people who met him, and certainly never talked about anything connected with bombs. After attending a couple of meetings, he said that he was moving to Russia on a work contract, and vanished as quickly as he had appeared.' Griffin was, on the surface at least, far more open to media enquiries. He said that Copeland had attended two meetings, at most three, but soon left for another organisation. However, despite promises to find out more, he, too, seemed to seize up.

*   *   *

As he became less involved in the BNP, Copeland grew increasingly depressed and alienated from the society around him. His family, and particularly his mother, were concerned about his well-being. Throughout his time in London she never knew exactly where he lived. She saw him only four or five times, usually at her parents' home in Hampton Hill, west London, and her only means of contacting him was by mobile phone. She got the distinct impression that he had deliberately cut himself off.

'I knew something was wrong in London,' she later recalled, acknowledging a marked change in his character. He had become openly racist, arguing with her, exclaiming, 'England for the English.'

Although he remained silent about his involvement with the BNP, he told her he had joined Combat 18. Mrs Copeland had never heard of the group and thought it was a football supporters' organisation.

'He'd become opinionated but I wouldn't argue. I'd say you've got your opinions and I've got mine. I would say I didn't want to know. He didn't like the area he was living in. There were a lot of blacks. If there was a group of Rastas on the pavement, he'd walk right through them. He didn't like people who didn't work, who lived off the State.'

Concerned at his obvious lack of friends and social life, Mrs Copeland repeatedly told him how she just wanted him to be happy, often saying how great it would be for him to have children and for her to be a grandmother. While she meant well, this surely must have added to his sense of loneliness and the failure he was feeling at this time. On another occasion, as she drove him to her parents' home in west London, he declared that he would never bring up a child in the way he had been brought up. He reeled off a list of resentments he had harboured for years. His parents had not let him play outside after dark; they didn't like him playing in the street; they had not let him go on all-night fishing expeditions at the age of twelve or thirteen; and they had refused to let him hang out with other children who gathered each evening near the local off-licence. He also criticised her for making him attend, six years before, the growth clinic, causing him the embarrassment and humiliation of having to endure a full body examination, which included a look at his genitalia. 'I was gobsmacked at what he came out with,' said Mrs Copeland. 'He was even angry because when he was seven I had refused to buy him a karate suit. I had no idea that he was so resentful. All I could say in reply was that he would feel differently when he became a father.' When they arrived at her parents' home, the aggressive attitude continued. 'He just didn't seem to care about anyone, but he wasn't rude to my parents. He always said please and thank-you.'

Lonely and largely friendless in east London, Copeland would spend most evenings sitting in his bedsit alone watching TV. Every month, shortly after pay day, he would travel up to Soho in central London and visit a prostitute. However, this did nothing to dilute his personal unhappiness and suicidal thoughts were never far away. While he would later tell police that he had suicidal tendencies for some time, he was, in his own words, 'a coward' and unable to take his own life.

Suicide may have been out of the question, but thoughts of death were never very far away from his mind. In late 1997 he moved across Newham to Bective Road in Forest Gate, a street of small terraced houses with a transient population. He had decided to move there to be close to work — by this time he had switched to Stratford tube station. The house had two bedsits on the ground floor and two upstairs. Copeland had the back ground floor bedsit next to Alan's, which was at the front. 'I recall he was a very quiet person who kept himself to himself. He came across as a bit of a macho person, but he never gave me any problems. I am gay myself and never had any derogatory remarks made about me. The only thing I can remember about David bad-mouthing someone was when he mentioned there was a smell in the house and he referred to the Asian boyfriend of a girl who lived upstairs.

I remember him referring to the boyfriend as "a Paki"'. I never thought he came across as an odd person at all. The only thing possibly that I did think was strange about David was that for a young man in his early twenties, he did not seem to go out, apart from going to the gym.'

In fact, it was at this address that he was to indulge in a habit that would remain with him until his moment of arrest — a fascination with chaos and destruction. The thoughts first kindled after the Atlanta bombings in the summer of 1996 were returning with a vengeance.

Fascinated and excited by such images, he began collecting newspaper and magazine articles on the subject, many of which he would pin up on his wall. He was not too fussy about the subjects, nor the politics of the perpetrators. He collected cuttings on IRA bombs, atrocities in Israel, refugees in the former Yugoslavia and pictures of pitiful, starving children in Africa. One particularly poignant photo depicted an aid worker cradling a gaunt-eyed, shrivelled black baby. It did not matter to Copeland where the pictures came from so long as they carried images of suffering people. Innocent people suffering from events over which they had no control. 'I'd get off on them,' he would later say. 'It's just evil, you know, I mean people suffering. I just liked them.'

Copeland also had a horror video of which he was especially fond. *Henry: Portrait of a Serial Killer* was, he told people, his favourite film. Made in 1990 and loosely based on a mass-murderer's confession, the film depicts a sociopath's sick and twisted world. Copeland would no doubt have read more into the film than simply its violence, probably identifying with the main character himself. Henry's first victim was his mother, who had humiliated him when he was a child. He also killed a friend's sister with whom he had found he was incapable of having sex. All this was not too far removed from the life of a young man who became convinced that his mother thought he was gay, whose parents had 'fucked him up', and who was unable to form relationships with women partly because of a concern about his sexual organs.

According to one reviewer the film is 'an understated, yet unforgettably chilling study of depravity, all the more disturbing for its composure.' Henry came second to Hannibal 'The Cannibal' Lector in *Total Film* magazine's poll of the 'Top 100 Madfellas of the Movies – the most evil film character ever'. Only managing number 7 was Anthony Perkins playing Norman Bates in Alfred Hitchcock's *Psycho*. Serial killer Henry slashed and murdered with a knife. Copeland's chosen weapon — bombs — allowed him to remain more distant from his victims.

Unfortunately Copeland's preoccupation with destruction didn't end with newspaper clippings or videos. He soon began to dream of carrying out similar atrocities himself. 'I wanted to carry out something similar,' he would later boast when asked for an explanation for his collection of cuttings. Thoughts of violence began preoccupying his life. He started collecting images from around the world, but rather than satisfying his desire for chaos, they only encouraged him further.

'It started off as a joke, you know,' he would later recall. 'I just laughed it off. Then, after a period of time I just kept thinking about it. In the morning, before I went to bed, in the daytime, and I just couldn't get it out of my head. And eventually I woke up one morning and I wasn't thinking about it any more, I was gonna do it. I was obsessed with it all. You know, it's just something that I wanted to do, had to do. I just bonded towards it, I can't explain it.'

The BNP offered Copeland an entry into the nefarious world of extreme right-wing politics and a political cause with which to justify his increasingly dark thoughts. It was not long before he was to continue his political voyage alone.

3

God's Nazi Soldier

'I'd just be the spark, that's all I plan to be.
The spark that would set fire to this country.'

David Copeland

COPELAND'S FASCINATION WITH VIOLENCE AND CHAOS showed little sign of abating as 1998 dawned. In fact, if anything, it was becoming more pronounced. His collection of cuttings, which he had begun a few months before, was growing out of all proportion. Scenes of famines, bombs, riots and mutilations were displayed prominently across his bedroom walls. Simultaneously, he began withdrawing from the few people he knew in London. One of these was Barnaby Ore who had been involved with the BNP since 1994. He had met Copeland on two occasions. The first of these had been in August 1997 when they had been in a BNP group in

Trafalgar Square, handing out leaflets in support of 'shooters' rights'. The second and last meeting was later that year at a BNP Christmas social with Tony Lecomber, the organisation's East London organiser. Shortly afterwards, Copeland stopped going to BNP meetings, telling Lecomber that he had secured a job abroad. This was not a total lie. He had, in fact, toyed with the idea of going to Russia, but for a holiday not for work. He never took that trip. Perhaps his disastrous experience of Thailand had put him off or perhaps he simply did not have enough money. But Copeland went on another trip abroad in 1998, the circumstances of which are still surrounded in mystery. He had told his father he was going to spend two weeks of his annual holiday in Poland. Not understanding the possible attraction of such a place, Stephen Copeland asked why he wanted to go there, but his son's reply was vague. Later, after the supposed trip, Mr Copeland asked how he had spent his holiday and again he received a non-committal response, leaving him at the time unsure whether his son had really gone to Poland or had spent the two weeks in London. Later, however, it emerged that Copeland had indeed gone to Poland, for some kind of what he called military training involving the use of guns. He has refused to say exactly where he went or the purpose or give any further details at all.

In that early part of 1998 the young man could not escape the images of chaos that permeated his mind. Lying in his room every night, Copeland would gaze at his collection of newspaper cuttings in a mixture of awe and anticipation. Slowly but surely he began envisaging his own atrocities, images of chaos and destruction caused by his own handiwork.

Getting hold of bomb-making designs was not a problem. It had been almost eighteen months since the Atlanta bomb and his first thoughts about embarking on a bombing campaign. It was simply the devastation, the fear and horror on the faces of those caught up in the blast, caught so dramatically by the TV cameras that were filming in the area at the time, that captured his attention. His immediate thoughts had been of a similar bomb at the Notting Hill Carnival. Now, he had decided it was no longer an amusing thought, a far-fetched fantasy that had tickled his imagination. He decided to make his own bomb.

He had learned through his friends in the BNP, and through the mass media, of the potential of the Internet. Entering the word 'bomb' into any one of the dozens of search engines would lead him to thousands of sites offering bomb manuals. As he did not have his own computer, Copeland visited an Internet café near Buckingham Palace, in Victoria, where he searched the web. It was not long before he stumbled across one of the dozens of sites offering *The Terrorist's Handbook*, almost 100 pages of bomb designs. From simple 'Molotov Cocktails' to 'High Order Explosives', 'Multiple Warhead Rocket-Bombs' to 'Mercury Switch Devices', *The Terrorist's Handbook* displayed them all. Copeland must have buzzed with excitement as he printed page after page. He might even have allowed himself a smile as he read the disclaimer in the document: 'Gunzenbomz Pyro-Technologies, a division of Chaos Industries (CHAOS), is proud to present this first edition of *The Terrorist's Handbook*. First and foremost, let it be stated that Chaos Industries assumes no responsibilities for any misuse of the information presented in this publication. The purpose of this is to show the many techniques and methods used by those people in this and other countries who employ terror as a means to political and social goals ... This makes one all the more frightened, since any lunatic or social deviant could obtain this information, and use it against anyone ... This is merely for reading enjoyment, and not intended for actual use.'

Copeland lost no time in studying the printed manual. He wanted to make a powerful bomb, one that would create a huge amount of damage and chaos, probably one similar to the Centennial Park device, which had first caught his imagination. As with his fascination with the images on his bedroom wall, Copeland was heavily influenced by a notion of power — his power as the perpetrator of terror compared with the impotence and helplessness of his potential victims. 'I was planning to build proper devices, main detonation devices with a powerful explosive — ammonium nitrate,' he would later admit. 'I got all the stuff together, a tiny bit at a time. I had to steal the nitric acid and all the other stuff. I had to run around London looking for it.'

One of these trips around London would be almost comical had the intent not been so serious. It also demonstrated a side of his character that was to become all too evident during his full bombing campaign, namely his inability to plan properly, to think ahead and to anticipate problems. Requiring nitric acid for the high explosive bomb he was hoping to make, he decided to steal a canister from Hays Chemicals in Greenwich, south-east London. 'It was a real heavy thing,' he was later to recount. 'First of all I picked it up over the wall. Then I rolled it over the bridge. You know I didn't have a car or nothing, so I got a taxi and made up some bullshit story about how I worked there.'

With the canister safely back home, Copeland set about trying to make a high explosive called mercury fulminate. He had read that, as well as nitric acid, two other chemicals were needed, mercury and ethanol. He had them both, so he followed the instructions carefully. However, the results were not what he intended. Instead of the planned results, the mixing of the three chemicals made a gooey mess. He tried six or seven times, mixing the constituent chemicals in different ways, but the result was always the same. Later, he was to learn from another manual, that a fourth chemical was needed. 'So then, you know, it really wound me up, 'cos it said you needed something completely different to make this. One manual was telling me one method, which I tried several times, you know just tinkering around with it, and it just wouldn't make nothing. So I got another manual and it said you needed flouric acid, which was extremely hard to get hold of. I tried and couldn't get hold of it. I didn't even know where to get hold of it. I was so wound up, I just wanted to give up. So for a few months, I just tried to put the thought to the back of my mind.'

*   *   *

As his first bomb-making attempt failed, Copeland switched his attention back to the BNP. He contacted Lecomber in the summer of 1998, telling him that he was interested in getting involved again. As with most of those in the BNP who came across Copeland, Lecomber was later reluctant to talk about his contact with him, saying only that Copeland wanted to get hold of some recent BNP publications. Claiming not to have any at his house, which in itself is hard to believe as he was editor of the party's monthly newspaper and a leading official in the organisation, he says that he directed him to the party's PO Box in Welling, south-east London. Whatever the true nature of the discussions between the two men, Copeland's relationship with the BNP seemed to be short-lived. The party had changed while Copeland was away. The BNP leadership was eager to capitalise on the Conservative rout at the 1997 election and working class disillusionment with New Labour, and it sought to remodel the party as a respectable alternative. This was not the BNP that Copeland wanted to join. He was an out-and-out racist and a secret, if failed, bomber. While he continued to have sympathy for its cause, the BNP was not the party in which he wanted to be active. He began to look further afield.

Barnaby Ore recalls getting phone calls from Copeland in 1998. The young man asked Ore where he could buy some Third Reich flags. Later that year he phoned again, saying he had received the flags, and adding that he had withdrawn his BNP membership. 'I asked him why,' said Ore, 'and he told me it wasn't paramilitary enough, and that he was expecting to go on camps. He told me he wanted to get involved with some other organisations and he wanted some other addresses, preferably something paramilitary. He asked for the address of the National Front, but I wouldn't give him it. He asked me what I would suggest, and I think I listed some address, an American bookshop.'

That summer, Copeland discovered Christian Identity, a right-wing fundamentalist religion that turns traditional biblical teaching on its head. While there are a number of slightly differing strands of Identity preaching, the most important develops the work of Englishman Edward Hide, who in 1871 claimed that the European race was the true descendant of the Lost Tribe of Israel. Reinterpreting the biblical book of Genesis, Hide developed a 'two-seed theory' of man's evolution. According to this view, Eve was seduced by a serpent and bore a son, Cain, who then slew his brother, Abel. Adam, meanwhile, the first white man, passed on his seed to another son, Seth, who went on to become the father of the white race. It was the descendants of Adam who eventually made their way to Western Europe and became the Anglo-Saxons, Celts and Teutonics. Cain's descendants however, if Hide is to be believed, are the Jews, the Seed of Satan. Other races, commonly called 'mud people' by Identity preachers, derive from a lower form of life: man before man. American Christian Identity followers have developed Hide's theory by claiming that the occupants of the *Mayflower* were these descendants, so making the United States God's Chosen Land. The Declaration of Independence, the Constitution and the Bill of Rights were simply God's desires for the Promised Land.

According to Leonard Zeskind, an expert on the American far-right, 'Identity sharply delineates a white Christian nation, appealing to those opposed to this New World Order. It opposes both multiculturalism from "below" and universalism from above. And the Bible provides a mythology of the nation's origins, particularly when wedded to more conventional stories about George Washington at Valley Forge. Believers assert dominion over a distinct territory, separate from that of non-Christians and non-whites. Their Biblical Law would govern, establishing God's Kingdom on Earth.' In such a society men and women would be divided along gender roles, races would not mix and homosexuality would be outlawed. In addition, laws would derive from the Bible, not the political preferences of the politicians of the day. 'It provides religious unity for differing racist political groups, and it brings religious people into contact with the racist movement,' asserts Zeskind.

As one might expect, Identity preaching differs greatly from mainstream Christianity, particularly over issues of racial equality and integration and the relationship between Christians and Jews. Believing that the Bible condones racial segregation, and so is God's Law, Identity followers argue that Christian ministers are violating God's Law by calling for all races to live together peacefully. Its view towards mainstream Christianity is not simply critical but openly confrontational, believing that the Christian leaders are liars, and agents of the Anti-Christ: 'The Anti-Christs in the pulpit have one objective, and that is to paralyze the people by obstructing their vision and proclaiming the Oracle of The Almighty,' said one Identity preacher writing in *America's Promise Newsletter*.

Copeland searched the Internet for sites relating to Christian Identity religion, finding two that particularly grabbed his attention. The first was Kingdom Identity, a right-wing fundamentalist religious organization based in Harrison, in the southern US State of Arkansas. The second belonged to Aryan Nations, a fanatical group based on a compound in the northwest state of Idaho.

Kingdom Identity teaching would have been politically in tune with Copeland's own thinking, especially on the issue of race. As Identity's Mission Statement clearly sets out:

'We believe that as a chosen race, elected by God, we are not to be partakers of the wickedness of this world system, but are called to come out and be a separated people. This includes segregation from all non-white races, who are prohibited in God's natural divine order from ruling over Israel. Race-mixing is an abomination in the sight of Almighty God, a satanic attempt meant to destroy the chosen seedline, and is strictly forbidden by HIS commandments.' The Kingdom Identity was no less strident in its views on homosexuality, another issue close to Copeland's heart. 'Homosexuality is an abomination before God and should be punished by death.'

Copeland was never much of a reader, but he certainly took in much of the Kingdom Identity material he obtained. During his confession, he would make several references to the Bible and this particular interpretation of it. Proclaiming that race-mixing is wrong, he told his interviewers: 'I think it's wrong all the mongrelisation with these races. You know what I mean if you read the Bible. I'm not really that religious. I do believe in God but I'm not a religious person. It pronounces, you know, it's anti-race-mixing, it's anti-black. He proscribes them as soul-less.' Kingdom Identity recently ran an ad in the *NAAWP* (National Advancement for White People) *National News* selling decals that say, 'Only inferior white women date outside of their race. Be proud of your heritage, don't be a race mixing slut!' While Kingdom Identity believes that the white race is superior to other races, it holds special antipathy towards the Jews. 'We believe in an existing being known as the Devil or Satan and called the Serpent, who is a literal "seed" or posterity in the earth commonly called Jews today. These children of Satan, through Cain, who have throughout history always been a curse to true Israel, the Children of God...' For good measure, Kingdom Identity literature depicts a Serpent with a Jewish head and adorned with the Star of David.

Copeland again sought justification of his own

homophobia in the Bible. 'If you look at any religious book that was ever written, if it's the Bible to the Koran, they all pronounce them as degenerates and should be put to death,' he told police during his interrogation, adding: 'I don't believe that they've got any place in society ... They have no use in society.' When pressed to explain his reasoning, he said: 'The whole point of animals is to breed. These people are just taking up space.' It was as though he was quoting out of Kingdom Identity literature. Months later, when he was to meet a fellow Nazi, Copeland was described as going on and on about the Bible. After his arrest, he was to describe himself as a Prophet, carrying out God's work.

Aryan Nations was an altogether more sinister organisation. Launched in the mid-1970s by self-styled pastor Richard Butler, it has become one of America's premier white supremacist groups. By 1994 it had chapters in 15 US States and international branches in several European countries. Not only has its compound become home to dozens of white supremacists, but its annual Aryan World Congress continues to attract some of the most violent racists around, including Klansmen, militant tax protestors and neo-Nazis. Like Kingdom Identity, Richard Butler is a follower of Christian Identity and believes that he and others of northern European descent are the true Israelites, God's real children. Believing themselves to be God's soldiers whose duty it is to fight for him on this earth, it is therefore unsurprising to find its followers have carried out many of the worst hate crimes in the US in recent years. Members of the Aryan Republican Army, a white supremacist group that was responsible for 22 bank robberies, were connected to Aryan Nations, one, Mark Thomas, being its Pennsylvannia state leader. Another terrorist group, The New Order, also had links to Aryan Nations. In the late 1990s four of its members pleaded guilty to a plot to blow up the headquarters of the Southern Poverty Law Center and poison the water supplies and bomb state buildings in several US cities. Nathan Thill was an Aryan Nations organiser when he murdered a black man in Denver, while one of Richard Butler's security chiefs offered a hitman $2000 to kill an informant. Another security chief who set up The Order II was sent to prison after his group bombed a federal building. There are numerous other examples.

Even Eric Rudolph, the man wanted by the FBI for the Centennial Park bombing, the incident which first caught Copeland's imagination, is a strong Christian Identity follower. He has been charged by police for the bombing of an abortion clinic in Birmingham, Alabama, in 1998 and suspected of involvement following two similar bombings against abortion clinics the previous year. According to the FBI, Rudolph learnt his Christian fundamentalism as a teenager, living with his mother as part of the 'Church of Israel', a group based in the Missouri Ozarks. He was later to be linked to several Christian Identity groups, including Richard Butler's Aryan Nations.

There are some other interesting similarities between the alleged work of Eric Rudolph and Copeland's own bombing mission. Like Copeland, Rudolph is considered a loner, drifting in and out of a succession of white supremacist groups. According to one newspaper report, 'he may have come under the spell of leaders who advocate racist and anti-government violence. But when he allegedly built bombs, federal officials say Rudolph acted alone.' Shortly after the bombing of the Birmingham abortion clinic, a letter claiming responsibility arrived in the name of the 'Army of God'. Similar letters were received after the two earlier attacks. The name 'Army of God' has been associated with anti-abortion violence since 1982, with it appearing on at least one bomb manual. However, federal authorities are convinced that no such organisation formally exists, but its name was simply invoked by Rudolph to represent the ideas and possibly the people who inspired him. At the time of the London bombings, a series of letters carrying the name White Wolves appeared. Perhaps this was no more than a coincidence.

Copeland was deeply affected by what he read. Though he never considered himself a religious person, he began adopting some of the Identity phrases and ideas he came across amongst the material he read. He began referring to black people as 'people of mud', without souls, while believing that he was one of the people chosen by God and in 'the seed line'. While it is doubtful whether he truly understood the biblical teachings of what he was reading, he certainly cherry picked those passages and ideas that not only corroborated his existing views but also gave a spiritual justification to them. He became a young man on a mission from God.

Biblical tracts were not the only material Copeland was reading during this period. Through one of the numerous Nazi book clubs in Britain he had purchased *The Turner Diaries*, a novel widely considered by many to be the modern-day *Mein Kampf*. *The Turner Diaries* is a fictional account of Earl Turner and an underground army, The Organization, in the USA that initiates a race war during the 1990s against a Jewish-controlled government, known in the book as the Zionist Occupation Government (ZOG), a phrase Copeland would later use himself. In the course of this war, the secret leadership of the underground army, known as The Order, oversees a truck bombing of the FBI headquarters and a mortar attack on the Capital building. The organisation itself is split into small cells. The whites win in the end after gaining territory in Southern California, murdering Jews and minority groups, and commandeering nuclear missiles to attack Israel.

Copeland would have found this book inspirational. For a man who hated blacks, Asians and gays, here was a story of one man fighting back. Given his fascination with mayhem, coupled with his desire to build and explode a bomb, he would have found political justification in the book, albeit in a crude and simplistic form, for his own move towards terrorism. He would have also learnt of the lasting impact of a terror campaign. 'But the real value of all our attacks today lies in the psychological impact, not in the immediate casualties,' reads a passage in the book. When Copeland finally carried out his bombing campaign, he was also hoping to send a wider message to society. 'My main intent was to spread fear, resentment and hatred throughout this country,' he would later boast. 'I'd just be the spark, that's all I plan to be. The spark that would set fire to this country. 'Cos every nutter out there, if he wants to get on the news, he's gonna have to blow something up. You know what I mean, they're all thinking about it. If you've read *The Turner Diaries* you know that in the year 2000, there'll be an uprising and racial violence in this country, then there will be a backlash [from the ethnic minorities]. All the white people will go out and vote BNP. If I was a white person with kids in London and they had all the blacks and Asians coming after them with knives and what have you, what are you gonna do, put up with it? No, you're not. Vote them out.'

While *The Turner Diaries* did not force Copeland to carry out the bombings, it certainly sharpened his political outlook on life. While The Organization waged its war against ZOG, they were continually conscious of the need to 'deal' with fellow 'white' Americans who, by their inaction or direct complicity, connived with the System. 'Today has been the Day of the Rope,' begins chapter 23 of the book. 'From tens of thousands of lamp posts, power poles and trees the grisly forms hang, each with an identical placard around its neck bearing the printed legend, "I betrayed my race".' Copeland shared this belief that white people who did not confront the System were actually part of the problem. When asked to defend his bombing of Brixton and the 'white' casualties, he responded: 'I didn't care about hurting them. If they want to live there, then it's up to them.'

On more than one occasion Copeland must have compared himself to the book's central character, Earl Turner, a 35-year-old worker in an electronics firm. The book is his diary, a record of one man's fight against the system he despised. In a tribute to him, the author ends the book by writing: 'Among those uncounted thousands Earl Turner played no small part. He gained immortality for himself on that dark November day 106 years ago when he faithfully fulfilled his obligation to his race, to the Organization, and to the holy Order which had accepted him into its ranks. And in so doing he helped greatly to assure that his race would survive and prosper, that the Organization would achieve its worldwide political and military goals, and that the Order would spread its wise and benevolent rule over the earth for all time to come.' For a young man who lacked confidence and had been considered an underachiever by most people around him, Copeland could at last accomplish something that would earn the gratitude of others in the future.

The race war envisaged by *The Turner Diaries* was not confined solely to the USA. In the spring of 1999, the book ends, an economic collapse signalled the chance for The Organization to gain dominance in Europe. 'That takeover came in a great, Europe-wide rush in the summer and fall of 1999, as a cleansing hurricane of change swept over the continent, clearing away in a few months the refuse of a millennium or more of alien ideology and a century or more of profound moral and material decadence. The blood flowed ankle-deep in the streets of many of Europe's great cities momentarily, as the race traitors, the offspring of generations of dysgenic breeding, and hordes of Gastarbeiter met a common fate. Then the great dawn of the New Era broke over the western World.' Perhaps Copeland, operating in the spring of 1999, thought he was living out the author's fantasy.

The Turner Diaries was written by Andrew Macdonald, the pen name for William Pierce, leader of the National Alliance and arguably America's most dangerous Nazi. A holder of a PhD in physics, Pierce has been active on the far right since the 1960s, when he joined the American Nazi Party, led by the late George Lincoln Rockwell. He became a leading member of the party after Rockwell was assassinated in 1967, serving as its Assistant Executive Officer and ideological leader. His connection with the group was to be brief, leaving in 1970 to join the National Youth Alliance, a rival Nazi group. Never a bit-player, Pierce reorganised the party under his leadership, renaming the group the National Alliance.

Today, the National Alliance is the best organised and most militant of the USA's white supremacist groups. Its membership is counted in the thousands, with the organisation now operating in over a dozen US states. Perhaps more significantly, its followers have influence in several other right-wing organisations. The National Alliance has a monthly magazine, *National Vanguard*, regular internal bulletins, an extensive Internet site, a book club with over 400 titles and even a short-wave radio station. More recently, Pierce has acquired Resistance Records, a white power music operation, which he hopes will sell 70,000 CDs every year. However, Pierce's influence stretches beyond his immediate organisational structure. In April 1995, at about the same time that Timothy McVeigh and Terry Nicholls were delivering the deadly truck bomb that was to destroy the front of a federal building in Oklahoma City, a 23-year-old National Alliance recruiter, Robert Hunt, rented a billboard just outside the main entrance of the huge Fort Bragg Army base in North Carolina, home to the 82nd Airborne Division. The message was simple, and its consequences deadly: 'Enough! Let's start taking back America! National Alliance.' Pfc James Norman Burmeister (20), Private Malcolm Wright Jr (21), and Spc. Randy Lee Meadows (21) took the Alliance message quite literally — a few months after the advertising board went up, the soldiers killed a black couple as they walked down a quiet street in nearby Fayetteville. All three soldiers were Nazis. In Burmeister's room, police found a Nazi flag and an assortment of white supremacist literature, including numerous National Alliance publications.

The Turner Diaries is not Pierce's only novel. In 1989, again using the name Andrew Macdonald, he wrote *Hunter*, a story of a lone killer who targets multiracial couples, Jews and gays. The killer's aim is to raise the political temperature in order to create better conditions under which a racist organisation can operate. The book is dedicated to Joseph Paul Franklin, a synagogue firebomber, who is serving multiple life sentences for the sniper murder of at least two black men. Pierce is uncompromising in his belief that a race war is necessary, that the System under which we live will not hand over power peacefully but must be forced to give it up. Writing in 1990, Pierce said: 'It is clear that if white males would respond to their rage in a direct, physical way, as skinheads do, then we would have no race problem, no Jewish problem, no homosexual problem and no problem with White race traitors in America. Our cities would be clean, decent, safe and White once again after a relatively brief period of bloodletting. The fact is,' he continued, 'that most white males will not take direct, physical action against their racial enemies. Still it is good that a few do, and that they act accordingly. Because they are so few, however, their actions cannot win the war for us. We must have soldiers of other kinds as well if we are to win. Ultimately, we will win the war only by killing our enemies.'

Pierce's two books were part of his strategy to advance his theory of race war. And it seems to have succeeded. Not only have more than 200,000 copies of *The Turner Diaries* been sold since it was written in 1978, but it has inspired a generation of racists across America and Europe. In 1983, *The Turner Diaries* inspired a real underground organisation known as The Order, the name of the secret leadership who controlled the Organization in Pierce's book. Led by Robert (Bob) J. Mathews, The Order carried out armoured car robberies to the tune of $6 million, murdered a Jewish radio host and a policeman, and killed one of its own members they believed was informing on them. The group was finally brought to book in December 1984, when its leader died in a fire resulting from a shootout with the FBI. Most of the other members received lengthy prison terms. At the time of their demise, The Order had begun a massive counterfeit currency operation, both to raise funds and to undermine the US economy, and had plans to poison the water supply of three US cities.

William Pierce and *The Turner Diaries* inspired Bob Mathews. According to the authors of *The Silent Brotherhood*, an account of The Order, 'Bob accorded Pierce a reverence approaching outright worship that he deigned to give no other man. When William Pierce spoke, Mathews became reticent, almost as if he was afraid to interrupt with thoughts of his own. It was decidedly unlike Bob Mathews.' Mathews had also been the Northwest representative for the National Alliance. The affection was mutual. After Mathews' death, Pierce praised The Order in his *National Vanguard* magazine for having 'set its sights on a full-scale, armed revolution, ending with the purification of the US population and the institution of a race-based authoritarian regime.' His editorial ended: 'How will the Jews cope with the man who does not fear them and is willing, even glad, to give his life in order to hurt them? What will they do when a hundred good men rise to take Robert Mathews' place?'

Several years later, *The Turner Diaries* was again widely suspected of inspiring domestic terrorism. The bombing of the Federal building in Oklahoma City in April 1995 almost exactly mirrored a scene from the book.

The impact of *The Turner Diaries* was also felt in Europe. It has been translated into several European languages, including German, French and Swedish, and it has inspired violence. In Sweden a Nazi organisation called White Aryan Resistance (VAM) was formed in 1990, a proto-terrorist group inspired by the notion of race war espoused by the book. In 1991 a group of four VAM members raided a Stockholm police station, stealing 36 Sig-Sauer automatic handguns, while other activists raided military dumps in search of explosives. The leader of VAM was identified as Klaus Lund, who had previously been sentenced for his part in the killing of an anti-racist in 1986. In August 1991, Lund and two associates carried out a bank robbery but were subsequently caught.

Even in Britain, which has seen little of the far-right domestic terrorism experienced in the USA or Sweden, *The Turner Diaries* has had an impact. While the occasional article about Bob Mathews and The Order was carried in British far-right publications during the 1980s, it was not until 1992 and the formation of Combat 18 that the US theory of race war really took hold. C18 was a joint US–British product. It relied heavily on the street thugs, largely drawn from the football hooligan world, that had characterised the British far right for 20 years, but now it incorporated US ideology. Terms such as ZOG and Race War became common in its literature. C18 even took the name 'The Order' for one of its magazines. In issue 4, it reproduced an article by Louis Beam on leaderless resistance, the theory of small cells of activists acting autonomously but following a similar strategy to prevent police infiltration.

Even the BNP, a political party supposedly committed to democratic means, was captivated by the book and the underlying message, so much so that William Pierce was the guest speaker at its 1995 Annual Rally. Coming only a few months after the bomb in Oklahoma City, Pierce revelled in the attention the book was receiving, telling the audience that he took the FBI assessment of *The Turner Diaries* as a blueprint for terrorism as a compliment. Today, a BNP organiser from Coventry, Mark Paine, runs the 14 Words Press, a mail order service that sells videos and other memorabilia relating to Robert Mathews.

'It was a sign of the times,' says Arthur, the BNP member who knew Copeland. 'I think at that time, virtually everybody had heard of *The Turner Diaries*. I think it has been said of John Tyndall's biography [*The Eleventh Hour*] that it's the bible of the BNP. That's quite clearly baloney. Equally, I don't think *Mein Kampf* is. *The Turner Diaries* is the closest, in that many people might not follow the strategy, but it's the book people are most enthusiastic about. Reading *The Turner Diaries*, you get a certain amount of satisfaction, of reading details of blacks, Jews, race-traitors and so on being killed. And when you are frustrated about the way society is going then that's a good tonic.' For Copeland, the book was more than just a good tonic. It was an inspiration for his plans, what he would describe to the police as 'his destiny'.

*   *   *

In the summer of 1998, Copeland moved from Forest Gate to a studio flat in Bermondsey, in south-east London. It was a dark, one-roomed bedsit in an old purpose-built block on the noisy, busy Jamaica Road. Living in such a place only added to the mental instability of this 21-year-old man. He had again decided to move to be closer to work, which was then based at the Bermondsey Underground station on the Jubilee extension line. Copeland acquired the room after visiting the Surrey Quays branch of Winkworths estate agents, where he is remembered for a number of reasons. He appeared timid and cautious, perhaps daunted by the complications of taking on a six-month lease. But eventually, after presenting references from his father, his family doctor in Yateley, his bank and employers, he secured a flat and moved in to it in June. Having told the estate agent that he was an engineer, there was some surprise when, on the day he moved in, Copeland telephoned from his flat using his mobile to say that he could not turn on the mains electricity. Over the phone the agent tried to talk him through the procedure, which only involved opening a small cupboard by the front door and flicking on a switch. Copeland still could not do it and the agent, to laughter in the office, had to go to the flat himself to switch on the electricity.

Once installed in the flat, Copeland added to his collection of newspaper and magazine cuttings, filling an entire wall with horrific pictures. He also had another go at bomb-making, but once again failed to think ahead. He decided to disguise his identity by using a false name. He had seen an advert for rocket fuses in a modelling shop, and wrote off to the company in Wareham, Dorset, asking for the fuses and Czech electrical match-head igniters, under the pseudonym, Mr T Smith. But it was rather a pointless subterfuge because he used his own address. This was not to be the last slip by Copeland.

Other equipment was bought locally — some from a local DIY store — while a trip across London secured him a large amount of liquid ammonium from a medical supply shop in west Hampstead. This was to form a booster charge for what he called a 'professional fertiliser bomb'. Despite his best intentions, Copeland failed yet again to make a viable device. Increasingly frustrated, he dropped the bombing plan, albeit temporarily. He poured the remains of the nitric acid down the sink and discarded the empty canister in the rubbish bin at the bottom of the stairs to his flat. He had initially tried to drop the canister down the chute, situated on the landing outside his front door, but it was, unsurprisingly, too big. He did not totally discount the idea of returning to his plans at some future date, and put some of the remaining ammonium nitrate in two glass bottles for safekeeping.

Trying to push thoughts of bomb-making to the back of his mind, Copeland returned to the far right, this time to the National Socialist Movement (NSM). Formed in March 1997, the NSM emerged out of a split within C18. With the original leader of C18, Charlie Sargent, exposed as a police informant on *World in Action*, while simultaneously awaiting trial for the murder of fellow C18 activist Chris Castle, his brother Steve Sargent and a few dozen supporters broke away to form the NSM. Sargent was the group's propagandist, fulfilling the same role he had occupied within C18. He produced *White Dragon*, a monthly newsletter that combined right-wing gossip, vitriolic attacks on multiracial Britain and observations about his favourite football team, Arsenal. It was, in comparison to the bulk of Nazi literature, more amusing and readable.

The NSM was one of the few openly Nazi organisations in Britain. 'The National Socialist Movement was formed in June 108 yf (1997 of the old calendar) for the purpose of championing the Cause of Aryan identity and Aryan freedom,' noted the first few lines of its *Aims, Strategies and Tactics*. 'Year 108 yf' means years after the birth of its hero, Adolf Hitler, a common feature of hardline Nazi groups and one also used by William Pierce's National Alliance. 'The flag of the NSM is the swastika, and the NSM proudly and unashamedly upholds the political creed of National Socialism.' Its aims were simply explained: 'To make known the truth about National Socialism — its noble idealism, and its principles of honour, loyalty and duty; to encourage Aryans to live in an Aryan way by striving to uphold the National Socialist values of honour, loyalty and duty; to encourage the creation of an Aryan homeland as a practical alternative to the decadent anti-Aryan society of our times, so enabling Aryans to live freely and healthily in accord with their natural and healthy customs; to build the foundations for a National Socialist revolution and thus create a National Socialist State.'

Its stickers often carried Swastikas and pictures of Adolf Hitler alongside the slogan: 'Adolf Hitler — Aryan Hero'. There was no disguising its politics. While it claimed to be a legal political party, its own literature espoused confrontation with the system in order to establish the Aryan State. 'This will require a revolution — the overthrow of our present anti-Aryan, multiracial, society and the creation of an Aryan homeland.' Interested parties were encouraged to become full members, and either join, or form, Active Service Units.

Steve Sargent had grown up in a racist family. His eldest brother, William, had been an organiser for the hardline British Movement during the same period, before taking up animal fighting and a life in rural Suffolk. Steve was the youngest of three brothers — his other brother was Paul David Sargent, better known among the far right as Charlie. Twice convicted for possession of drugs, Charlie grew up in the world of skinhead music and football violence, rubbing shoulders with the leaders of the Chelsea Headhunter hooligans even though he himself was an Arsenal fan. In 1992 Charlie formed C18, initially as a fighting squad for the BNP. Within a year it took on a life of its own, a life that was good to Charlie. Controlling the C18 mail order business, Charlie got rich on its pickings, especially its CD operation, which brought in, by his own estimation, almost £200,000 in three years. It all came to an end in late 1996 when fellow C18 activists fingered him as a police informer. In a desperate attempt to retain control, Charlie lured another C18 supporter into a trap, getting his close friend, Martin Cross, to stab him to death. Both men were sent to prison for life.

Steve Sargent was by far the quietest of the three brothers. While his brothers used their fists, Steve acquired a reputation for wit and intelligence, combining both talents in the production of C18 literature. Like Charlie, he had been brought into the far right through the world of football hooliganism, first with his local team Barnet and then later while following England abroad. While Sargent was rarely involved in fighting, he did surround himself with a motley crew of villains and thugs, none more so than a group based on the Harold Hill estate in Romford, Essex. This group earned an unenviable reputation following their harassment of a local Asian family — acid was thrown in the mother's face, the children were taunted on the way home from school, and the wheel nuts on the father's taxi were loosened. The family finally decided to move when their family dog was killed and thrown through their front window. Sargent claims never to have met Copeland, but on hearing of his arrest did admit to friends in the NSM that he had heard of the name.

While Sargent was the propagandist, the organisation's leader was Tony Williams. At first glance, Williams seems untypical of the Nazis Copeland would have encountered in the BNP, being considerably older and certainly wealthier than many activists. Though only in his mid-40s, Williams' connection to the far right spans almost three decades, having joined the NF as a teenager in the 1970s. By the early 1980s, he was already a branch organiser for Ipswich, but that was only the beginning. A sign of Williams' importance in the British Nazi scene was graphically shown in 1982 when, at the age of only 26, he was given the honour of escorting the ashes of the veteran Nazi Savitri Devi to their resting place at the home of the American Nazi Party in Arlington, Virginia. Embroiled in the internal feuding in the 1980s National Front, Williams reappeared as a secret backer of C18 and particularly an associated publication, *The Oak*, produced by John Cato, leader of the National Alliance (UK). Williams emerged from the shadows in 1995, speaking at a C18 meeting in the East Midlands. A close friend of the Sargents, he stayed loyal to them during the split in C18 in 1997 and helped to bankroll the NSM.

It was with Tony Williams that Copeland was to have most contact. Controlling the NSM mailbox, Williams opened and then answered Copeland's first letter enquiring about the group, to which Williams responded by sending out the initial NSM information pack, and an application form which Copeland filled in and returned. The new recruit was given membership number A640740, suggesting that the party numbered many thousands, whereas the reality was that it had only eight full members, paying £20 a year, and between 70 and 80 supporters, each paying annual subs of £10. Copeland started to receive regular NSM bulletins and Williams' own magazine, *Column 88* – the digits standing for the initial letters of Heil Hitler.

While Sargent supplied the propaganda and links with the street thugs and Williams supplied the money, neither man was the political brains behind the NSM. This work was done by the group's original leader, David Myatt, a man with a longer and more bizarre history than Sargent and Williams put together.

Born just after the War, Myatt spent much of his childhood abroad, first in Tanzania where his father worked for the British Government and later in the Far East. After an upbringing in overseas public schools, Myatt returned to England in his mid-teens to complete his education. His childhood instilled in him a thirst for travel and over the next 30 years he spent considerable time abroad, largely retracing the path of his earlier life. 'It gave me a perspective that perhaps I wouldn't have had otherwise,' he was to later admit. However, it also instilled a loneliness that is apparent in the man and his writings.

His political opinions were formed as he turned 16. Reading books about Nazi Germany, Myatt became engrossed in the 'Loyalty, Honour and Duty' displayed by the Germans of that period, particularly of the SS, Hitler's elite troops. Admiring the 'heroic warrior nature' of National Socialism, Myatt set about discovering the ideas behind Adolf Hitler, his search eventually bringing him into contact with Colin Jordan, the British leader of the World Union of National Socialists. Jordan was soon to launch the British Movement, a hard-line alternative to the newly formed National Front. Myatt threw himself into political activity, though he was never entirely content. Even at that young age, he was proud to consider himself a National Socialist at a time when others were publicly distancing themselves from that title. After dropping out of Hull University, where he was studying physics, Myatt moved to Leeds where he took up full-time politics. In January 1974 he formed the National Democratic Freedom Movement (NDFM). It lasted less than a year, but during its short life its members were involved in a series of violent attacks on black people, trade unionists and socialists. For one attack, Myatt was sent to prison.

With time to mull over his short political career, Myatt became disillusioned with the far right, though more with the leadership than the ideology. The leadership, he thought, was woefully inadequate. Believing that they weren't idealistically motivated, Myatt regarded the 1970s as a period of missed opportunities. Turning his back on political activity, he joined a monastery, believing that he might have a vocation as a priest. The eighteen months he spent there was a period of reflection, an opportunity to gather his thoughts, but he eventually decided that the Church was not for him: 'I had a great struggle between my political beliefs and my religious dogma. In the end I decided that the religious dogma of the Catholic Church was not compatible with what I felt.'

After a period of travelling, including a visit to the grave of his father in East Africa, Myatt returned to the political fray a harder and more determined man. By this time he was close to finalising his theories, which were, if anything, a twisted or 'revisionist' version of National Socialism. Rather than treating Nazism as purely political ideology, Myatt saw the religious, philosophical and spiritual dimensions that he believed had been overlooked by others. He regarded Nazism as a harmonising influence that linked man and his environment in a 'natural way' through irrational mystic bonds of racial kinship and the 'folk community'. In many ways this theory was an updated version of the pre-war Fascist theory of 'Blood and Soil', which argued that identity was created by one's racial heritage and links with nature and the Fatherland. However, Myatt's emphasis on the religious, even Messianic, aspects of National Socialism, is evident in the way he described the struggle in spiritual terms. This struggle, he believed, is a holy race war. 'For the Destiny of the Aryan to be fulfilled,' he wrote, 'there has to be a holy war against all those who oppose National Socialism.'

However, there was a dark side to Myatt, hidden from even his closest political friends. David Myatt established the Order of Nine Angles (ONA), a hardline Satanic church in 1985. Espousing 'traditional Satanism' and rituals involving human sacrifices, Myatt and the ONA are considered dangerous even by those within the Satanic fraternity. For Myatt, Fascism and Satanism are inextricably linked. On joining the ONA a ceremony of worship of Adolf Hitler and National Socialist ideology is performed in front of a swastika and a framed picture of the Führer himself. One ONA ritual, Mass of Heresy, contained in the Black Book of Satan, includes the chanted chorus: 'We believe Adolf Hitler was sent by the gods to guide us to greatness; We believe in the inequality of the races and in the right of the Aryan to live according to the laws of the folk.'

The ONA was part of a loosely-aligned international Satanist–Nazi network, linking groups in Britain, New Zealand and the USA. These included the Fraternity of Balder, the Order of the Left Path, Ordo Sinistra Vivendi and the Black Order. This Occult–Fascist Axis revered Third Reich Satanism and called for a modern Nazi renaissance. These sinister esoteric socialists proclaim the 'Demonic revolution', to usher in the New Order on the collapse of the Old; a New Order that will 'awaken the Dark soul of man, that he might live as a totality with the Light and the Dark returned to balance. These esoteric societies recognise Fascism (whether called by that name or not) as the political expression of primal truths. They include the Black Order of Pan-Europa, Fraternity of Balder, Order of Nine Angles,

Abraxas Foundation, Blood Axis. All such groups are playing their part in the unfolding of Aeonic destiny and the approach of Ragnarock. Fenrir is about to be unleashed.'

Despite his best attempts to keep his Satanist views hidden, it was not long before this link seeped out. The consequent adverse press publicity caused Myatt to once again disappear from view in 1985, this time claiming that he was becoming a Buddhist. It was not until 1992 that Myatt re-emerged, this time flirting on the edges of the newly formed C18. He began advertising his political writings in *The Oak*, the magazine produced by John Cato and funded by Tony Williams. His strident views and obvious intelligence caught the eye of Steve Sargent and it was not long before the two became political friends. 'We have to stop dreaming of winning national power by playing the unfair electoral game of our opponents,' he wrote in one of his National Socialist newsletters, 'and start being practical.'

'The primary duty of all National Socialists is to change the world. National Socialism means revolution: the overthrow of the exiting System and its replacement with a National-Socialist society. Revolution means struggle: it means war. It means certain tactics have to be employed, and a great revolutionary movement organised which is primarily composed of those prepared to fight, prepared to get their hands dirty and perhaps spill some blood. To succeed, such a revolutionary movement needs tough, uncompromising, fanatical individuals.'

In C18, and later the NSM, Myatt saw the raw material from which a revolutionary movement could be built, men who had discarded the electoral path and were committed National Socialists. Moreover, men who were prepared to use violence to achieve their goals. Violence did not scare Myatt — he had been in jail twice and referred to it as 'an educating experience. It taught me not to be afraid of anything the State could throw at me,' he added. Even the seemingly indiscriminate violence of C18 was not offputting: 'I don't see anything inherently wrong with it. It's a question of using that material, of harnessing it in a productively useful way.' He was particularly interested in the younger skinhead followers of these organisations. 'These mostly young Aryans have the right instincts; they have the right feelings about life. Their often rowdy behaviour, their tendency to like brawls, is natural and healthy because it is part of the warrior heritage. Indeed, the skinhead cult was, and is, natural, instinctive Aryan (and working class) rebellion against capitalist bourgeois respectability and the multiracial society. As such these Aryans are by nature and instinct inclined towards National Socialism, and may be said to already be in an instinctive way, National Socialists. To be National Socialists, all such people need is some understanding of National Socialism, and some guidance so that they can use their toughness, their aggressive spirit, in a revolutionary way.'

Myatt saw himself as the educator. His language was colourful, direct and confrontational — just to Copeland's liking. One document circulated from one of his many ONA and National Socialist mail boxes and written under the pseudonym, Godric Redbeard, was *System Breakdown: A Guide to Disrupting the System*. 'This work aims to provide a brief guide to the strategy and tactics National Socialists need in order to create a revolution and create a National Socialist State,' reads the introduction.

The document details how this National Socialist society should be brought about. 'First, a revolutionary situation must be created by such things as direct action and sabotage. Second, the practical means to take advantage of such a breakdown, and any revolutionary situation, must be in place.' It goes on to call for the disruption of everyday services from water to sewage, sabotage to the National Grid and traffic chaos. 'Members of the direct action groups are at the forefront of the struggle,' it concludes. 'They are heroic warriors, fulfilling their Destiny as Aryans, and anyone who acts against them is scum. We are fighting a war for our very existence — the time for playing games is over. Now and in the near future there are only two kinds of Aryan — hero or coward. The hero is the National Socialist who fights for Aryan freedom and an Aryan homeland, who fights to end Zionist domination.'

Copeland would later use the word 'destiny' to describe his bombing campaign. That was not to be the only word or phrase he picked up and adopted from National Socialist literature. He also liked to call people natural 'predators', a label that was repeatedly used in NSM material.

Between 1994 and 1998 Myatt produced almost 30 issues of his newsletter, *The National Socialist*. In them, he outlined his critique of the present society, how it was controlled by the Jews and how it was to be overturned. In *Special Edition #2 — Aryan Revolution*, Myatt makes a Declaration of War. 'We can no longer simply fight skirmishes with our visible, often communist enemies on the street as we no longer have the time or the freedom to indulge ourselves with playing the electoral game our Zionist foes and their lackeys have rigged and whose rules they will change when it suits them. We must recognise that we are fighting a real war. We have real enemies, who will use any means and any weapon in order to win. Our choice is a simple one — fight for freedom and for victory, or do nothing and endure the oppression of the System. Men fight, when war is declared, while cowards make excuses. We declare war on the whole anti-Aryan tyrannical System that exists in every country where Aryans are in the majority — on the governments, organisations and people who aid and abet this System and who support, actively or by inaction, the governments that support this System. Anyone who is not with us, actively or covertly, is our enemy — for that is the nature of war.'

This war was to be, according to another of his newsletters, a holy war. 'We are not interested in compromise with such enemies as we could not compromise with such vermin, such is the magnitude of their crime and such is their treacherous nature. We want freedom! We want vengeance! Our holy war will be bloody, as many people will be injured and killed. Some of those injured and killed may well be civilians, and thus "innocent". But in all wars there are some innocent victims, for that is the nature of war. Nothing significant and lasting is ever achieved without some suffering, some hardship or some loss.'

Much of Myatt's political writings were available on an Internet site belonging to Herve Guttuso, a French Nazi who had been living in England for several years. Guttuso combined his work for Combat 18 and later the NSM with being the leader of the Charlemagne Hammerskins, a violent skinhead organisation that was loosely affiliated to the Hammerskins Nation, an international Nazi skinhead organisation with chapters across North America and Europe. On Guttuso's Hammerskin's site, which itself was attached to a larger NSM site, Myatt's political writings were much in evidence. Alongside highly racist and anti-semitic cartoons and propaganda, any surfer logging on to the site would have also been able to download *The Turner Diaries* and *The Terrorist Handbook*, the political inspiration and the practical manual for Copeland's bombing campaign.

By the time Copeland joined the NSM, Myatt was no longer its leader. A few months previously, his Worcestershire home was raided by police investigating racist material on the Internet. On the same day, police in Essex raided the Chelmsford home of Steve Sargent and Herve Guttuso. The Essex raid resulted from an extradition request by French police who were investigating the Internet site of the Charlemagne Hammerskins, a French skinhead group led by Guttuso. Along with much of Myatt's more militant National Socialist writings, the site contained threats of murder. Pressure on the authorities to act had increased when four Frenchmen loosely linked to the group had been convicted for digging up the body of a young girl, having sex with it and mutilating it. In the end both men escaped prosecution. At the same time as his house was raided, Myatt's Satanist links were exposed in the anti-fascist magazine *Searchlight*. Fearing adverse publicity, he resigned as leader of the NSM.

*   *   *

Holed up in his Bermondsey bedsit, Copeland's health was taking a turn for the worse. Perhaps his failure to make bombs added to his frustration and subsequent ill-health. In his own words he became 'stressed and depressed', adding: 'I was suffering from everything. I was like a nervous wreck.' He says he started to have what he described as 'panic attacks', the first occurring when he was in a bus. He described it as like being hit suddenly across the head and he had difficulty breathing. Although the symptoms passed within a few minutes, there were to be more of them. His father recalls: 'Sometimes we'd go into a café, say, and he'd suddenly feel not well, getting hot and flushed. He'd have to get out, into the fresh air. I think he was having these panic attacks because he couldn't sleep at night.' It is now believed that these 'panic attacks' could have been the first signs of schizophrenia.

Copeland could not cope. He decided to move back to Yateley, to what he called 'the sticks'. He handed in his notice to his employers, Drake and Scull, and returned to the estate agents to see whether he could cancel the lease. The landlord demanded that he see out his contract and pay until Christmas, a full three months away. Copeland did a flit, leaving the flat without telling anyone. The estate agent was, unsurprisingly, furious, using Copeland's month's deposit as part-payment and then chasing him up at the family home. Despite letters and telephone calls, he got nowhere. Eventually he gave up.

Mr Evil

Copeland's father says he never knew his son had broken the lease and still cannot understand why he should have felt so much stress. Stephen Copeland believed his son had a good job, paying him, after stoppages, about £300 a week. He did, however, admit his son had a cavalier attitude towards money, saying that he always got cash out of machines and would often leave money, sometimes hundreds of pounds, lying around the family home. According to his father, Copeland's job did not require too much exertion, and far from being stressful, there were long stretches when there was little work to be done, often because of industrial action by fellow workers. Mr Copeland said: 'The job may have been getting to him because there were so many rules and regulations. At times you used to pull your hair out in even trying to be able to do any work, let alone physically getting on with it. We'd be standing around a lot, and I think he got bored and it sort of ground him down a bit.'

While Stephen Copeland was obviously concerned about his son's well-being, he was also very worried about losing his shotgun licence. He enjoyed regular outings with a friend to the local clay-pigeon range, and was worried that if police discovered that his son was back at home, all this would be put at risk. He had been refused a licence once before because of his son's criminal record. Relations between father and son, never very good since Mrs Copeland had walked out, became even more strained after Copeland's return.

4

Copeland Prepares
for Bombing

*'I've got things to do. I've got something I'm doing
at the moment. It's a secret. I kept saying
something's gonna happen soon. Something's gonna happen.'*
David Copeland

BACK IN YATELEY, Copeland calmed down for a time. He'd
been prescribed sleeping tablets and had even started to look
for work locally. Anything would do. Even casual roofing or
floorlaying, as he had done for a time before. His inability to
find work increased his bitterness and his racism. At that
time there had been a lot of media coverage of ethnic
cleansing in the former Yugoslavia. Copeland believed
British people also had a right to ethnically cleanse
immigrants.

'You know, the British people didn't ask these people

over,' he would later assert. 'They were brought over as cheap labour. Now every white man and woman has to work as cheap labour. It's just totally wrong. You've got so many poor white people in this country. It wasn't so bad thirty years ago, 'cos the councils and whatever were still all white and they looked after their own. But now you get all this bullshit, everything has to be equal. It demeans the white man in this country now. People like me are looked upon as second-class citizens.'

Throughout his time in London, mail, including that from extreme right-wing organisations, continued to be sent to the family home. Sometimes his father had taken letters to him at work in London and sometimes Copeland had gone home at weekends to collect it himself. This was to remain the case up to the time he was arrested for the bombings.

His brother Jon remembers going to his father's house one weekend and meeting David who asked him if he wanted to go on a march and hand out some leaflets.

Although Jon declined, his brother gave him some literature which Jon later put in a rubbish bin. 'I think he phoned up a few people, to see if they wanted to go on a march,' Jon told us. 'But I don't think he was successful with anyone from Yateley. We thought it was just a bit of a joke, him trying to get people going off on a march. We didn't even know if these marches were actually going on.'

Copeland had decided on confrontation. Having tried and failed to make an explosive device on his own in London, he toyed with the idea of forming a small cell. 'I thought about trying to recruit a group,' he was to say later. 'But you just can't trust anyone.' As well as paying £20 to become a full member of the NSM, Copeland also sent its leader Tony Williams another £20 in postal orders for a £6 NSM T-shirt and 400 NSM stickers. After receiving them, Copeland telephoned Williams and asked if there were other NSM members in his area. 'I explained to him that there were other members in his area, but not an area co-ordinator, and would he be interested in this position,' said Williams later. 'He seemed quite happy to do this. I explained that first I would contact an established local member to meet him.' That man was Kirk Barker, a NSM activist with an unenviable repution for violence. Williams wrote to Barker informing him of Copeland's interest in the group and requesting he arrange a meeting. This Barker did, in a small pub in the centre of his home town of Basingstoke.

Whether Copeland knew it or not, in Barker he would have found one of the most violent Nazis in Britain. Barker, married with four children when he met Copeland, became a racist after leaving school. He said: 'I started to dislike blacks as a result of a number of them coming from Reading and causing trouble in the town. Also, when I left school, I had trouble getting a job and was turned down for jobs by black or Asian employers. I thought the jobs I applied for were being taken by black or Asian men or women.'

A long-time skinhead, Barker had become active on the far right in the 1980s, being close to the group who ran the skinhead organisation, Blood and Honour. Formed in 1987, Blood and Honour was an umbrella organisation for bands and skinhead followers across the country, putting on concerts and producing records. Initially formed by Ian Stuart Donaldson, lead singer of the racist band Skrewdriver and unarguably the world's most famous Nazi skinhead, Blood and Honour was passed over to a Milton Keynes-based group led by Neil Parish in 1989. Barker, a close friend of Parish, was to become a major player in the music scene for the next four years, usually as a leading member of its security operation, Skrewdriver Security.

It was a lucrative period for Barker and his friend Parish. Concerts often attracted several hundred people, each paying as much as £10 to enter. In addition, albums, T-shirts, magazines and flags were part of the extensive merchandising operation that brought in as much as £1,000 a week. As a leading member of security, Barker accompanied

Parish to concerts and meetings across the country. Like Parish, Barker also joined the BNP.

Perhaps unsurprisingly, given his size, Barker was not averse to violence and quickly earned the reputation as Blood and Honour's armourer, providing coshes, knives and CS gas to others on the scene. On 23 November 1991, he was to combine violence and music. Returning home from a concert in Baldock, Hertfordshire, Barker was among a group of Blood and Honour supporters involved in one of the horrific and unprovoked race attacks of the time in nearby Buntingford, when five Asian waiters were attacked outside their restaurant in the early hours of the morning. As the staff were closing up for the night, a van pulled up beside them and a number of skinheads jumped out, viciously attacking them with beer bottles. The van drove off, only to return minutes later. The vehicle drove at the waiters who had to leap on to a grass verge to avoid being run down. The skinheads then attacked them with baseball bats. One tried to escape to a nearby house to get help, but before he reached his destination he was knocked unconscious with a baseball bat blow to the head. When he came to, he remembers being dragged by his feet back into the road.

When the police later searched the van they found an assortment of weapons, including CS gas, a machete, baseball bats, knuckle dusters, clubs and knives. There was also a huge quantity of National Socialist propaganda and a Nazi flag. Along with Barker, several of the leading skinhead organisers were in the van — Neil Parish, Blood and Honour organiser; Tony Morgan, the BNP organiser for Wales; Steve Jones, lead singer of the skinhead group, English Rose; and Nick Marsh, who along with Barker, ran Skrewdriver Security. Four of the eleven were sent to prison, with Barker receiving the stiffest sentence of three years for driving the van that had tried to run down the waiters. Summing up, Judge Joseph Gosschalk told the court that the racist element of the crime was an aggravating factor. In sentencing, he described the incident as a 'cowardly and vicious attack ... there must be an element of deterrent to others who might be tempted to do what you did.'

Even before Barker began his sentence, he was in trouble again. While awaiting trial for the Buntingford attack, he was arrested and later convicted for possession of CS gas before a skinhead concert in London, in September 1992. Barker was to lower his profile when he came out of prison, but he never changed his politics or severed his close friendships with several C18 leaders. In 1996, he and a few other skinheads formed the British Hammerskins (BHS), 'an organisation for skinheads, run by skinheads'. As with several other organisations of the time, the BHS was obsessed with US theories of race war.

The meeting between Barker and Copeland was brief and unproductive for both parties. Barker recalled later that the NSM's leader, Tony Williams, wrote to him to ask if he would meet Copeland. 'Williams wanted me to see whether Copeland was OK and that he was not a left-wing infiltrator. He told me that Copeland wanted to set up a unit in Hampshire and Williams wanted to know whether Copeland was suitable to become involved within the movement.' Barker telephoned and they arranged to meet at 1.00 pm on the following Saturday outside Basingstoke railway station. He told Copeland that he was easily recognised 'because I'm big and have tattoos on my head.' The pair met up as planned and went to The Hare and Hounds public house in Flaxfield Road. 'I remember Copeland being quite well spoken and he seemed quite intelligent,' recalled Barker. 'He told me that he didn't drink alcohol, so we both had soft drinks. We spoke about the BNP and the NSM. I told him I'd got into trouble over politics, and that I didn't want to get actively involved again. He told me he wanted to get more involved in the NSM and mentioned Odinism and Paganism to me. I told him I found that quite interesting and then he told me that he was a Christian and he started going on about the Bible. He seemed intense and fanatical about Christianity.' Disturbed that he was with 'a religious nut, who was banging on about Jesus and the Bible', Barker says he tried to make an excuse to leave the pub, but Copeland asked if he could go with him to his house to pick up some nationalistic literature and some racist stickers. 'I told him I was a bit busy because I didn't want him coming to my house,' said Barker. 'I told him I'd meet him for a drink during the week at Farnborough. I then phoned him during the week and told him that I couldn't meet him. That's the last contact I had with him.'

Barker's unease about Copeland does not appear to have been passed on to Williams. A few weeks after the meeting, the NSM leader was contacted by Steve Sargent, who was an honorary member. Sargent told him that Barker had met Copeland, had found him quite satisfactory and was recommending him as a member. On February 25, seven weeks before the first bombing, Williams wrote an official letter to Copeland headed 'NSM unit formation' in which he detailed the then 22-year-old's promotion to Unit Leader for Hampshire and Wiltshire. Enclosed with the impressive letter was a list of names and addresses of members and supporters in the area. Williams says that Copeland then telephoned him and asked for phone numbers for people on the list. 'I told him that I had not got any that were not on the list. He then asked a few strange questions about Christian Identity ideas. I told him that I wasn't personally interested in that. I confirmed his post as Unit Leader.'

Unfortunately for the police, in their keenness to get evidence to charge him they failed to pursue Copeland's right-wing links. In addition to Kirk Barker, there were other extremists in Hampshire and nearby Surrey, including several servicemen. If Copeland's meeting with Barker was aimed at setting up a cell of people along the lines of the leaderless resistance groups outlined in *The Turner Diaries*, then Copeland was probably in contact with some of the others in the area. There are many omissions in the account he gave to the police. He never revealed that he had met Kirk Barker or, indeed, his association with the BNP, or his contact with Tony Williams of the NSM. We have also discovered that Copeland was seen in a pub in Aldershot known locally as a 'squaddies pub', used almost exclusively by soldiers. It seems inconceivable that he just wandered into it. Quite who he was meeting and what was being discussed, remains a mystery. However, at about the same time, *Searchlight* revealed that two members of the Parachute Regiment, based at Aldershot, were linked to the NSM. It is not inconceivable that Copeland, as the new NSM organiser, was meeting some of his members.

Soldiers would also know something about explosives and making bombs. Although Copeland says he carried out the bombings himself, there remains disbelief that he could have constructed the devices entirely on his own. Some of the materials he handled are dangerously volatile, especially when mixed together. Did he have help? People who had been in contact with him while he had lived in London were amazed that he could have had sufficient technical knowledge to construct bombs. One of those who had shared the same house as him was amazed when told by his landlord that police wanted to speak to him about Copeland, who had by then been charged with the London nailbombings. 'I don't know how he managed to make bombs because I remember one day he had a puncture on his bicycle and did not know how to repair it. He had to phone someone on his mobile to ask how to do it.' Members of his family do not think he could have done everything by himself and weeks after his arrest detectives were still in the area, trying to flush out his contacts to see whether they had the technical know-how. According to one police officer: 'It doesn't matter how good and detailed the bomb manual is, you still need someone sitting on the other side of the table, explaining exactly how it should be done, so that you don't blow yourself up.'

Two Hampshire men traced by detectives some time after Copeland's arrest provide interesting details of their impressions of encounters with him as the NSM's 'regional co-ordinator' in the weeks and months leading up to the nailbombings.

The first is Howard, unemployed, a friend of Kirk Barker, and involved in far-right politics for eight or nine years. After seeing a NSM sticker on a lamp-post in Oxford Street in central London, Howard sent off £10 to became a supporting member and was eventually contacted by Copeland, who was described as being responsible for social events in the Hampshire area. The pair eventually met up in January 1999 at Farnborough railway station, and went to the nearest pub, The Ham and Blackbird. Copeland wore his baseball cap and Howard thought it odd that he kept his bomber jacket zipped up to the neck although it was not chilly in the pub.

Howard recalled: 'I found it strange that he was the organiser of social events and drinks etc, because I quickly found out that he didn't drink, and he didn't really talk about the NSM at all or even introduce himself as its regional organiser. The main thing we talked about was religion. He said he was very heavily into it. I remember asking him if he was a Christian. He replied that he wasn't and was more interested in the religious "right", and he always got his information on the way to live from his Bible.'

Surprised by Copeland's manner, Howard asked him about his personal life: 'He told me he was going to go for three months to America. I asked him if was going to take his family with him. He said something to the effect of not having any friends and his parents were dead. He said he was a completely free agent as he didn't have any real friends or work colleagues either. I asked him if he knew people I had known in the BNP and he said he didn't. You would have expected him to have known people in our area if he had been a member of the BNP as I had been. He asked me a lot of questions about my views on the BNP. Was I disillusioned with them? Did I find them patronising? Did they use me in any way? My views were that a lot of the money was going to the rich people in charge of the party. It seemed very odd to me that someone who was so into religion had an interest in the BNP, because the two really do not go hand in hand.'

Howard's meeting with Copeland lasted for about an hour and when they parted, there was no agreement for more contact and Copeland did not even ask for his phone number. 'We were not on the same wavelength really as I was looking for a mate to socialise with in my area who shared the same interests. My overall impression of Copeland was that he was very much a loner. I find it hard to believe that he could have been a member of the BNP as most of the BNP people I knew and met were all happy-go-lucky and we could all have a chat and a laugh. He would not have fitted in at all because he came across to me as having no personality.'

What Copeland thought of Howard is not known, but at this time he was having much more contact with an eighteen-year-old called Anthony, whom he tried to recruit to do some 'paki-bashing'.

Although Anthony and Copeland had both been to the same school, they did not know of each other there because of the four-year difference in their ages. But in late 1997 or early 1998, they met at a local pub, The Monteagle Arms, now called The Poets Corner, and, according to Anthony, became mates. 'I remember David used to travel to the pub on his bike. I never knew any of his mates although he used to speak to a couple of people in the pub. He used to leave early, so he could ride home on his bike after he had had a few beers. I remember he used to get 'mouthy'. He used to stare at people when he was drunk and often offer them outside for a fight. This was totally opposite to his normal character which was shy and quiet. He mostly kept himself to himself.'

The pair lost contact for much of the latter half of 1998, but met up again before Christmas, seeing each other on about ten occasions over the weeks leading up to Copeland's arrest. 'From the time I first met him until the last time that I saw him, I could see definite changes in his behaviour,' said Anthony. 'He started off being shy and at the end his behaviour was aggressive. I remember he got into a fight before Christmas. He said someone from Farnborough had been bad-mouthing him and this guy was in the pub. He went up to this guy on his own and had a word with him in the pub and then left it until kicking out time. I was with David in the pub's car park, and David went up behind this guy and pushed him from behind. The bloke turned around, punched David in the face and then David retaliated by giving this guy a good pasting. The guy was on the floor and David then walked away over to where I was and he was then really calm, saying something like, "That's what people get when they mouth off about me." This was probably the only time I saw him losing it, although he remained aggressive. He used to say to me, "Do you fancy going up to London and doing a bit of Paki-bashing?" He asked me to do this three or four times, but I never went and I don't know if he did either.

'As for David's personal relationships, I never knew him to have any, and if he did, I never met them. I never saw him with any girlfriends or even talking to a girl. I used to say to him, "Why don't we go to Farnborough or Windsor and pull a few birds," but he was never into it. I used to think maybe he's a bit bent, but he never spoke about it.

'Just after Christmas I remember David saying that he wanted to get a bit of money together to go to America. I thought he meant for a holiday, but he told me that he wanted to join the Ku Klux Klan. I just laughed when he said this. I knew he was racist as he'd made that quite obvious over the Paki-bashing and stuff like that. I also knew he was a member of the National Socialist Movement and was its regional leader. I had heard about the National Front and the British National Party but I hadn't heard of the NSM. He said it was an organisation that once in a while got together and that it was different from the National Front and Combat 18. The way that he spoke, he wanted to form his own group, but whether or not he did this in the end, I don't know. He said he wanted to go out and do stuff. He would always use the words "hurt them". I assumed he was basically fucked up in the head. The words "hurt them" mean to me that he wanted to go to London or all around the country and do stuff like "drive-bys" – I mean like a couple of guys getting out of a car and bashing up either blacks or Pakis. I don't know if he ever did this.

'About two months before he was arrested, he asked me to join the NSM and I did. There was no paperwork or anything like that. He just told me that I was now a member. He asked me to do a few things for him, like putting stickers up on lamp-posts and shops in and around Yateley and surrounding areas. These stickers said "White Pride", "Join the NSM", "No surrender to the IRA". All I did was simply put up stickers.' According to Anthony, Copeland kept referring to the NSM leader Tony Williams. 'He used to say, "Tony's phoned me requesting a meeting, so I can't come round." [Author's note: Williams has denied ever meeting Copeland.] There was one time that David didn't like talking on the phone. In fact, he never liked it. He thought that his telephone was bugged and he used to say that things could get quite dangerous. I think he was also cautious about being recognised as he was always wearing a plain black baseball cap, so much so that I never even knew what colour his hair was and for all I knew, he could have had long hair.'

*   *   *

Copeland was causing other problems at home towards the end of 1998. Unsuccessful at finding a job locally, Copeland had persuaded the Jubilee Line contractors, Drake and Scull, to take him back. He remained at home, annoying his father and having violent arguments with his younger brother Paul, who was back from university for Christmas. Eventually Copeland was asked to leave, and he was forced to find a place of his own. After looking in the local newspapers, he found a room in nearby Farnborough, and with help from his elder brother Jon in the New Year he left Yateley, taking everything he wanted with him. His father threw out the rest and told a workmate that he had virtually disowned his son.

Copeland's new work in London was mostly at Bermondsey, but occasionally he worked at Westminster Underground station, right by the Houses of Parliament. Relations with his father had reached a new low. At lunchtime and for other breaks, they went to the local Bermondsey café, Rose's, but they usually sat apart and the café owners did not even know they were related. Rows between the pair were witnessed by Paul Mifsud, another engineer who had just started work with the father-and-son team. Their jobs involved balancing the flow of air and water systems along the new Underground line, with the young Copeland acting as their assistant. The three were to work closely together in the five months leading up to Copeland's arrest.

Mr Mifsud is of Maltese origin and is in his thirties, happily married with children. He is a calm person, interested in meditation and, at over six foot tall, he towers over the Copelands. From the outset, he found David Copeland very strange. 'The word that comes to mind is angry. You meet this young man and within a couple of hours he's coming across as very angry,' he told us months later. 'He was angry at childhood events, frustrated with life and totally insecure, an icy man. He had a need to shout at the world to get noticed. He was awkward to work with and after a week his dad told me I could get rid of him if I wanted, but I saw a twenty-two-year-old man, full of anger, and I thought if I got rid of him, where's he going to go? So I tried to help him in the job and as a person. It now goes through my mind, should I have helped him or not?'

Copeland also had physical problems. 'Dave has a bad body odour problem,' Mr Mifsud told police. 'He has told me that he doesn't wash or use deodorant and we have had many arguments over the months about the problem, because he really did, and does, smell. It's strange because sometimes after such an argument, he would come to work the next day in a clean shirt, having used deodorant, but this would last only a day or so, until he went back to not washing and smelling badly.'

Much of the BO problem was caused by Copeland invariably wearing the same clothes — a black baseball cap, a dark blue zip-up bomber jacket, blue denim jeans or black combat trousers, and black boots.

Mr Mifsud said he thought Copeland had a strange way of walking, with the backs of his hands pointing forward. 'Dave is very nervous when crossing the road, which, to some point is almost comical. Obviously in London you have to be careful in view of the large number of cars. But Dave will really hesitate before crossing the road, and then he almost runs across. He seems to have a permanent frown about him. He always looks very intense, angry and focused.'

Mr Mifsud told us he could have decided to keep his distance, but he chose otherwise. Interested in psychology and personality development, Mr Mifsud found Copeland fascinating, as he did his father. So, instead of rejecting David Copeland, he sometimes encouraged him to talk about himself, his problems and the way he had been brought up. It was a hard job, as Copeland rarely opened up about himself. Over the weeks, however, Mr Mifsud found that, to an extent, he could relate to the younger man, who he found immature, unloved and insecure.

'While Dave works with his father, they don't get on at

all well,' Mr Mifsud told police on the day of Copeland's arrest. 'They do speak, if they have to, about work matters and very occasionally they will speak about some members of their family, but I feel there is no love lost between the two of them, from both sides. I recently overheard an argument between the two, where I think Steve tried to hit Dave. Steve has said that he has disowned Dave and they just don't get on. Dave has said to me that he doesn't want to know his brothers or his mother. He doesn't have a girlfriend and has not had one since I've known him. He strikes me as a real loner. He has told me that he thinks his parents, in his words, had "fucked him up" because they thought he was gay. He said his parents shouldn't have had him if they weren't prepared to support him. He gave as an example that they should have bought him a car. He was very, very angry and I think he really believed that his parents owed him a living.'

Mr Mifsud offered Copeland advice. As the young man had been thinking of moving back to the capital, Mr Mifsud suggested that he look around Balham or Tooting in south London. The idea was rejected by Copeland because he said there were too many blacks there. 'He said he couldn't stand young black youths on the streets and wouldn't want to live near them.' But Mr Mifsud says that, although there were discussions about race and David's sexuality, the young man said little that he would describe as racially derogatory or insulting. 'His hatred was for everyone and everything,' said Mr Mifsud. Copeland had also revealed that he used the services of prostitutes, and Mr Mifsud tried to reassure him that eventually he would find the right girlfriend. Working and talking to both Copelands, he thought at times he was acting as a counsellor between the pair, trying to patch up their differences. But it was an impossible task.

General discussions between Mr Mifsud and David Copeland about political issues did not get very far. 'He spoke about the conflict in Serbia. He said he sided with Serbia and had thought about joining them to fight on their behalf.' His other heros were 'strong dictators', such as Hitler, Stalin and Saddam Hussein. 'Over the months,' said Mr Mifsud, 'I gave up trying to reason with him to change his views. He is very set in his ways. He will not change his views on anything or for anyone and is very argumentative.'

There were also displays of his bad temper, with violence always close to the surface. One such occasion, when a joke was made about him being homosexual, drove Copeland into a fury. It happened when he and Mr Mifsud were in a café that they visited fairly regularly together. Someone made a remark about them having forgotten their handbags. Copeland reacted aggressively, and the man who had made the remark backed off, apologising that it had only been a joke and no offence had been intended.

Copeland was continuing to have 'panic attacks', when everything would go black. He stopped going to barber shops because he 'felt uncomfortable', and started cutting his own hair using a pair of clippers he had recently bought.

Some of what he said appears to have come straight from National Socialist Movement literature. According to Mr Mifsud, Copeland 'felt it was in human beings' nature to be a predator and to kill'. One NSM newsletter article entitled 'The Aryan Way' rejects the turn to constitutional politics by groups such as the BNP and declares that Aryans 'are predators, natural hunters. Instead of acting like dangerous predatory Aryans, instead of living and acting like Aryan warriors, we have become "political" and worse, "politically respectable", instead of going out, armed and dangerous, and fighting and killing our enemies, we have handed out leaflets. Nature favours the ruthless, the predatory, the adaptable and the strong. We either become Aryan again, and predatory, and thus ruthlessly fight for our freedom and our future, or we become submissive, give up our freedom and have our race become extinct.'

Copeland also talked about serial killers. 'He seems to have a fascination for serial killers and has occasionally talked about them,' said Mr Mifsud. 'He has spoken about a film, *Henry: Portrait of a Serial Killer*, and has said that it is a good film, a role model for him. He treated the character almost as an idol.' With hindsight, other observations were ominous: 'A couple of months ago or so, Dave said something like he didn't want want to live like a 9-to-5 body in the rat race. He said he would rather risk going to prison for robbing a bank or dealing kilos of heroin than live like that.'

If Mr Mifsud's timing of that conversation is correct, it coincides with Copeland's discovery that he could indeed make a viable bomb. It would not be a high explosive device, but it would, if placed correctly, kill or maim people.

Copeland started detailed planning and preparation six weeks before the first blast. He lived in a small nondescript room, next to the bathroom, on the first floor of a semi-detached house in Sunnybank Road, Cove, on the outskirts of Farnborough for which he paid £60 a week in rent. The house is owned by a Baptist Church and managed by the Reverend Dr Chris Russell. Tenants came and went every few months. When Copeland was there, he shared facilities with two other young people, Alison and Graham. All three had separate rooms and shared the living room, kitchen and bathroom, but they rarely saw each other, and they did not even know each other's surnames. For a few weeks there was a fourth tenant, a German, called Friedrich, a friend of Dr Russell's son who was then in Germany — Copeland referred to him as 'Fritz' or 'the Kraut'. Each tenant's room had its own lock and each tenant was responsible for their own cleaning, which meant no one else saw inside Copeland's room. He had added to the cuttings and horror photographs he had brought with him from his room in Bermondsey, and also displayed prominently on the wall was a large red Nazi flag. He also had a pet — a large white rat he called Whizzer. Before buying it, he had asked Alison if she minded. She said she did not, so long as Copeland kept it in a cage.

Alison told us she and Graham did not like Copeland, and had no idea what he got up to. He seemed to have had no visitors at all, and by that stage he had virtually cut himself off from his family. After his mother had walked out of the family home, he had kept in touch with her by phone at her parents in Twickenham, occasionally visiting her, but even this limited contact ended in 1997 when he moved to London. His elder brother, Jon, with whom he had been close, never visited, and his father only went to the house on two or three occasions during the months his son was there to give him a lift by car to the Jubilee Line, if they were both working the same night shift together. Mr Copeland never even went inside the house, let alone his son's room. It is just one of the many deep regrets that Mr Copeland and Jon harbour about David. They think that if only they had seen something of what he was up to, then they could have reasoned with him, and maybe the bombings would never have happened.

Although Copeland's earlier attempts at bomb-making had ended in failure, he still retained his copy of *The Terrorist's Handbook*. There was also other equipment from Bermondsey, including the igniters. During one lonely evening spent sitting in his room, the thoughts of bombs re-emerged. 'I was just bored one night, and I thought I'd read through that manual. I didn't really read through much of it. I found a bit that explained how to make a pipe bomb. And then, you know, it was easy after that. The idea started floating around my head again.'

Thoughts quickly turned to action. There would be one bomb a week — the first at Brixton in South London, which he believed to be the focal point for the black community; the second was for Asians in Brick Lane in the East End; and the third aimed at gay people in Soho. He said he knew the bombings 'would just piss everyone off'.

The issue of race would never have been far from Copeland's mind as he mulled over his bombing plans. The public inquiry launched into the police handling of the murder of black teenager Stephen Lawrence was coming to an end and the media, which for months had been covering the unfolding story, went into overdrive. Racism within the police, among the five whom it was alleged committed the killing, and within society at large preoccupied the media throughout the early months of the year. For a young man who avidly bought newspapers and watched TV, Copeland could hardly have escaped the details of the Lawrence murder.

Stephen Lawrence had been murdered while waiting at a bus stop in Well Hall Road, Eltham, south-east London, in April 1993. Six years, one trial and several internal police investigations later, the murderers remained at large. On coming to power in May 1997 the new Labour administration promised a Public Inquiry, hoping that at last, a degree of justice would be done for the parents of Stephen Lawrence.

Whatever Copeland personally thought of the murder, he would no doubt have been angered by the publicity surrounding the case. If he felt anything like the leaders of Britain's far right, the public outpouring of guilt and shame would have sickened him. 'Stephen Lawrence Murder Not a Racist Killing' ran a headline of the National Front newspaper, *The Flame*, claiming that Stephen was a victim of gang violence. *The League Sentinel*, the irregular publication of the highly secretive Nazi group, The League of Saint George, cast doubt over Stephen's innocence, asking whether he was carrying a knife at the time of the attack and had previously been a suspect in an earlier stabbing of a white youth. One NF supporter even attacked Stephen Lawrence's memorial, resulting in a short prison sentence. At the next Nazi music concert, fellow extremists gave the NF man their support by holding a collection.

Turning the murder on its head, the BNP attempted to portray those behind the Inquiry as the real racists, hell-bent on whipping up white guilt as a means of extending the 'multiracial experiment'. Copeland would no doubt have agreed with one article in the BNP magazine *Spearhead* that attacked the anti-racist crusade emanating from the Lawrence Inquiry: 'How can a supposedly idealistic ideology be espoused by people whose bottom line is money and power? Because, in truth, the real motive force of "anti-racism" is very far from being idealistic. The logical, and intended, conclusion of "anti-racism" is the genocide of every distinct racial grouping, and the substitution of a melange world of near-slaves; it is in reality the supreme and most pernicious form of racial hatred.'

Copeland's own sense of persecution and frustration would only have been increased a few weeks later when police raided the homes of 14 supporters of the violent Nazi group, C18. Eight police forces were involved — London, Lancashire, Merseyside, Kent, Thames Valley, Humberside, West Yorkshire, and South Wales. Among the most high profile of these arrests were two serving soldiers — one of them a member of the Parachute Regiment based in Bulford, Wiltshire, and the other in the King's Regiment, based in Preston. Commenting on the raids, a Ministry of Defence spokesman said: 'The MOD has been fully co-operating with the civilian authorities throughout these investigations. There is no home or hiding place for racism in the Army. Our action here graphically demonstrates that.' While there was obviously little coincidence that these raids occurred so soon after the Lawrence report was published, allowing the police and army to claim a propaganda coup, it was part of a longer term investigation into C18 being conducted by the security service, MI5.

The first few months of 1999 were not a period a confessed racist would have enjoyed as the press, politicians and community figures fell over themselves to demonstrate their anti-racist beliefs. The general atmosphere of the day must have disgusted Copeland. Any hope of achieving his racist society through the ballot box must have seemed more distant than ever. It was probably with this realisation in mind, mixed with a sense of outraged anger, that Copeland continued his planning.

Copeland saw himself as a young man on a mission, an avenger. He had just been appointed the NSM's Unit Leader, and for the next six weeks he was busy obtaining explosives, more equipment, experimenting with devices and testing smaller versions of devices. He later claimed to have spent £1,500 on different fireworks, bought from three shops in Farnborough, one of which was a joke shop. At first he bought 'Flash and Thunders' and then switched to 'Air Thunders'. He usually cycled around town, but sometimes he bought so many fireworks that he needed taxis to get home.

One such journey in March to 25 Sunnybank Road was recalled by Timmy Rossiter, one of the drivers with A-Line Taxis in Farnborough. Copeland had bought a huge amount of fireworks from Raison Brothers, a shop that also sells fishing equipment and crossbows, and had asked one of the staff to order a taxi for him. In addition to three large boxes of fireworks, Copeland had his mountain bike with him. Mr Rossiter helped the young man load everything into the back of the cab. Thinking Copeland's boxes contained fishing gear, he asked him if he was going fishing. Copeland replied: 'Something like that.'

Nothing more was said for a time until the passenger broke the silence by asking questions about the black cab, inquiring how much it had cost and asking whether it was difficult to drive. Copeland disclosed that he was an engineer on the Jubilee Line, that he had been working nights and was making a lot of money, as much as £1,200 a week. The true figure was about a quarter of that and Mr Rossiter knew he was boasting. Copeland then related that his bike had been stolen a couple of weeks earlier, after he had left it at Farnborough Station. The police had recovered it and after a bit of bother finding out where the police had it stored,

Copeland had finally got it back. He told Mr Rossiter that 'his faith in the police had been restored'. As with the vast majority of other people Copeland met at that time, Mr Rossiter remembers him as an ordinary, normal young man, although a bit scruffy.

A Farnborough vet, Caroline Clough, also met Copeland around this time and was amazed to learn later that the young man who had visited her was the nailbomber. When we told her that we had heard that Copeland had visited her, she said his name meant nothing to her, as she was more likely to remember someone from his pet and the name of the animal. As soon as a rat called Whizzer was mentioned, she remembered Copeland, and expressed great surprise that such a person could have carried out such appalling acts. She, too, recalled him as being rather scruffy, but he really cared about his rat, as he had perservered in getting help for it. First he had taken Whizzer to a vet's surgery, and then, because the rat was suffering from a skin complaint, he had made a separate appointment with Ms Clough who is a veterinary skin specialist. Whizzer was treated with a special shampoo and the cost of the whole consultation was £14.58. Ms Clough said that she had seen pictures issued by police of the Brixton bomb suspect but had not recognised him, and then she again failed to make the connection when he was arrested locally, even though she remembered at the time wondering whether he or any of his family was known to anyone at the surgery. The consultation was on 27 March, exactly three weeks before the first bomb. Even when he was heavily involved in buying materials and equipment so he could kill and maim people, he cared sufficiently for Whizzer's welfare that he found time to take the pet for treatment.

Jon Copeland recalls how as well as the rat, his brother loved the family cat, Suzy. 'It was the most horrible cat you've ever known. She wouldn't go to anyone in the family. She'd just run away if you approached. But she'd always go to

David and sit on his lap, while he stroked her. It was strange ... I didn't really see him much for a few months. When he came back from London, there was a change in him. He was a bit reclusive. He stayed in his room. I tried to get him out for a drink on a number of occasions, but he didn't want to know. He just kept himself to himself. He wasn't talking about blacks, Asians and gays to me. He was just subdued. I saw him at my father's house a few times when I took my young daughter round, and he was very nice to her, always attentive and loving. Now I look back at it, I think it a bit strange that he likes pets and kids more than adults.'

Anthony Sales had also met him. Before joining the Royal Navy, Mr Sales rented the room at Sunnybank Road before Copeland, moving out at the end of 1998. He had left some of his belongings in black bin liners in the loft, and returned to the house to collect them in early April, two weeks before the first bomb. He met Copeland and the pair had a conversation about various matters, with Copeland asking about life in the Royal Navy. Apart from appearing rather scruffy and making clear that he did not like what he called 'Pakis', Mr Sales did not think there was anything unusual about him.

He was never to see inside his old room. If he had, he would have found it had been turned into a Nazi shrine with a large poster of Hitler's deputy, Rudolf Hess and a colourful, well-produced National Socialist Movement calendar showing lots of 'Sieg-heiling' blond-haired Germans. Then there were all those sick photographs and newspaper cuttings of murders and other atrocities.

Some of these were new. One photo showed a woman with a knife still sticking in her head, who had been attacked on a train. The accompanying cutting said the assailant had fantasised for years about knifing a woman in the head. He was sent to Broadmoor, to be detained indefinitely under the Mental Health Act. Another cutting, from a February newspaper, was of the Old Bailey trial of a 24-year-old who 'chopped up his lover and ate her thigh with pasta and cheese sauce'. He admitted manslaughter on the grounds of diminished responsibility and was sentenced to life imprisonment. Interestingly, his favourite film, just like Copeland, was *Henry: Portrait of a Serial Killer*. A copy of the video was also in Copeland's room, as were copies of Hitler's *Mein Kampf* and *The Turner Diaries*, and a large quantity of racist literature.

Copeland's mind was now concentrated on his forthcoming bombing campaign. Sitting at his dressing table, watched by his pet rat, he worked on his bombs at night, often into the small hours, perfecting their design and power. To allow fumes to escape, he kept the windows open, even though the nights were cold. He emptied the explosive powders out of the fireworks, carefully separating them into different piles. Then after mixing very small quantities together with black powder, he used his cigarette lighter to test their explosive strengths. The burn marks he made are still on the table.

Having decided on what he thought was the correct proportions of explosive, he packed the powders into a small length of narrow pipe, in which he had drilled a hole to carry an igniter. After glueing up both ends, and attaching a timer device, he had a small pipe-bomb, ready for testing. Copeland made three such experimental bombs, cycling at night the short distance to Rushmoor Common where he set them off in woods on old Army land, without apparently disturbing anyone. Satisfied with the results, he then set about getting more equipment from Farnborough shops for the big bombs he was to explode in London.

To carry the heavy devices to their targets, Copeland bought three sportsbags, a Head bag for Brixton, Reebok for Brick Lane and Nike for Soho. He bought lengths of four-inch-diameter drainage pipes that he sawed into three pieces, each about a foot long, and into which he would pack the explosives from the fireworks. He also bought electrical gear, big old-style alarm clocks, sandwich box containers and a range of different-sized nails, up to ten inches long. Thousands of nails, about five kilos, were packed around each pipe bomb. He was ready to wreak havoc.

Two years previously there had been another attempted bombing campaign. In January 1997 three Danish C18 members posted bombs hidden in video cassettes to a number of targets in Britain. One was intended for Sharon Davies, the former Olympic swimmer-turned-TV presenter, whose 'crime' had been to engage in a relationship with the former black athlete Derek Redmond, a cardinal sin for the racially conscious far right. The pair had previously been the subject of a death threat in a Combat 18 magazine. The bomb plot was foiled after police, acting on a tip-off from an informer at the very highest level of C18, notified the Danish authorities, who immediately began tailing the main protagonist, Thomas Nakaba. While Nakaba was sentenced to eight years imprisonment, police were unable to nail the London man named as the man thought to be responsible for masterminding the plot.

Early in 1999, Copeland was not alone in preparing for racial violence. Not too many miles away from his Farnborough home, another racist was about to strike at Britain's multiracial society. Stuart Kerr, aged 20, was, like Copeland, linked to an array of far-right groups, including C18, BNP, NF and the NSM. He, too, was conducting his own private war. For two months, he and another racist had carried out a campaign of violence against an Asian-owned corner shop in Chichester. Windows and lights in the shop in Stockbridge Road were smashed on a number of occasions. The owner, Chandrakant Patel, became so concerned about his family's security that he moved his wife and three daughters out of the building at weekends. It was during one such weekend that Kerr and an accomplice threw two petrol bombs at the shop. Unknown to him, the attack was caught on video. The police had been called in the week before and had installed a CCTV camera. Kerr fled towards Chichester town centre where he set a police car alight. He was caught soon afterwards, but not before he had repeatedly slashed his arms.

Kerr's bedroom, like Copeland's, was a shrine to Nazism. Pictures of Hitler adorned the walls, along with National Front stickers and derogatory slogans defacing a West Ham team photograph. Among the Nazi literature were copies of the BNP publications *Spearhead* and *British Nationalist*, C18 information bulletins and the C18 White Wolves magazine *The Wolf*.

Kerr was arrested just days before Copeland's first bomb, but did not appear in Chichester Crown Court for sentencing until November 1999. Judge Anthony Thorpe gave the maximum prison term possible — 12 years — telling the court: 'Members of the ethnic minority group rightly look to the courts for protection from the vile and despicable hatred that is peddled by racist bigots. In the past, I suspect they have felt they have not been afforded the protection they rightly deserve and I have great sympathy.'

Meanwhile, Copeland could not resist dropping hints about his own plans. Devoting more and more time to his final bomb preparations, his work on the Jubilee Line became increasingly erratic, and he often never turned up at all, claiming he was ill. Paul Mifsud was unconvinced by these excuses and suspected his workmate was up to something. The pair had worked together for several weeks, and Mr Mifsud believed, probably rightly, that he had become the person closest to the lonely, angry young man.

The conversation with Mr Mifsud was recalled later for police by Copeland: 'I'd been telling (him) that something's gonna happen soon, and like I've got things to do. I didn't actually say I'm gonna blow anything up. What I said was I've got something I'm doing at the moment. It's a secret.' Asked how long he had been giving him these warnings, Copeland replied: 'I never actually told him I was planning this, but I kept saying something's gonna happen soon. Something's gonna happen.'

5

The Brixton Bomb

'If no one remembers who you are, you never existed.'
David Copeland

COPELAND'S BOMBS WERE POLITICALLY MOTIVATED. He claimed: 'I am a Nazi. I believe in a National Socialist state for this country, for the entire world, the Aryan domination of the world. I believe in a master race.' To achieve that racist dream world he followed a strategy propounded by the extreme right wing, that a race war could be started by attacking Blacks and Asians, provoking them to a fight back. 'I would be the spark that would set fire to this country,' said Copeland, echoing the far-right literature he read.

But there was also a more deep-rooted personal desire. He craved fame and notoriety, just as when a child he had sought approval and recognition by going that bit further than anyone else. 'My main intent was to spread fear, resentment and hatred throughout this country — murder, mayhem, chaos, damage, to get on the news. It's a top story really. I wanted to be famous in some sort of way. If no one remembers who you are, you never existed.'

Copeland's landlord, Reverend Dr Chris Russell, like many others who came into contact with him, cannot believe that he managed to do the bombings alone. For one thing, he thought him 'not too bright' and therefore incapable of planning a bombing campaign and of constructing powerful devices. He also looks back with amazement at Copeland's behaviour on the days of his first two bombs. It was part of Dr Russell's routine to go to 25 Sunnybank Road early every Saturday afternoon to collect the rent. He saw Copeland just before he set off to plant the Brixton and Brick Lane bombs. 'He was his normal usual self,' said Dr Russell. 'If you or I was going to do something like that, we'd be on edge beforehand. He was nothing like that.'

Copeland had started to build the Brixton bomb the night before, wearing gloves so as not to leave fingerprints. He had already glued up one end of the four-inch pipe, so it was difficult to put in the flash powder he had extracted from the fireworks. He pressed it down using a pestle. He was surprised at how much explosive he could pack in. Then he glued up the other end, opening his windows wide to clear the room of fumes and also to speed up the drying of the glue. He had put an igniter to act as a detonator inside the pipe with the explosive, leaving a hole in the pipe so that wires could be attached.

In the morning, he assembled the rest of the device. He put the pipe bomb in a cardboard box, surrounding it with hundreds of differently sized nails. He padded out the box with tissue paper, to stop the bomb and the nails moving about. Wire led from the container to a transparent plastic sandwich box and the battery-powered timing device, which consisted of an old-style alarm clock with the minute hand removed. A nail had been hammered into the clock face so that when the hour hand reached 5.30, it would activate an electrical circuit that would ignite the detonator in the pipe and set off the bomb.

Copeland set off for Brixton shortly after seeing Dr Russell. He explained later that he had planned to wear some form of disguise, and had visited a shop at an earlier stage to see what was on offer. But when he returned on the day before his planned bomb, it was to find that the shop had sold out of his chosen disguise. Instead, he decided to wear a light-beige coloured baseball cap bought a few days before, rather than the usual black one he wore all the time. He described it later as a 'stupid' cap. His failure to use a proper disguise and to have worn such a distinctive cap was to lead to his undoing. Leaving the house on the Saturday afternoon, Copeland wore a dark navy blue Harrington jacket with a tartan lining, green combat trousers and black boots. He slung the heavy Head bag on to his back, with the strap across his chest, running from his right shoulder to under his left arm. He cycled the mile and a half to Farnborough railway station and caught a London-bound train. As he sat in the carriage, he imagined the bomb exploding prematurely and blowing him up. He did not worry.

He got off the train at Clapham Junction, the nearest rail station to Brixton. He was far too early. He had primed the bomb for 5.30 pm but it was just after 3.00 pm, so he went into a café for a drink to kill time. Twenty minutes later he went to the taxi rank outside the station and took a black cab to Brixton. As he neared the destination, Copeland was surprised to see so many white faces, having thought that, being white, he would have stood out like 'a sore thumb'. He commented on this to the driver, who explained that Brixton was now very much a multiracial area. He got out of the cab in the centre of Brixton, next to Lambeth Town Hall and wondered for a moment whether he should have gone to Peckham, which he knew had proportionally more black people and where he knew he would definitely appear like a sore thumb. However, he was in Brixton and it was seen throughout the UK as the centre of the West Indian community. He did not particularly want to injure white people, but he thought they should not be in such a black area in the first place.

As he walked around Brixton with his bomb, looking for a good place to plant it, he again thought of it exploding on his back. He visualised a flash, but was to say later that he did not care. 'In a way, I think I was hoping it would explode, killing me, 'cos I'm a coward. I've had suicidal tendencies for a long time, but I can't end my own life. I just didn't care [if it exploded]. If it did, it did. I just didn't care. I was just like a robot.'

Copeland walked along the main street towards the Underground station but before reaching it, he saw a busy bus stop at the junction with the street market in Electric Avenue. The bus stop was outside the Iceland supermarket, reckoned to be the busiest of the chain's UK stores. He thought it could be an ideal place for his bomb. He noticed a trader with a tray of CDs, tapes and cigarettes and thought that he would put his bomb bag down next to him, and pretend that he was waiting for a bus. However, he decided to look for other sites and walked along Electric Avenue, past the stalls selling fruit and vegetables, electrical goods and bric-a-brac. He decided as he walked back along Electric Avenue that the bus stop would indeed be the best place to leave the bomb. He would not be noticed and he would hurt more people there. But he was still far too early. There was much more than an hour to go.

Having picked his spot, Copeland walked back towards Lambeth Town Hall. He needed the lavatory and went inside the library and asked the staff there whether he could use the toilet. They told him the toilets were not open to the public and suggested that he went to a nearby pub. Copeland did as told and, without buying a drink, politely asked one of the barmen if he could use the toilet. Getting approval, he relieved himself and then went to sit in a small paved garden area opposite the Town Hall. He took off the heavy bag and sat on a wall. As he waited, two people approached him and said they were conducting a survey to find out people's views of Brixton Police. Would he help? Copeland was happy to oblige. Answering their questions killed more time. After they had finished, thanking him for his co-operation, he says that he got bored. Finally, after slinging the bag across his back again, he set off for his target.

Back at the bus stop outside the Iceland store, the trader with the CDs had disappeared. The street-wise Copeland thought, correctly, that he must have been unlicensed and had probably left for a few minutes because the police or market officials were in the area. Copeland took the bag from his back and laid it on the pavement next to the shop window and the bus-stop, close to the Iceland entrance. He took off the gloves he had worn while carrying the bag. The street trader returned to his pitch and did not appear to notice either Copeland or his bag.

With the bus stop crowded with Saturday shoppers, Copeland knew people would be hurt, maimed and probably killed. He wondered whether to stay to watch the bomb going off, and thought he might even join in afterwards to help the injured. However, he later said that he had never fantasised about killing people: 'I don't get off on that. I fantasise about the chaos and disruption that's caused.' Although there was between thirty and forty minutes until the bomb was set to explode, Copeland waited only briefly before casually walking off, back along Brixton Road and into Acre Lane. He went into a mini-cab office and took a cab back to Clapham Junction. He returned by train to Farnborough, cycled home from the station and watched TV news that evening to see what happened.

The Head bag was noticed by the trader shortly after Copeland had left. At first he thought it belonged to someone waiting at the bus stop, but after five minutes, with no one standing next to it, he carried it round the corner into Electric Avenue and put it between two stalls where he could have a better look at the contents. He unzipped the bag and saw the two boxes. Others joined him and they saw that inside the plastic box were batteries and parts of an old alarm clock. Two coloured wires led into the cardboard box, which they saw was full of nails and shredded paper. They realised that it might be a bomb.

Calmly, another trader, George Jones, and a fourteen-year-old boy, Gary Shilling, carried the bag away from the stalls and put it on top of some pallets, propped against the brick wall at the side of the Iceland store. Gary suggested putting the bag inside a large metal rubbish container to deaden the impact of any explosion, but Denis Costello, an ex-soldier who has the fruit and vegetable stall on the other corner of Electric Avenue, shouted at him to leave it where it was as the rubbish bin could spread shrapnel. Panic was increasing, but no one could be sure that it was a bomb. The stallholders were reluctant to leave their pitches. One man, seeing what looked like a very nice new Head bag sitting on top of the pallets, went up to it, despite shouted warnings that it was a bomb. He removed the device and made off with the bag. Another person who ignored warnings was a cab driver who parked his vehicle next to the pallets. The Iceland security guard went to investigate the commotion, saw the bomb and ran back inside the store.

'He was like Corporal Jones out of *Dad's Army*, saying "Don't panic, don't panic",' said the store manager, Paul Maskill. 'I thought he was joking but he'd gone back outside and there was a bit of a crowd gathering, so I went outside.' To get a closer look, Mr Maskill went right up to the bomb, until his face was just inches away. 'People were saying to me that it must be a bomb,' he said, 'but my impression of a bomb is like six sticks of dynamite, tied together with an alarm clock on top. This was in a brown shoe box with a plastic bag on top of it. I didn't really believe it was a bomb, but judging people's reactions around me I felt the best thing to do was to dial 999.'

Mr Maskill ran back to the store, called the police, and then returned outside, joining others who were trying to keep people away from the device. Some refused to listen. 'For some reason, people were asking me questions about it,' said Mr Maskill. 'I seemed to be in charge of it. I was just praying for the police to turn up. I just couldn't wait for them to get there, to relieve me of this problem, this burden that I had.' Eventually the police arrived, but they parked on the main Brixton Road. Mr Maskill went to tell one of the officers where the bomb was. 'He got out of his car and followed me round the corner, and as we went round the corner, it exploded. It went very dark, and I could picture a flash, and I could smell a burning, like the after-effects of Guy Fawkes' night.'

The time was 5.28 pm and the blast was heard a mile away. The wall of the Iceland store took much of the bomb's impact. Hundreds of nails were sprayed around the area, injuring 42 people, including eighteen black or Asian people. Nails stuck in bodies. One four-inch nail penetrated the outer layer of the brain of a 23-month-old toddler, the son of a teacher. Two people lost eyes. There were several fractures. The injuries would have been greater, but for the cab parked by the bomb on the pallets. It was blown across the road, nails smashing into its side. Shards of glass from broken windows added to the injuries.

Paul Maskill remembers running from the scene, then coming to his senses inside the Iceland store: 'I had a moist feeling at the top of my legs and I thought I'd wet myself. I put my hands down there and they were covered in blood. I thought something's gone badly wrong down there. I looked at my trousers and they were all shredded as if in a cartoon on the television. Then I put my hands to my head, and I felt a nail sticking out of my head. I just couldn't comprehend what was going on.'

Mr Maskill was lucky to be alive. In hospital, he discovered he had been hit by a total of eight nails. In addition to the one in his head, there were three in one of his legs, one in his groin and three in his chest. He was off work for eight weeks and then returned to the store, but after three weeks he needed another five weeks off. Realising that it was emotionally too much to continue working in Brixton, he was transferred to another Iceland store. Months later, he was still suffering from the traumatic event. He suffered terrible guilt because his girlfriend is black and from Sierra Leone. She had fled that country's political violence for what she believed to be a more civilised England.

*   *   *

In the immediate aftermath of the bomb blast, no one could recall whether there had ever before been such a devastating, indiscriminate, no-warning attack in a predominately black neighbourhood. Given the confusion and the nature of the explosion, the responses were predictable. The Home Secretary Jack Straw described it as 'an outrageous and mindless act. Our sympathies go out to the injured and their families and to the families of the injured policemen.' Scotland Yard's then head of crime for south-west London, Commander Hugh Orde, visited the bomb scene and said: 'Whoever is responsible obviously has no regard for human life. I would consider them to be extremely dangerous.'

The Metropolitan Police rapidly put into motion a pre-planned procedure for dealing with such a major incident. A meeting of some of the top brass was convened, a senior investigating officer appointed, and the investigation was dubbed Operation Marathon. Such code names are chosen at random from a computer list. It was just coincidence that the one picked suggested that the investigation was to be long running.

The police had no clear idea of who had caused the

explosion, telling the media that they were keeping an open mind as to the bomber's motives and investigating all avenues. Over the next two days a number of different theories or motives were put forward, but most were quickly discarded.

Earlier that day, Brixton had played host to a demonstration against the conflict in Kosovo. It had been organised by the Lambeth 'Stop the War Committee', considered by some as being pro-Serbian. However, the Serbian Information Office was quick to point out that in all the years of conflict in the former Yugoslavia, Serbia 'hasn't broken a single pane of glass in this country'. Animal Liberationist campaigners were another group that came under suspicion, the theory being that they had targeted either the Iceland store or the Boots store across from it, on the other corner of the junction with the High Street. A group calling itself the Animal Rights Militia had made death threats against vivisectionists, while another group, the Justice Department, had said they, too, were prepared to harm people involved in animal experiments. The Animal Liberation Front spokesman, Robin Webb, said there was no reason for either store to be targeted, as Iceland had been the first supermarket to have a meat-free section and was the first to ban genetically modified foods, while Boots had sold its animal testing laboratories.

Other speculation included black-on-black gangland warfare. Parts of south London, particularly Brixton, had been hit by Yardie violence, usually turf wars over drugs, but such attacks were on individuals and not indiscriminate. There was no point in drug dealers using a bomb in a street to injure or kill. Guns are their favoured weapon to wipe out a rival or an informer or exact revenge for a deal that had gone wrong.

The IRA and other Republican groups were also quickly dismissed. Nail bombs had been a common IRA weapon in Northern Ireland and one had been famously used in

London, but that had been back in 1982 and the target had been military, when four Household Guards and seven horses were killed in Hyde Park. True, the IRA had in more recent years attacked commercial targets, but these had been spectacular, huge bombs in the City of London and Canary Wharf causing hundreds of millions of pounds' worth of damage. The IRA ceasefire was still on, and if that was to be broken, the belief was that it would be with another such spectacular bombing. A nail-bomb in a crowded street in a working-class area was simply not their style.

It was also thought unlikely that this was a copy cat act following the sentencing the week before of the Mardi Gra [sic] bomber Edgar Pearce. He had pleaded guilty to planting dozens of different explosive devices in London and the Home Counties over a three-year period. Although innocent members of the public had been injured, none very seriously, his campaign had been one of extortion against Barclays Bank and Sainsburys, with letters warning of further bombs if cash was not handed over. In the aftermath of the Brixton bomb, Iceland and Boots said they had received no such warnings or demands of any kind.

From the outset most speculation centred on a racist motive for the attack. The McPherson Report on the inquiry into the murder of the black teenager, Stephen Lawrence, was still provoking very strong reactions, particularly from those on the political extreme right who regarded the report's conclusions as outrageous. Could the bombing have been part of a racist backlash against the report, with Brixton targeted because it was viewed as a primarily black area? The black rights campaigner, Lee Jasper, was in no doubt. He told *The Guardian*: 'A nail-bomb in the Brixton market could only be intended to inflict the maximum damage possible to the black community. If this is an act of racial terrorism, it is the most severe escalation we have ever witnessed in the UK.' In the same newspaper, Gerry Gable, publisher of *Searchlight*, was even more accurate with his analysis. 'If this was racially motivated,' he said, 'it was the work of a loner. There is no far-right-wing group with the inclination or the capability to do this.'

With the extreme right the likely perpetrators, attention immediately focused on C18, which had coincidentally held a concert in Coventry that very same evening, with the London contingent leaving the capital in mid-afternoon. When news of the Brixton bombing spread at the concert, some were delighted. While few opposed such a racist act, the mood was one of mystification, with no one admitting to any prior knowledge that Brixton was going to get bombed.

The lack of information from the intelligence agencies was to prove a great hindrance to the police. Scotland Yard's Anti-Terrorist Branch had been put in charge of the investigation because it had 'the skills and expertise for dealing with this type of incident'. While this statement was essentially correct, all the more recent high-profile terrorist activity tackled by the branch had depended on back-up intelligence. Although the police maintained the open mind policy in terms of the possible motives behind the bomb, the gut feeling of Anti-Terrorist Branch officers was that it had indeed been a racial attack. But with little positive intelligence to work with, the detectives were stuck. The Anti-Terrorist Branch had dealt with mainly Irish terrorists and animal liberation groups, and even with those groups their role had been reactive, responding to events and depending largely on intelligence from other agencies. It had little or no experience of dealing with racists.

MI5, the Secret Service, and its operational arm, Special Branch, have the job of monitoring and gathering intelligence on extremist groups, ranging from the extreme right to the extreme left. There is supposed to be liaison with the police, the National Crime Squad and the National Criminal Intelligence Service (NCIS), but, in reality, the arrangements and procedures do not always work according to plan. A certain amount of rivalry, distrust and mutual contempt has developed between CID detectives and MI5. While Scotland Yard officially maintains that co-operation between the different agencies works well, this is not the case on the ground. This was particularly evident in the mid-1990s when the Anti-Terrorist Branch was grappling with IRA teams intent on causing spectacular explosions in the capital.

MI5 and Special Branch were obtaining very good information about IRA active service units being sent to Britain from both Ireland and Northern Ireland. The IRA men were followed and addresses they used were kept under observation and sometimes bugged, but often the Anti-Terrorist Branch were either kept in the dark entirely or not told until a late stage of the operation. This was for two reasons. First came the need to protect the identity of informants — if information leaked out prematurely that MI5 or Special Branch knew, for example, that a particular IRA man had moved secretly to Britain under a false identity, then the hunt would be on by the IRA to find out who had tipped off the authorities. Not only would the informant's life be in danger, but a good source of information would be terminated. Much better, so the thinking went, was to act on a need-to-know basis, so that information would be limited to as few people as possible. Second, there was a fundamental difference in tactics — MI5 preferred to follow and monitor Irish terrorists, letting them run, in order to find out who their contacts or helpers were on the mainland. The police would not be told until their help was needed, either when it became clear that an actual bombing was being mounted, rather than explosives or guns simply being moved, or because so many IRA men were being watched that it had become too much for MI5 and Special Branch to handle on their own and more eyes were needed.

Problems would arise as soon as Anti-Terrorist Branch police joined an operation. Their inclination was to arrest as many of the terrorists as they could and charge them with conspiracy to cause explosions, but that was impossible without proper evidence and what had been gathered by MI5 or Special Branch was often unusable in court. Although their 'watchers', often ex-soldiers who had served in Northern Ireland, kept surveillance notes of a suspect's movements, these were not up to police standards and could be picked apart by clever defence lawyers. MI5 notes were primarily for intelligence purposes and not designed to provide solid evidence that would stand up in court. It also did not help police prosecutions when it emerged in court that some of the MI5 watchers also had criminal records. The police believed that sloppy MI5 and Special Branch methods had resulted in the acquittals of guilty men or in failure to prosecute in the first place. They resented having to pick up the pieces of what they viewed as inadequate investigations. For its part, MI5 did not particularly mind if all that resulted was the disruption of a terrorist operation, the stopping of a bombing or other outrage, rather than arrests. Although they failed to understand police frustration, MI5 consistently came up with good information about the IRA and other Republican groups.

However, as far as the extreme right wing was concerned, it was a different matter. MI5 and Special Branch tended to concentrate on gathering intelligence to aid the policing of demonstrations and to gain information on fund raising. But their efforts on even this relatively simple kind of operation were sometimes woefully inadequate. One middle-ranking detective relates that it was Special Branch's job to advise operational police in advance on the size of forthcoming street demonstrations. 'Getting such information before demonstrations is important because you can then plan to have the right number of police there, in case of trouble,' he said, 'but often they couldn't even get that right. They would say ten thousand people were expected and only five hundred would turn up. At others, they'd estimate only a few and no trouble, and there'd be thousands there and violence with counter-demonstrators. If they couldn't get that kind of thing right, why expect them to come up with anything useful on a right-wing bombing?'

The general MI5 assessment was that Britain's racist organisations were not sufficiently organised to present a major threat to society. London Special Branch was even more scathing of the extreme right's ability to cause trouble. In a series of quarterly bulletins on political extremism produced over the past few years, it has repeatedly dismissed the threat from the extreme right. MI5 did, however, view C18 slightly differently and while it ignored the rest of the right wing, it kept a close eye on this former BNP-linked group. Although C18 was considerably smaller and less influential than it had been in the mid-1990s, when it was attracting whole branches away from the BNP and running the highly lucrative Blood and Honour music scene, it remained a threat.

While three Danish C18 supporters were imprisoned for their part in the letter-bomb campaign in January 1997, police were unable to gather enough evidence to prosecute Will Browning, the man alleged in Denmark to have masterminded the campaign. Will Browning's involvement in the racist right began as a teenage skinhead in Jersey. The only child of a broken home, Browning was first arrested for fighting at the age of ten. Within a year he was in trouble again, this time being sent to a secure school where he spent most of the following four years. At the age of sixteen he moved to London, becoming an apprentice in his father's carpentry business, but violence was never far away, and at the age of nineteen, he was jailed for three years for attacking a gay man in King's Cross.

His aggression propelled him to the fore of C18 and saw him involved in many of the group's most vicious attacks. In 1992, he ambushed a left-winger who was flyposting, stabbing him repeatedly in the back and legs with a screwdriver. Two years later he tried to stab an anti-racist football fan in the face, again with a screwdriver, this only weeks after he had led a C18 attack on a group of Chelsea fans, which had left four people in need of hospital treatment. Nor were his targets confined to Britain. In October 1995 Browning was alleged to have led a ten-man C18 team to Sweden with the intention of attacking a leading activist in a rival Nazi group. Though the target fled before the British Nazis arrived, Browning was undeterred. The following year Nakaba claimed that Browning asked him to accompany him to Gothenburg to shoot the Swede.

Browning was obsessed with the idea of race war. In 1996 he and a small team became increasingly frustrated with what they perceived to be the lack of activity of the C18 leadership, which was now scorned by much of the right for being a talking shop. Browning hatched the Danish bomb plot, and although the bomb campaign failed, he soon had a new target for his anger. When close friend Chris Castle was stabbed to death in a planned ambush at the hands of deposed C18 leader Charlie Sargent, Browning promised vengeance. When it was revealed that Sargent had been passing information on to the police, Browning swore not only to get even with Sargent, but to target the establishment.

The post-Sargent C18 was radically different from what it had been before. Declaring himself a 'left-winger', Browning claimed that C18 was now the true revolutionary anti-establishment group. Caring little about the rest of the far right, whom he referred to as 'nonces, misfits and weirdos', he abandoned previous recruitment policies and thoughts of far-right dominance. People were either with him or against him. This strange political stance alienated him from the rest of the far right and, one by one, groups and individuals distanced themselves from C18. None of this seemed to bother Browning and in the autumn of 1998 he was again alleged to have started planning a bombing campaign. In October, British police received a tip-off from German intelligence that Browning and another C18 member had travelled to Germany to discuss a possible bombing campaign with hardline German Nazis. According to the information received, Browning wanted the Germans to gather together the materials, while a British C18 supporter would be flown over to assemble the bombs.

Adding to police concerns over C18 were the group's growing links with international violent extremists. In Sweden the group formed an alliance with the Aryan Brotherhood, a prison-based organisation involving several people convicted of murder. Its leader was Nicolas Lodfahl, a strong supporter of C18 and friend of Will Browning. In the summer of 1998, while on weekend leave from prison, he sent a bomb to the Swedish Interior Minister. In Northern Ireland, C18 had established some low-level links with the Loyalist Volunteer Force (LVF), an extreme Loyalist paramilitary group. In July 1998 nearly thirty C18 supporters travelled to the LVF heartland in Portadown to celebrate 12 July, the most important date in the Protestant calendar.

As a result of rising concern about its activities, the homes of fourteen C18 supporters, including two soldiers, were raided in an MI5-orchestrated operation only weeks before the Brixton bomb. The raids were part of a concerted effort to disrupt any plans the group harboured of causing trouble. Browning was not arrested and the authorities hoped that seeds of doubt would be sown about his reliability.

A couple of weeks later, as a confrontation with Serbia over Kosovo loomed, Browning and two C18 colleagues attempted to travel to Slovakia where they were to use a Blood and Honour concert as cover for an international Nazi meeting with affiliated groups from Scandinavia, Germany, Serbia and Slovakia. Browning never made it to the concert. He and the other English Nazis were stopped by Austrian police on their arrival in Vienna and handed over to waiting MI5 officers. Browning was told in no uncertain terms that while he might have got away with the Danish plot, any repeat attempt would be stopped. Though acting in a foreign country, MI5 was working in close partnership with the Austrians and the Slovakians. When Browning and his group reached the Austrian/Slovakian border later that evening, police prevented them from entering. The harassment of Browning continued. A few days after his return from Austria, MI5 officers sent him a bunch of flowers.

Although nothing emerged from the raids that gave any indication that C18 was planning a Brixton-type outrage, and with little other useful intelligence coming in, the possibility of C18 being behind the bombing was not ruled out completely, although it was considered highly unlikely. While there was an initial fear that Browning might have been wound up sufficiently to carry out a bombing campaign, the assessment was that this was unlikely. Police surveillance on him in the months leading up to April 1999 had been extensive and Brixton did not seem to fit in with Browning's intentions of striking the establishment. Much more likely, the police reasoned, was that the bombing had been done by a renegade member or small cell of activists operating independently of the leadership.

After the Brixton bomb, the police appealed to the local black community for help. Among those who responded was Mike Franklin, chair of the Lambeth Police consultative committee and vice-chair of the London-wide police racial advisory group, set up in the aftermath of the Stephen Lawrence murder. This group liaises with Scotland Yard's CO24 group, the Racial and Violent Crime Task Force, headed by the popular Deputy Assistant Commissioner John Grieve, who had previously been in charge of the ATB (Anti-Terrorist Branch). Mr Franklin attended several briefings and news conferences over the bombings and was surprised that Mr Grieve was not present at any of them. With the ATB taking charge it seems that CO24 was kept away from the centre of the investigation.

Mr Franklin took the view that the priority was to catch the person or people responsible for the Brixton bomb, rather than speculate at that stage about the motive. That could be left until arrests had been made. However, he also believed that the police should be as open as possible, and argued that the public should be told of any claims of responsibility. In fact, there was a series of such phone calls, strengthening beliefs that extreme right-wing elements had carried out the bombing. The first of these came 36 hours after the explosion when a 999 operator took a call from someone purporting to be from C18. Intriguingly, the call was traced to a phone box on Well Hall Road, Eltham, in south-east London, where Stephen Lawrence had been stabbed to death. It was close to another phone box used by Stephen's friend, Duwayne Brooks, when he called police after the stabbing.

At a news conference on the Monday following the bombing, the head of the Anti-Terrorist Branch, Alan Fry, would not be drawn on the phone call, simply repeating that he was keeping an open mind, but adding that there was no evidence or intelligence to support the claim. Later in the news conference he appealed for anyone with any kind of information to contact the Anti-Terrorist Branch Hotline. Then he returned to their main problem: 'We have had no intelligence, before the events of Saturday afternoon, and we have no current intelligence.'

By the next day, still without that key intelligence, the lone racist bomber theory was gaining strength as Mr Fry told the BBC's *Crimewatch* programme that the person responsible could have been a renegade member of C18. The same programme announced the offer of a reward of £10,000 for anyone with information leading to the arrest and conviction of those responsible. By the end of the week the reward money had increased to £30,000, comprising offers of £10,000 each from the Metropolitan Police, Lambeth Council and *The Voice* newspaper.

After the first phone call claiming responsibility, three others quickly followed, but police refused to give any details, having no idea whether they were genuine or from other groups or individuals jumping on the bandwagon. Also undisclosed at the time was that other information had been passed to the police prior to the Brixton bomb, but it seems that its importance and possible link was not recognised until some time later, when it was eventually passed to the ATB.

Detectives learned that a chilling warning from a group calling itself the White Wolves had been sent to ethnic minority newspapers and magazines as well as some left-wing figures. The newspaper *Eastern Eye* received a message two days before the Brixton bomb. Crudely stencilled, it was headed 'Statement by the Command Council of the White Wolves', and began: 'Notice is hereby given that all non-whites and Jews (defined by blood, not religion) must permanently leave the British Isles before the year is out. Jews and non-whites who remain after 1999 has ended will be exterminated. When the clock strikes midnight on 31/12/99 the White Wolves will begin to howl, the wolves begin to hunt. You have been warned. HAIL BRITANNIA.'

Although Copeland was to deny knowledge of the White Wolves, he adopted their belief, shared by others on the extreme right and by some religious sects, that the dawn of the new millennium would signal death and destruction.

The White Wolves letter was not the first example of racist hate mail. Abusive letters, circulars and death threats have long been a part of far-right activity in this country. Frank Bruno's mother was the victim of one such hate campaign. In 1995 she began receiving letters of abuse, shortly after her name and address appeared in *The Stormer*, a tatty newsletter produced by West London C18. This was soon followed by phone calls and death threats. Two leading C18 followers, Mark Atkinson and Robin Gray, were later sent to prison for producing *The Stormer*, with the judge concluding that the two men could be held responsible for this hate campaign. A couple of years earlier, several hundred anti-semitic letters were circulated to Jews across the country around the Jewish New Year. Sometimes hate mail was part of a co-ordinated campaign by far-right groups, while on other occasions it was the work of a lone individual who held a grudge against a political or ethnic opponent in their locality. The co-ordinated campaigns seemed to come in peaks and troughs. The emergence of C18 in 1992 heralded a wave of letters and threats to political opponents, trade unionists, black and Asian people. Another wave of hate mail was dispatched in 1995 when C18 activity was at its peak.

Finding those behind the White Wolves letter proved difficult for the police. It was obvious that the culprit or culprits had some involvement in the right wing — the letters were sent to specific targets, which could only have been of significance to those active on the right. Among the recipients were *Searchlight* and the *Campaign Against Racism and Fascism*, two specialist publications campaigning against racism. Another, a local East Midlands newspaper called the *Mansfield Chad*, would have only proved a target for those who remembered its front page exposés of local far-right violence back in 1993.

However, there was no known organisation by the name of White Wolves. One possibility was a section of C18 that went under the name White Wolves. It had been established in 1995 by Del O'Connor, a leading figure in the organisation. He had come up with the name White Wolves C18 as a means of distinguishing the northern group from the London group. 'It was to give us our own identity,' he told people around him. T-shirts, stickers and even a magazine bore its name. However, it was still part of C18 and police information discounted its involvement in the bombing.

Del O'Connor had been active in Nazi politics since the skinhead heydays of the 1970s. Born in south London, he grew up among the right-wing following of the Chelsea Headhunters and skinhead bands from across London. He bypassed the NF, preferring the more militant British

Movement and in doing so involved himself in violent attacks against his political opponents. Like many of the others in the far right, O'Connor had been bullied at school and his involvement in politics gave him an opportunity for payback.

By the 1980s, O'Connor had become a leading figure on the skinhead music scene. A very close friend of Ian Stuart Donaldson, the lead singer of Skrewdriver, O'Connor was at one time the leader of Skrewdriver Security. By the late 1980s he had joined the Ku-Klux-Klan, eventually heading its security section. His involvement was to be shortlived — the KKK leader, Alan Beshella, was exposed in the press as a convicted child molester and the KKK folded soon after. Disillusioned, O'Connor switched allegiances to C18 in 1993, shortly after coming out of prison where he had served a two-year sentence for violence. Aside from organising activities in the north, O'Connor played a pivotal role in establishing C18's links across Scandinavia. He was, however, never far from trouble. In the summer of 1997 he was arrested and imprisoned for a vicious assault on a bouncer in a Swedish bar.

For the police investigating the nail bombings, eliminating O'Connor from their enquiries was proving difficult. He had disappeared from his Wigan address at the beginning of the year and had not been heard of since. It was rumoured that he was in the USA, but finding him there was not straightforward. More worryingly, it appeared that he had split from C18 after becoming increasingly disillusioned around the time of his disappearance. While it was thought unlikely, the police were not discounting the possibility that he was the lone wolf behind the bombings. MI5 would have remembered that O'Connor accompanied Browning to Germany six months before where a bombing campaign was discussed.

Further evidence that the police had to look beyond C18 came only hours after the C18 caller claimed responsibility.

In at least one, and possibly two, separate phone calls, one to a press agency, someone purporting to be from the White Wolves claimed the bomb. Two days later, *Searchlight* received a call from a telephone box in Whitehall, saying that the bomb was the work of the White Wolves and not C18. The caller was young, his voice squeaky and rushed. After delivering his one sentence he hung up. Again, no doubt a coincidence, but on the day the call was received, Copeland was working no more than a few hundred metres away on the Jubilee Line extension at Westminster Underground station. The next day *Searchlight* and other organisations received their second White Wolves stencilled letter. Written in the same format as the first, it read: 'C18 did not carry out the Brixton bombing. We, the White Wolves, did.'

By the end of the first week following the bombing, and despite much speculation about the motive, the police were no closer to finding those responsible. However, they had been making greater progress with conventional police work, which had started immediately after the Brixton bomb went off.

The market traders and others who had handled or seen the device before it exploded gave police good descriptions of what appeared to be a fairly simply constructed bomb. That view was confirmed by forensic examination of the debris, which included batteries, wiring and fragments from an ordinary manual Acctim brand alarm clock that had been adjusted so that it could be used as a timer. A total of 1,244 nails of different sizes were recovered, some stuck in victims and others embedded in wood and other objects in the market. Traces of the explosive residue showed that it had been firework material rather than the high explosive or the sugar-and-fertiliser mix favoured by organised terrorist groups. Fragments of the device were sent off for a much more detailed examination by forensic scientists, but that would take time. In the early days, all the evidence on the ground matched what had been gathered elsewhere — the police were dealing with an extreme right-wing breakaway group or an individual.

The big break for the police came with the hold-all containing the bomb. If the device had stayed inside the bag it would have been blown to bits. Luckily for the police and the public, the bomb had been removed and the bag stolen. The man who had taken the bag as it lay on a pile of pallets propped up against Iceland's wall in Electric Avenue was shocked after the explosion. It had gone off shortly after he had run off and, uninjured, he had had a lucky escape. He realised amid all the confusion and panic, that he might appear to have been more involved in the bombing than he was, so he went back to the scene and left the hold-all on the pavement outside Boots, alerting people that it had contained the bomb.

The police appeal for information about anyone seen with such a bag came to nothing. It looked fairly new, but tracing its retail origins would be a difficult job, not least because it could not be easily determined that it was a genuine Head hold-all, rather than an easily obtainable counterfeit one. If it had been handled by only one person other than the bomber, the bag could have revealed good fingerprint evidence, but too many people had touched it and it was thought likely that the bomber would have had the sense to wear gloves or to have wiped the bag clean before planting it. However, the bag was to provide a vital clue when tied in with that other increasingly used police tool, closed circuit television (CCTV). In the mid 1990s several IRA bombers had been jailed as a result of being caught on CCTV cameras that linked them with the scenes of explosions or points on their route to the bomb targets. The Mardi Gra bomber, Edgar Pearce, had been picked up on a CCTV camera actually planting a device next to a bus stop at a shopping centre.

In a bid to crack down on street crime and drug dealing, Brixton has one of the country's largest concentrations of

CCTV cameras. More than thirty community-funded cameras cover Brixton streets, controlled and monitored twenty four hours a day by operators in a large room in Lambeth Town Hall. If they see anything suspicious on one of their screens, the security staff can move the cameras remotely and zoom in to obtain a closer look. At least three cameras cover the bomb scene, and everything is automatically recorded on tape. Quite separately, many other premises have their own CCTV cameras and video recorders, including Brixton Underground Station, just a few yards from the bomb scene. McDonald's has three cameras, two of which pick up people on the pavement, while the Iceland store also has a camera pointing outside.

Within hours of the bombing, police had obtained all the recordings for that Saturday afternoon. The expectation was that the bomber must have been caught on one or more of them. It was simply a question of viewing all the tapes and looking for someone carrying a dark hold-all bearing green Head logos, and then, having singled out the suspect bomber, releasing the tape with a public appeal. But the exercise was to prove more difficult than first thought.

There were several hundreds of hours of tape to view. Not only would this take up hundreds of man-hours, but the quality of the images was far from ideal. Many cameras were at rooftop level and this, coupled with the constant re-using of tapes, resulted in the images of people at street level being ill-defined. None the less, viewing commenced with officers looking for anyone with a dark-coloured hold-all. As it had been the main shopping day of the week, many people were carrying bags. Identifying hold-alls as opposed to other bags was difficult and finding bags with Head logos was out of the question because of the blurred or indistinct images. There was also the problem that bags can be carried in different ways. Because the streets near the market were crowded it was difficult to see anyone carrying a bag by hand because other people were in the way, and it was equally difficult to see someone carrying a bag over their shoulder unless the camera was positioned behind them. If the latter was the case, it was impossible to get a useful facial image. Several possible suspects were seen on the videos and tracked from one camera position to the next, but most were eliminated, either being seen to have left the area with their bags, or not to have been anywhere near the market.

Concentrating viewing on where the bag had been left was initially impossible because detectives remained uncertain exactly when or where the bag had been left. Trying to work out its movements backwards from the pallets where it had exploded was difficult, since none of those who had handled it wanted to admit that they had done so because it could have appeared that they had been trying to steal it. Eventually detectives succeeded in tracking the bag back from the pallets to the bus stop near the Iceland entrance.

But there was no guarantee that the bomber had left the hold-all there. It had been moved so often that no one could be sure it had not been moved before being left near the bus stop. And if the bomber had planted it there and then left by bus, it would probably be impossible to identify him because the camera covering that area was on the other side of the street and the view of the pavement would be obscured by the bus. There was another problem. A bus had broken down nearby, which made it even more difficult to see anything, or anyone, in the vicinity of the stop. Nevertheless, officers concentrated their viewing on what they had of that area, and they struck lucky with pictures from the Iceland video.

The Iceland camera is attached to a large monitor screen just inside the entrance to the store and pointing outside. Anyone going into the store or passing by the entrance can see themselves on the large screen. The camera picks up some of the pavement immediately outside the door, but it does not cover the area to the right where the bomb bag was planted. Hoping that the bomber had not left by bus, but had walked past the store entrance, the tape was studied intently. Many people had crossed the doorway before the explosion, and although none of them was carrying a hold-all, one officer spotted someone on the screen nearly an hour before the bomb went off.

It was a young man walking by wearing a distinctive white- or cream-coloured baseball cap. The officer had viewed other videos and remembered seeing that same baseball cap on someone carrying a hold-all on his back. Now the Iceland video, timed at 16.32 pm, showed the young man without a bag . Where had the bag gone? Could this man be the bomber? All the video footage shot in Brixton was scoured for anyone wearing a white baseball cap. Such a person was picked out several times at different locations and there was no doubt about it. He had been seen carrying a bag around the area for nearly an hour before he was suddenly seen without it at the Iceland entrance. On one tape he was seen walking down Electric Avenue past the Iceland store and the market stalls with the bag on his back, possibly trying to decide where to leave it. He had not been spotted at first on that tape because he had been filmed from the front and it is virtually impossible to see that he has a bag on his back. Both his hands are free and it is only with freeze-framing of the tape that a bag strap is seen across his chest.

The police had their suspect. But there were some puzzles. Detectives could not understand why he had walked around the area for so long beforehand. He must have known it was likely to be covered by video cameras, and the chances of being picked up by them would increase the longer he stayed in the area, but he appeared to have taken no steps to avoid them, even the very obvious one at the Iceland entrance. How had he travelled to and from the area? Was he wearing some kind of disguise? The answer to the last question would have to wait. The pictures obtained of the suspect were not good enough to release as part of a police appeal to the public for information. They were too fuzzy and had to be enhanced. The best place in the world for that was at NASA in the USA. The operation to fly the tapes to and from the USA was being prepared.

Then, the second bomb went off.

6

Brick Lane and Panic

'It's great, isn't it? It's all happening.'
Copeland on the murder of the BBC TV presenter
Jill Dando and his first two explosions

'Our main line of attack must be on the immigrants themselves,
the Black and Asian ghettos. If this is done regularly,
effectively and brutally, the aliens will respond
by attacking Whites at random, forcing them off the fence
and into self defence. This will begin the spiral of violence
which will force the Establishment's hand on the race issue.'
White Wolves document

IN THE DAYS FOLLOWING THE BRIXTON BOMB, Copeland not only prepared for his next attack but added to his collection of horrific pictures. He pinned up on the wall in his room some of the photos and newspaper reports of the Brixton blast, among them a large reproduction of the X-ray photograph of the toddler who had a nail embedded in his skull. This photograph had been issued by police, and Copeland must have smiled at the headline — 'Who did this?' Appealing for information, the police release went on: 'Are you suspicious of anyone or have you heard the slightest rumour about who may be responsible? There is a substantial reward for information which leads to the arrest and conviction of those responsible for this vicious atrocity.'

The reward became a topic of conversation between Copeland and the German tenant, Friedrich, who had moved into the small front bedroom above the front door in 25 Sunnybank Road in March. Friedrich was on the teaching staff of a local school. He hardly ever saw the other tenants, Alison and Graham, but had talked a lot with Copeland in the evenings, although he had never seen inside his room. 'I soon realised that he had strong aversions against such persons who were not like him — foreigners, mainly those with dark skins. His aversion was also against northern English people. In my opinion, he was a Nazi, because he was against every group to which he did not belong. When I described for him the persecution of minorities – Jews and other thinking persons – he did not yield. Despite his obvious aversion against minorities, no preparedness towards violence was recognisable in him. I found him very ready to be of help, and we also talked about things which interest me in London. I would describe him as unemotional.'

Friedrich cannot remember if he saw Copeland on the day of the Brixton bomb, but recalls that they talked about it two or three days later. 'Dave and I talked of the reward. Jokingly, he mentioned that we could each accuse the other to obtain the reward. He was very interested in any news of the Brixton attack on television, but he did not give any opinion on it, apart from saying later that such events can happen in multi-cultural areas.' Friedrich moved out of number 25 on the following Saturday. Asked later if he remembered any unusual incidents, he stated: 'For about ten days before there had been a strong smell of excrement near Dave's room. Due to the unfriendly, unhygienic and unclean conditions, I decided to move out. Dave was not the main reason for my decision.'

The Brixton bomb also came up in conversation with Copeland's 'mate' Anthony, who appears to have been the person closest to him in Hampshire at this time. Copeland had called at his home on the Thursday, and Anthony recalled: 'I brought up the fact that the Brixton bomb had gone off. I seem to remember he said that they deserved it, but he never said or did anything to suggest that he was in any way responsible. He was calm and expressionless. He only stayed about ten minutes at most. Before he left, he said he would call me again the next week, but I never heard from him again.'

During the day before, Wednesday, 21 April, Copeland went to the Littlewoods store in Farnborough and bought his second bomb hold-all, a Reebok. He had always planned a series of bombs to go off at about the same time on successive Saturdays. But he only decided to plant his second bomb at Brick Lane, in east London, on the Friday, the day before. He regarded Brick Lane as the heart of the Asian community, just as Brixton was the symbolic centre for the West Indian community. While he had never been to the area himself, he had seen a TV news report that said people there wanted to call the area Bangla Town, just as the Chinese district in London was called Chinatown.

The Brick Lane bomb was built in exactly the same way as the Brixton bomb. Copeland filled another foot-long drainage pipe section with firework explosive the night before, let it dry and then assembled the rest of the device in the morning. Early in the Saturday afternoon he set off by bicycle from the house in Sunnybank Road for Farnborough Station, wearing the same clothes as the previous Saturday, light-coloured baseball cap, dark bomber jacket, green combat trousers and black boots. But halfway there he realised he had forgotten his train pass. He returned home and, because of the hitch, re-primed the bomb for half an hour later, 6.00 pm instead of 5.30 pm. He also used a phone box near the house to call for a taxi, using the name Cooper. The call was logged at 3.10 pm and the driver apologised for being a few minutes late, but Copeland told him it did not matter. Getting into the cab, Copeland hit the door with his heavy bomb bag and apologised. When they arrived at the station, Copeland gave the driver a big tip, cheerfully saying, 'Keep the change, mate.'

The week before, Copeland had got off the London train at Clapham Junction, but on this Saturday he continued to the terminus at Waterloo. He withdrew £200 from a cash machine and then went to a lavatory at the station, paying 20p. Although he only wanted to urinate, his homophobia and fear that others would look at his genitals made him go into a cubicle. Then he headed outside and asked the taxi driver at the head of the station cab rank to take him to Shoreditch Station, close to Brick Lane. The driver did not like the look of him, but had to carry him as he was for hire and at the front of the taxi queue. Copeland held tightly on to his bag during the journey. The fare was £4.20 and, paying with a £5 note damp with sweat, he again told the driver to keep the change.

There was a hitch in Copeland's planning. The famous Brick Lane market is held on Sundays, not Saturdays, a mistake he realised only when he arrived in the area. He had expected throngs of people, but found very few around. He saw a few blond-haired tourists, Germans or Swedes, who he thought must have made the same mistake as him. Walking about, he wondered whether to abort his mission, detach the wires and go home to return the next day when his bomb would be bound to catch Asians. But time was moving on and with no obvious place where he could easily dismantle the device, he decided to abandon it. He chose Hanbury Street, just off Brick Lane. Seeing two vans there, parked close together, he walked between them so he could not be seen, and dumped the bag.

For the first time, he decided to call the authorities. He intended claiming the bomb as the work of the Nazi group, C18. He found a telephone box, dialled 999, but then, instead of talking, punched in the digits 2-1-8, the number 2 representing the initial letter C. What the operator made of this, if anything, is not known. However, the call is a further demonstration that there was more to Copeland than being a simple lone bomber.

Once again, Copeland did not stay to witness the effects of his bomb, choosing instead to take a taxi back to Soho in central London. By now he had decided that his next target would be homosexuals, his other great hate after blacks and Asians. He walked around Soho, deciding where would be the best place for his third bomb and decided to get rid of his light-coloured cap, stuffing it behind the water cistern in a cubicle of a public lavatory. Then he returned home via Waterloo.

In Hanbury Street, just as in Brixton the week before, someone spotted the new Reebok bag. Gerald Lynch had driven to the area at 4.30 pm, parking his red Ford Sierra outside the police station in Brick Lane. While searching for a restaurant, he saw the bag lying on the ground in front of a white Ford transit van outside No. 32 Hanbury Street. With no obvious owner, he thought it had been lost, so he picked it up and decided to take it to the police station. However, the police station was closed, so he put the heavy bag in the boot of his car, opened it up and looked inside. He saw a cardboard box filled with nails, on top of which was a sandwich type plastic box. It looked to him as though the bag belonged to a workman. He decided to walk to the nearby Leman Street Police Station, but because the bag was so heavy he left it in the boot of his car. He intended to tell police what he had found, inviting them to return with him to collect it. Unfortunately, Leman Street Police Station was also closed. It was only then that Mr Lynch remembered the Brixton bomb explosion the week before and decided to telephone the police. He dialled 999 on his mobile phone from outside Leman Street Police Station. The call was logged at 5.58 pm.

Although the two police stations were closed, the police had extra patrols out in areas viewed as vulnerable, including Brick Lane. A message was sent to two officers, PCs Boon and Jamieson, to drive to meet Mr Lynch at Leman Street. Just before they received the call, the bomb went off in his car.

The explosion in Brick Lane blew the Sierra apart. Nearby vehicles and buildings were damaged and windows of shops, offices and restaurants blown in. Fortunately, because there was no one next to the car, the injuries were less severe than at Brixton. Even so, several people were cut by flying glass and suffered from hearing damage, including perforated eardrums. Six people, all Bangladeshis, were taken to hospital but only one was detained overnight.

Emdad Talukdar, who works in the Asian studies department of an educational charity, was lucky. He had been very close to the car, but, after seeing a friend walking along Brick Lane, he went over to greet her. Moving away from the car may well have saved his life. He remembers a big flash, and a thunderous roar: 'I saw the car jump four feet in the air. The boot lid flew up about 25 feet high. There was a huge fire and it went dark with the smoke. We ran into a side street and then I realised I had been hit. My head was bleeding.' His friend, who was also his doctor, pulled out a large shard of glass embedded in his head, and stemmed the flow of blood. Dr Hosne Haq said later: 'We thought we were about to die. There was glass flying everywhere and a huge fire. I thought a building would collapse on us.'

The windows of two restaurants were blown in. Shahid

Ahmed was serving in the Sweet and Spicey: 'All the windows at the front of the restaurant shattered and I went deaf. I ran down into the basement to get away. I have never been so frightened.' One of the customers, Eddie Ezzra said: 'The explosion threw us off our feet. I heard someone say, there could be another bomb, so we all ran away.' The explosion also ripped through the Café Naz. 'There was masses of fire and smoke,' said the owner, Muquim Ahmed, who was with his wife Rashmi and young daughter, Monique. 'My wife fainted at the shock of it all and my daughter was screaming hysterically. We were lucky not to be injured.'

*   *   *

The Brick Lane explosion dashed any hopes that the Brixton bombing had been a one-off. It also meant that any lingering doubts about the motives behind the first bomb were dispelled. The second bomb, coming exactly a week after Brixton, meant that minority communities were under attack from the same group of racists or the same individual. But the police lacked leads.

While they were no closer to finding the authors of the White Wolves letters, Del O'Connor had been all but eliminated from their enquiries, as information received back from the FBI seemed to indicate that he was still in the USA. However, the day after the Brick Lane bomb, a new lead had emerged in the press. Towards the end of 1994 a publication carrying the imprint White Wolves had been circulated anonymously among far-right activists. The 15-page document carried a chilling call for race war, and its recommended course of action was alarmingly similar to the two bombings. It was a document unlike any that had been circulated for many years. While groups such as C18 had regularly advocated race war, the authors of this seemed far more serious. The document lacked the immature abuse that regularly characterised C18 material and instead was a reflective and honest assessment of the far right's failure over the past 20 years, containing language rarely seen on the right.

'Every nation has the absolute right to defend itself, its land, its identity,' it read. 'A nation is a living thing, not just a collection of individuals, and just as a nation can thrive so it can die. So who are we to target? Not necessarily the politicians or media who have waged the undeclared war. They are paid well for their treachery and are, in the main, replaceable. Besides, the public wouldn't understand such actions as relevant to them, so wouldn't take sides.

'Instead, our main line of attack must be on the immigrants themselves, the Black and Asian ghettos. If this is done regularly, effectively and brutally, the aliens will respond by attacking Whites at random, forcing them off the fence and into self defence. This will begin the spiral of violence which will force the Establishment's hand on the race issue.

'The British people will fight, but not if we offer them only the soft voting option. WE must point them in the right direction by taking the necessary action to start the spiral of violence which will ultimately include even the reluctant, forcing them to fight. The victory will come from them once they have no other option, but the initiative must come from us. There are a dozen Belfasts and a hundred Londonderrys in Britain today, they're just waiting for a spark.

'It is true that the immigrants are innocent of any recognised crime individually, but collectively they make up an invading army which threatens the birthright of children and the unborn generations of our folk. Their presence spells the death of our people, so if they must be forced out with extreme violence, then so be it.'

The White Wolves document detailed possible attacks and counter-surveillance tactics. It advised supporters to form cells of two to five people, but to continue life as normal. 'If you are already a member of an established Nationalist party, stay with it. A sudden exodus of a group of keen members prior to [White Wolves] activities would be a dead giveaway.'

This document was classic leaderless resistance and reflected the growing influence of US white supremacist ideas, which had permeated British Nazi thinking since the early 1990s. The document concluded: 'We do not believe that we alone can win the Race War, but we can start it!'

There were alarming parallels between the document and the bombings. The choice of Brixton and Brick Lane as targets were of the sort recommended in the White Wolves document. The theory of the 'spiral of violence' was obviously in the mind of the bomber(s) and the 'simple clock-timer bomb' diagram drawn in the document bore some similarities to the timing device used in both bombings. It was not impossible, police thought, that the perpetrators of the bombings had been planning this for years.

If no one was caught, there would inevitably be another bombing. No one had died in the first two explosions, although the Brixton injuries had been horrendous. If these bombings continued, someone would eventually be killed. But which area would be hit next? Would it be Southall, home to the Punjabis, or the Jewish community of Golders Green? People who had studied Nazi groups knew that homosexuals could also be next on the list. That view was shared by some groups of gays, who over the years had also received threats from the extreme right. Some contacted Scotland Yard and were alarmed to learn that the Anti-Terrorist Branch had not considered that gays were at risk. Journalists on the weekly *Pink Paper* decided to issue a warning to the gay community to be on its guard and look out for possible bombs. It went to press on the Tuesday evening with a front page devoted to the story, under the headline 'Gays in Fascist Bomb Alert'.

Panic began to set in, and it was not confined to the

London area. Minority groups in other parts of the country, fearing that the bomber would be finding London too difficult, wondered whether they would be next on the list. They contacted their MPs for help. Downing Street and Home Office pressure on the police increased.

Anti-Terrorist Branch detectives were still hampered by the lack of good intelligence from MI5 and Special Branch. Informants in the extreme right-wing groups had failed to come up with any useful leads. Police hopes of catching whoever was responsible for the Brixton bomb were resting on the video pictures of the suspect, which were being enhanced in the USA. It was hoped they would be ready for release as part of a public appeal by the end of the week. Meanwhile, just as they had done with Brixton, police set about methodically gathering evidence from the Brick Lane bomb.

They had a very good description of the bag and its deadly contents from Gerald Lynch, who had taken it to the police station after finding it in Hanbury Street. He said it had been a black Reebok sports bag with red handles, containing a sandwich-type plastic box and a cardboard box with hundreds of nails inside. It matched the description of the device given by people who had seen the Brixton bomb before it went off, and confirmation that the devices were virtually identical came from forensic examination of the debris at Brick Lane. This showed the device had contained the same kind of fireworks explosives and an Acctim brand alarm clock had again been used as a timer.

Once again, however, police could find no witnesses who had seen anyone carrying such a Reebok sports bag. As to when it had been left in Hanbury Street, one witness, Harry Mansfield, was able to help. He had walked along the street heading towards Brick Lane very shortly after 5.00 pm and had not seen anything out of the ordinary. A few minutes later, he had retraced his steps and, walking back along Hanbury Street, he saw the sports bag. He actually remarked that it could have been a bomb, but he continued on his way.

There were far fewer video cameras in Brick Lane than in Brixton and scanning of the limited footage showed no sign of the bomber. Again, as with Brixton, mystery remained about how the bomber had got to and from the scene. Although the Brixton suspect had walked around the area for about an hour before planting the bomb, he had not been picked up by the video cameras at the tube station there. Similarly with the second bomb, there was no sign of a suspect at the tube stations near Brick Lane, Shoreditch and Aldgate East. The police were looking for some other form of transport.

The man who could have provided police with the answer was the taxi driver who had taken Copeland to Brick Lane. He had a clear memory of the unusual fare he took from Waterloo to near Shoreditch station. Like many others who knew Copeland or had had some contact with him, the taxi driver told us he wanted to remain anonymous, to be known only by his nickname, Rino, fearing that he could be traced. Rino had worked until late on the Saturday night and did not learn of the Brick Lane bombing until the next day when he heard about it from radio news and from a Sunday newspaper report. He mentioned to his wife that he had taken someone close to the bomb scene. She said that it might have been the bomber and that Rino should perhaps contact the police. But he did not do so. He had been fairly close to two earlier big London bombs, in the City and at Canary Wharf. Both had been carried out by the IRA and Rino believed that a similarly well-organised group must have also been responsible for the Brixton and Brick Lane bombs. By comparison, the man he had carried in the back of his cab had not looked or acted like a bomber. He had been alone, too young and too scruffy to be a bomber. Rino could simply not connect the young man with the bombing, and so decided not to contact the police.

Rino's information would have been very useful to the Anti-Terrorist Branch detectives in a number of ways. His description of his fare matched the pictures the police were obtaining of the Brixton bomber. It was known that he had not used Brixton Underground station, so it was possible he was avoiding travelling by Tube because he knew that each station had several video cameras on which he would be picked up. But, more importantly, if he had travelled to Brick Lane by taxi, then that could have been how he had travelled to and from Brixton. Checks could have been made with local mini-cab firms and appeals put out to London black cab drivers. And there was significance in Waterloo, where Rino had picked up the bomber. As the vast majority of its trains are from points south of the Thames, the probability was that the bomber had travelled in from the south, and that was where his home would be. It also meant that he could have travelled by rail to Brixton, too.

However, Rino and the other individuals who had contact with Copeland cannot be blamed for failing to contact the police at an early stage. The public perception of those who carried out bombings was that they were part of organised groups, not lone youngsters. That impression had not been dispelled by the police and, of course, they had not yet issued the video and photos of the Brixton bomb suspect. When that happened later in the week, Rino responded immediately, but others who saw the pictures and were much closer to Copeland than taxi drivers still failed to make the connection.

Meanwhile, Copeland was enjoying himself. He had carried out two bombings, which had attracted a lot of publicity. He pinned more newspaper cuttings and photos of his exploits on the wall of his room in Farnborough. Among them was a colour photo, cut from a newspaper, of Emdad Talukdar, showing him pointing to where he had been hit in the head by a sliver of glass in the second explosion. Two other events excited Copeland, too.

Three days after the Brixton bomb, in a suburb of Denver, Colorado, two eighteen-year-olds, filled with hatred, had

Top: The face of evil. David Copeland: racist, bigot and killer.

Above: Copeland pictured in a baseball cap talking to police. He is shown next to John Tyndall, the BNP leader, bloodied after fighting broke out at the BNP's 15th Anniversary rally.

Left: Copeland's National-Socialist Movement membership card.

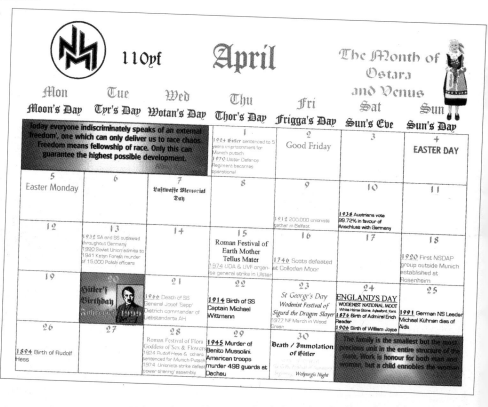

Above and opposite top: When the police searched Copeland's flat after his arrest, they found all manner of offensive right-wing material, including a Nazi calendar, extracts from which are shown here and opposite.

SEX IS NATURAL BUT REMEMBER YOUR DUTY TO THE FAMILY AND AN ARYAN FUTURE

Below: A meeting of white power activists, all giving a Nazi salute.

Only *inferior* White women date outside of their race. Be proud of your heritage, don't be a race-mixing Slut!

Kingdom Identity Ministries

These stickers were distributed across the country by various right-wing organisations. The terrifying message speaks for itself.

WE ARE BACK !

National-Socialist Movement

Racist - And Proud of It!

We of the *National-Socialist Movement* are racist - and proud of it! We of the NSM speak for the ordinary Whites of this country.

We of the NSM believe that *racism is right* - that racism is the will of Nature. We believe it is natural and necessary for us to be proud of our race, our racial heritage, our traditions.

We of the NSM believe it is natural and right for us to want to live among our own racial kind, according to our own traditions.

We of the NSM want to keep alive our White traditions and our White way of life.

We believe it is wrong for us to be forced to live in an anti-White multi-racial society. All the major political parties - Labour, Tory, Liberal - support this multi-racial society and its anti-White politically-correct policies.

All other organizations are in favour of this multi-racial society which has *outlawed* our natural and ancient rights and traditions - such as the ancient right to carry and use weapons in self-defence.

Our present multi-racial society has taken away our ancient rights and traditions because it is determined to make us - the White people of this country - into a submissive and passive people.

We of the NSM are having none of this! We are proud, and tough - like our warrior ancestors!

We of the NSM are fighting to create a Whites-only homeland where we can live among our own kind according to our healthy traditions.

To find out more about the NSM, write to:

National-Socialist Movement

Below and left: **A National-Socialist newsletter, plus other NS letters to and relating to Copeland. Material such as this was found in Copeland's flat, and was one of the terrifying influences that led to his devastating reign of terror...**

National-Socialist Movement

8 February 1999

Greetings Comrade Kirk

I hope this letter finds you well and in good Aryan spirits.

My reason for writing is to ask if you would help a local Full member who wants to get active in the cause and bring a few comrades together from the area. I 've spoken to him over the phone and he seems a good type and on the level.

He is:

David Copeland

If you could give Dave a ring, perhaps you could share a pint out and let me or Steve know that he's the sort that could be trusted with a list of our local activists. I've told him to expect a call from one of us soon. We seem to be getting a hell of a lot of guys interested in your area and with someone willing to get things together who is local things could only get better.

Anyhow, thanks for all your support. and I look forward to hearing how you get on.

Yours ever
Heil Hitler!

Tony Williams
Leader

enc: 4 x bundles stickers

National-Socialist Movement

25 February 1999
Our Ref: TW/A/640740

Dear Comrade David

Re. NSM Unit Formation

I hereby appoint you to the position of NSM Unit Leader (under sections 1.4, 5.3 and 5.4.1. of the NSM Constitution). This position is probationary. Welcome to leadership, responsibility and accountability to your comrades!

This is a senior position and I will expect a Report on your progress by 25 March. If everything is satisfactory then Unit status will be then be confirmed by Official Certification (see 5.6).

You are advised to read the enclosed Constitution and Rules of the NSM carefully as you will be expected to abide by these. please advise me of the name you wish to use for your Unit (eg. Hampshire NSM, South Central NSM, Candor Legion etc. etc.), giving a second choice in case the first is unacceptable. Unit letterheads can be obtained from us which you can then photocopy. If you wish to adopt a symbol for your Unit please send good artwork (colour or b+w).

You will be responsible for the NSM's development within the counties of Hampshire, Wiltshire, Berkshire and Surrey. You may wish to send out a bulletin to your Unit members and supporters (subject to 5.3.5.) announcing its formation. You may use the above BCM number for the heading if you do not wish to use your own address. Obtaining a Unit PO Box should be an early objective. You must send a copy of any circular to me at the above address. Naturally, your religious beliefs are your own matter and should not form a part of any circular. If printing is a problem, then this can be done by us to your design and content, which should ideally be sent to us typed. Alternatively you may wish to write individually. A list is attached for this purpose which is strictly confidential For Your Eyes Only. Also enclosed is an enquiry received the other week from Yateley. Do not disclose my phone number to anyone, but please give me a ring if you need any advise.

Remember, you are not expected to go out and recruit the general public. Your first duty is to the comrades within. Person to person recruitment is always best. Get your comrade's ideas about what they want from you. Keep them happy, advertise socials regularly even if only a couple turn up, and things will take root and grow over time. Do not rush to the local press with worthless sensation seeking publicity. Stay honourable. Use your initiative, within the terms of the Constitution, and advertise trips to local historic sights, exhibitions, talks etc. When you have regular meetings established and more than five turning up, book a pub room and I would happily give a talk myself, or send another official.

I look forward to hear how you are getting on - have good times, learn and good luck!

Yours ever
Heil Hitler!

Tony Williams
Leader

enc: Your order, NSM Constitution
P.S. A booklet of common Questions & Answers on NS should be out soon.

David Copeland

AND WHAT OF DAVID? WELL HES BEEN MOVED SIDEWAYS BY OUR BASTARDIZERS FOR MENTAL ASSESSMENT TO BROADMOOR, CLEVER AH ? NICE AND QUIET, NO UNCOMFORTABLE PRESS OR MEDIA SPOTLIGHT REMINDERS TO THE SUSCEPTIBLE ENGLISH PEOPLE REGARDING OUR CONTINUING WIDE OPEN DOOR POLICY FOR IMMIGRANTS AND ASYLUM SEEKERS TO POUR IN, AND EVEN MORE, VERY IMPORTANT NO ENCOURAGEMENT TO ANY OTHER YOUNG ENGLISH PATRIOTS TO LET MORE BOMBS, OFF UNDER OUR IMMIGRANTS AND PERVERTS; AND EVEN WORSE UNDER US POLITICAL BASTARDIZERS? THE FACT THAT OUR BASTARDIZERS HAVE ACHIEVED BY STEALTH WHAT HITLER FAILED TO DO! THE INVASION OF ENGLAND BY MILLIONS OF UNWANTED BLACK AND ASIAN ALIENS; AND THEIR ARROGANCE WHEN ELECTED, OE WE ARE NOW IN CHARGE, AND WE DECIDE WHAT WE DO; NOT THE ENGLISH VOTER!

THIS IS DEMOCRACY IN MODERN, MODERN, ENGLAND LADS, THE ATTITUDE BEING ENGLAND MORE FOR THE ISLAMICS AND BLACKS; THE ENGLISH HAVING PASSED THEIR SELL BY DATE ARE EXPENSIVE AND DEMANDING; IMMIGRANTS BEING MUCH MORE SUBSERVIENT AND LESS EXPENSIVE KNOWING HOW MUCH OUR BASTARDIZERS PROTECT THEM.

YOU THINK WE ARE JOKING ?? JUST GIVE THESE STATEMENTS ABOVE A FEW MINUTES LOGICAL THOUGHT THATS ALL WE ASK, ARE WE IMAGINING THE SLOW INEXORABLE ISLAMIC BASTARDIZATION OF ENGLAND AND ITS ENGLISH PEOPLE? SCOTLAND FOR THE SCOTS WALES FOR THE WELCH, FINE! AND THE ISLAMICS WANT THEIR OWN SEPARATE PARLIMENT? LIKE THEY WANT THEIR OWN STATE IN CHECHNYA CHEEKY SLIME BASTARDS THE RUSSIANS DO WELL TO PUT THEM DOWN PERMANENTLY. AND FINALLY DO YOU LIKE WHATS HAPPENING TO YOU; THE ENGLISH PEOPLE, IN YOUR OWN COUNTRY? DAVID DIDNT, AND LIKE ST GEORGE REACTED LIKE THE GOOD PATRIOT HE IS.

England for the English? Not anymore !! Its for everyone else"!

AND THE BURDEN ON ALL OUR SERVICES, HOSPITALS, SCHOOLS, HOUSING, ETC BY THE DAILY INFLUX OF ALIEN IMMIGRANTS AT THE ENGLISH TAXPAYERS EXPENSE IS BLOODY CRIMINAL !

Above: A right-wing cartoon and message praising the acts of David Copeland.

Right: Pictures issued by Scotland Yard of the suspect bomber. Copeland is wearing his 'disguise', a light-coloured baseball cap. These pictures led to Copeland's identification, his arrest, and to him advancing his Soho bomb by a day.

CB 9123   COPELAND. 02

Dear Mr Mclagan

    I can not express my
INNERCENSE or GUILT in any
letters I write due to a
bullshit law, which i find
extremily hypocritical coming
from a DEMOCRATIC
goverment
    I will be consulting my
solicitor about this I would
wish to carry on and open
a line of communication
with you.
        Yours Sincerly
        D Copeland

PS: Sorry about any spelling mistakes.

2/8/99

In replying to this letter, please write on the envelope:
Number CB9123 Name COPELAND
                  H.M. PRISON BELMARSH
                  WESTERN WAY
Wing H8U 1   THAMESMEAD
                  LONDON
                  SE28 0ER

Dear Mr Mclagan

    Sorry, i havent wrote
to you lately, it would be
better if i didn't write
atall, i would prefer you to
come and interview me in
person, i would wish you to
come and see me sometime
after my next court apperaing
contact my lawyer to find out
the details.

    Yours Sincerly D Copeland

VF004 (No. 243) 29/4 H.M.P. Maidstone

7/11/99

Mr Mclagan,
        Im trying to get you
to visit me hear at broadmoor,
try from your end as well, im
up in courts, see you there it will
be interesting, You are being prevented
from visiting me for political reasons
only, the Zog are trying to cover up
sweap me under the carpet, as you are
a media person and there for part of
the Zog malybe universionally you could
pull some stoings with your Jewish
masters, I think you are a 'good
journalist and want to find out the
truth,

        Dave

        D Copeland.

**Letters from Copeland to
the authors sent from
Belmarsh and Broadmoor
after his arrest.**

27/1/2000

DAVID COPELAND
8296
LUTON

Dear Sir,

I'm writing this letter to draw attention to my mistreatment at the hands off incompetent doctors here at broadmoor,

It would be good to do a programme on this establishment as there are lots of things that go on in here.

Even thou i do not act like a skitzo i have been diagnosed one, I believe it is political as they couldn't get me in here fast enough and get me drugged up to the eyeballs on drugs, shortly before my trial.

People come in here normal and are turned into vagatables some off them are petty crooks, I have seen this with my own eyes, this is what they are trying to do to me,

Ive got my legal team trying to get a Judicial review to stop them from drugging me as the drugs have slowed me down so much its taken 1 hour to write this short letter if the drugs are not stopped

---

27/1/2000.

I will have to try and get my trial put off for another year as it would be unfair to me to go to trial like this,

that I would like to say that i do not suffer from any of the symptons associated with skiteophrenia but still in drugged

the powers that be are trying to not me off without giving me a trial as it will be embarrasing to them

DCopeland

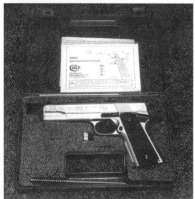

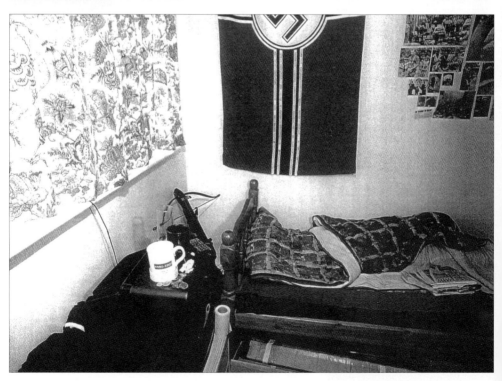

Pictures taken of Copeland's room after his arrest. Note the crossbow in the corner, and the pictures of various atrocities pinned on the wall. They also found this gas-powered pistol that Copeland, thankfully, never found the opportunity to use.

walked into their school, Columbine High. They carried bombs made from fireworks, just like Copeland's. They also carried guns, including a semi-automatic carbine, two 12-gauge shotguns and a mini-assault handgun. Eric Harris and Dylan Klebold killed twelve pupils and teachers, particularly singling out those who said they believed in God. Then, two days after the Brick Lane bomb, had come the murder of the BBC presenter Jill Dando outside her home in Fulham.

These two events and the two London bombings were discussed by Copeland, his father and Paul Mifsud during a break while working at the new Bermondsey tube station. The two older men were saying that it seemed as though London, having got over IRA bombings, was now under attack again. David Copeland's contribution to the conversation was brief and, with hindsight, significant. 'Yes, it's great, isn't it?' he exclaimed. 'It's all happening.'

Other Londoners also appeared to be being inspired by the high-profile bombing incidents. Although neither Copeland nor anyone else but the police knew it, another lone racist with home-made bombs and far-right connections had been arrested on the other side of London on the day of the Brick Lane explosion. Quite why Scotland Yard played down the incident has never been explained. James Shaw, a 57-year-old security guard, had been detained by police following a dispute with a bus driver who had thrown Shaw and his friends off his bus when he caught them smoking and drinking. Police found two explosive devices inside Shaw's carrier bag, and when they went to his home in Brentford, west London, they found race-hate literature, pictures of Hitler, swastikas and references to the Unabomber and the Mardi Gra bombings. They also discovered a list of religious buildings, including synagogues.

A Scotland Yard statement at the time gave minimum information, saying only that three men had been arrested after a dispute in Chiswick and adding that it was not thought to be linked to the Brixton bombs. There was a brief reference to Anti-Terrorist Branch assistance in the case. There was no mention of racism, of Shaw's bombing plans or of anything found in his home. Predictably, no newspaper carried anything about the arrests. Details of the arrest and what he planned did not emerge until many months later at the Old Bailey. Shaw's bombs, small bottles with fuses in their caps, were to be placed on railway lines to disrupt services. 'He is a loner who lives an isolated life,' said his lawyer at the Old Bailey when Shaw was given a nine-year jail sentence. 'He has a pathological interest in bombs and hates everyone. He hates everyone equally.' Even long after he was sentenced, Scotland Yard would not elaborate on how the Anti-Terrorist Branch had 'assisted' them.

Keeping silent about Shaw's arrest and what had been found at his home may have been an attempt to prevent adding to the growing sense of panic amongst ethnic minority communities. Releasing details at that time could have indicated that the nailbomber they were hunting probably had more political motivation than the police wanted to suggest.

The nailbomber had struck on successive Saturdays at almost exactly the same time. It was too much of a coincidence. It meant the police were now dealing with a serial, racist bomber who, if he was not caught, would inevitably kill someone. Scotland Yard started to plan for a huge police operation for the next Saturday, which would be the bomber's next attack, if he stuck to his pattern.

Advice, guidance and warnings were issued to the representatives of concerned or vulnerable groups, including those from ethnic minorities, gays, and the Jewish community. On 29 April, there was also a meeting of the Met's Race Lay Advisory Group (RLAG) set up by Scotland Yard to liaise with community leaders in the wake of the Stephen Lawrence affair. This meeting degenerated at times into a bad-tempered affair, with some of the community representatives, expecting more of a discussion, resenting what they viewed as being talked down to by some police officers.

Community organisations planned patrols in some parts of the capital, notably Southall in west London and Golders Green and Stamford Hill in north London. Posters were issued from area police stations. One showed two hold-alls and posed the question 'Which contains the bomb?' Another featured a picture of two eyes and the caption 'bomb detectors'. The gay newspaper *Pink Paper* hit the streets of London on the Thursday morning with its front-page story warning that gays could be the next target. It is claimed that this spurred the police into warning some gay establishments in Soho, including the Admiral Duncan pub, but other well-known gay venues in London were not visited. Scotland Yard planned for uniformed police to be out on the streets in strength in vulnerable areas on the third Saturday. If the bomber struck again, officers would have to be available to help the victims.

Many police forces have introduced schemes where officers receive training on how to handle the victims of disasters and serious violent or racial crime. In London there are now several hundred officers who have completed a six-day training course, spread over two weeks, at Hendon police college in north London. Once trained as family liaison officers, they can be called upon to look after the interests of victims in both the short and long term, offering help and advice in a number of different ways, ranging from helping with hospital visits to passing on information about the progress of police investigations. Of those who have received the full training, about one hundred in London are dedicated, full-time family liaison officers. However, at the time of the bombings, there were far fewer police officers qualified for this kind of liaison and welfare work. The training had only just been taken over by the Racial and Violent Crime Task Force (CO24).

With more public casualties expected, an emergency plan

was rushed through. Extra officers had to receive training in dealing sensitively with the injured, their families, and with the relatives of anyone killed. The normal six-day training period was impossible as arrangements could not be made in time to bring together officers from every London borough as well as trainers from Avon and Somerset, race crime victims, social workers, and Victim Support representatives. Instead, a one-day training session for 186 more officers was arranged for the Friday. Although still inadequate, it was to turn out to be invaluable.

Outside London, police forces were also alerted to possible dangers, especially in areas with a high concentration of black and Asian people. Security at shopping centres and markets in many of Britain's larger cities was stepped up.

Fears of a wider campaign were heightened five days after the Brick Lane bomb when a letter, sent in the name of the White Wolves, arrived at the offices of the Mansfield Unemployed Workers Centre. It carried a chilling warning that May Day, only a few days off, was going to be a dark day. The letter, which had been posted in Nottingham, contained the codeword, Nemesis, the same as had appeared on the original White Wolves letters that had been dispatched a few days before the Brixton bomb. Shortly before the letter arrived, the Centre had been attacked and had one of its windows smashed. With the annual May Day festival only days away, the local Trade Union movement was put on alert. Their fears seemed well-founded as the night before events were due to take place, police found material consistent with that found in bombs in an abandoned car in Chesterfield, the site of the main May Day march in the area. Police had picked up the car on the outskirts of Mansfield and, realising that it had been reported stolen earlier that day, gave chase for several miles. As the stolen car arrived in Chesterfield, the two white male occupants fled, never to be seen again.

Throughout the early part of the week following the Brick Lane bomb, police were preparing to issue the video pictures and stills of the Brixton suspect. A great deal of effort was being put into this public appeal for information, so much so that three journalists from BBC's *Panorama* were given short shrift by Anti-Terrorist Branch officers when they went to Scotland Yard on the Thursday morning. The visit had been arranged that morning, after *Panorama* had obtained important information that the programme makers believed could help the police investigation. *Panorama*'s editor Peter Horrocks, was joined by producer Andy Bell, and Nick Lowles, one of the editors of *Searchlight*, who was contributing to a planned programme. The team had learnt that former National Socialist Movement leader Dave Myatt was believed to have written the fifteen-page White Wolves document, which had called for indiscriminate attacks on black and Asian communities and also carried simple bomb designs. The journalists also carried information suggesting that a closer look at the leadership of the NSM was needed. It later emerged that Copeland was one of its organisers. The *Panorama* team had expected to be seen by a senior officer, but it was an ordinary detective constable who was sent down to the ground floor entrance to see them. She listened to what they had to say, but took no notes in front of them.

The pictures obtained of the Brixton suspect had been sent twice to and from NASA in the USA, and the resulting images, though still not very sharp, were far better than the originals. They were shown to Special Branch officers, but no one had any idea of the bomber's identity. They were not shown to any contacts in any extreme right-wing groups out of fear that the suspect would be tipped off and learn too early that he had been caught on camera. The police believed it was important to issue the pictures in one massive publicity operation. The aim was obviously to catch the bomber, but if the publicity resulted in him abandoning his bombing campaign, then so much the better. The pictures were so good that, with help from the public, they would get their man and lives would have been saved. How much serious consideration was given to how the bomber would react on seeing pictures of himself is not known.

On Thursday lunchtime, Scotland Yard released the video and stills taken from it during a news conference by Assistant Commissioner David Veness and the head of the Anti-Terrorist Branch, Deputy Assistant Commissioner Alan Fry. They received instant massive coverage, beginning at lunchtime with radio and TV news programmes. The broadcasts were repeated throughout the day and into the evening. The pictures were carried on the front page of all editions of the London *Evening Standard* and on many national newspapers' front pages the following day.

Preparations were also well under way for the huge police operation on the third Saturday, when detectives believed the bomber would strike again. A special watch was to be kept on the big London railway stations and known extremists were also under surveillance. However, Copeland remained one step ahead of the chasing pack.

7

The Soho Bomb
and Arrest

*'I knew it would piss everyone off especially Blair,
Mandelson and all them lot ... I could see the people
I was gonna maim and kill. I didn't feel joy about it.
I didn't feel sad. I just didn't feel anything.'*

David Copeland

AFTER DELIVERING HIS BRICK LANE BOMB, Copeland had
travelled by taxi to Soho to decide in which gay pub he
would leave his third bomb. After blacks and Asians,
homosexuals were always going to be his next target. His
hatred for them was intense. He was to say later that killing
and maiming homosexuals was, unlike the earlier bombs,
'personal'. His genitals, the focus of medical concern at his
birth, had continued to worry him well into his adult life.
Fears that they were too small may have contributed to his

unease about relationships with women. Indeed, he had had only one girlfriend, and that never became serious. As a result many, including his family, had questioned his sexuality. In denying any homosexual leanings, his hatred towards gay men became even more bitter. Copeland had talked over his problems with his workmate, Paul Mifsud, who had tried to reassure him that he would eventually meet the right person, but Copeland had been unconvinced and continued to resort to prostitutes. He believed homosexuals were degenerates, with no place in society. Bombing them would make them suffer, reinforce his own heterosexuality and also hit at those he hated in Government. 'I knew it would piss everyone off,' he said, 'especially Blair, Mandelson and all them lot.'

He had not decided to target Brick Lane with his 'Asian' bomb until the night before. While his 'homosexual' bomb had always been destined for one of Soho's gay bars, he had not decided which one, a problem that had not been resolved by his reconnoitre at the weekend. He decided to return on a weekday, after telling Mr Mifsud about a porn video he had bought in Soho. He believed it featured bondage and torture, but when he viewed it he saw it was about coprophilia. Angry with the shop where he had bought it, he told Mr Mifsud that he would return it after he finished work early on the Thursday afternoon. That same week there had been police raids on some Soho premises and Mr Mifsud joked with Copeland as he left at 2.00 pm that he might find the shop had closed down.

In Soho, Copeland returned the video and asked people which of the area's gay bars was the best. He decided on the Admiral Duncan in Old Compton Street. However, while in one sex shop, he heard a radio news broadcast that was to change his plans dramatically. The newsreader said that Scotland Yard had issued video footage and photographs of the Brixton bomb suspect. A startled Copeland left the shop, bought an *Evening Standard*, and was even more shocked.

There on the front page, under the big headline 'NAIL BOMBS', were two photographs of himself with the subheading 'Do you know this man?' The entire front page was taken up with the pictures and the story, which began: 'These are dramatic closed-circuit TV images of the man police believe is responsible for the Brixton nail bomb. In an urgent appeal for public help, Assistant Commissioner David Veness said it was the Yard's "number one priority" to trace the man. Mr Veness said: "He must be caught and we need the help of the public. Someone knows him, someone knows that they went to school with him, works with him, associates with him, has seen him".'

Copeland knew the game was up. Someone would recognise him, even though he had not been wearing his usual black baseball cap at Brixton. While most people would probably have reacted by either giving themselves up or by going to ground, Copeland decided otherwise. Such was the depth of his hatred for homosexuals that he was determined to complete his mission, but instead of doing the bombing on the Saturday evening, as everyone expected, he would bring his plans forward. The only problem was that the third bomb was not ready. It would take up to 24 hours to assemble and prepare, and all the flash powder and necessary parts were in Farnborough. He decided to head there, pick up everything necessary, and return to London, as it would be too risky to stay overnight in his room. He would have to stay in a hotel and construct his bomb there.

On the journey home, Copeland felt people were looking at him, recognising him, and he was worried that by the time he got to 25 Sunnybank Road, someone would have alerted the police and officers would be waiting for him. It was a risk he had to take to make gays suffer before he was caught. At No. 25 only one of the other tenants was home. It was clear Alison had not recognised him as the bomber. Upstairs in his small back room, it took him about half an hour to pack what he needed — a length of four-inch-diameter pipe, firework explosives, clock, igniters, wires, glue and tools. It all went into the Nike hold-all he had bought in Farnborough earlier in the week. He had everything apart from connectors to join wires to batteries, but he could easily get them in the morning from an electrical shop.

As Copeland left the house, bag slung over his back, he was dressed in black, according to Alison. Black jeans, black jacket, black boots, black bag. Under his zipped up jacket, he wore his Euro '96 T-shirt. He set off for Farnborough railway station on his mountain bike, but he got a puncture. There was no time for him to fix it or return home, so he wheeled his bike to the station, left it chained up there, and took a train to London. He decided to stay in Victoria, an area he knew well. This was where he had visited the Internet café to get instructions from the web on how to make bombs and also where he had been one of the group of BNP militants who had raided the nearby Politico's bookshop.

In Victoria, Copeland went to the Airways Hotel in St George's Drive. Giving a false name, he paid £40 in cash for room 204 on the first floor, with a shower and small balcony above the main entrance. But the room was available only for the Thursday night. The hotel was full on the Friday, as it was a bank holiday weekend. Safe inside the room, Copeland immediately got to work building his third bomb. He glued one end of the pipe, and put it outside on the balcony to cool down and dry. Once it had set, he put flash powder inside adding in some magnesium to make it a little more powerful. Having packed the mixture down tightly, he glued up the other end of the pipe and again put it out on the balcony to set. It was well past midnight when he finished, and he went to bed, sleeping soundly.

*   *   *

Earlier that day, after Scotland Yard's issuing of the video and stills, and during the next day, known right-wing extremists received visits from the police or MI5. They included an east London activist who had moved to the NF from the BNP. Another BNP member with C18 connections was ushered into a car as he waited for a bus to take him to work. He had been a friend of Stuart Kerr, who was then in custody for a fire-bomb attack on an Asian corner shop in Chichester (he was later sentenced to twelve years), while over in west London another C18 man was pulled off the street in similar fashion. In all these cases, the authorities were asking for information or trying to get the extremists to grass on their mates. Even if they failed to recruit them as informants, the hope was that they would be scared, knowing that the police were on to them.

Following the appeal to the public, calls started to flood into Scotland Yard on Thursday afternoon. The first useful information leading to the bomber came from Rino, the taxi driver who had taken Copeland from Waterloo to Brick Lane. Rino saw the pictures on TV that evening while at work and immediately recognised his fare. 'That's when it clicked,' he told us. 'That was the guy I had in the cab. I said there's no doubt about it. Although the pictures weren't great, you could see it was him. It's a shame the pictures didn't come out sooner, 'cos I would have made the connection.'

Rino's main memories of Copeland had been that he was a scruffy-looking young man, he had asked to be taken to an unusual place and the conversation had been strained on the way there. He recalled other details that even now, months later, still make him shiver. He now understands why the £5 note that Copeland had paid him had been so hot and wet with sweat after being held in his hand throughout the journey. Rino remembered more about his passenger's bag: 'He held on to it for dear life. He did not let it go. It was between his legs, so it didn't move. Normally someone puts their bag on the floor and you can hear it slide across the floor as you go round corners. But it didn't move at all, so I knew he was holding on to it, and he didn't sit back at all. He sat rigid, which is not a very comfortable way to ride in a taxi.' Rino believes that Copeland was worried about the bomb exploding prematurely. 'It's frightening to think it could have gone off at any time. I try not to think about it. My wife was seven months pregnant at the time, and I've got a little boy, so it doesn't bear thinking about.'

Taxi drivers are viewed by police as reliable witnesses, so when Rino went into Bishopsgate police station in the City of London at 10.00 pm on Thursday and told his story, Scotland Yard was contacted and his information was recognised as very significant. Rino usually works until after midnight, but a senior Anti-Terrorist Branch detective asked him to stop work immediately and go home, where he would be seen first thing in the morning and a longer statement taken.

Armed with Rino's detailed information, police started to look for the bomber on the CCTV taken at Waterloo on the previous Saturday. A hold had been put on all the CCTV footage from London's main tube and railway stations for both the previous Saturdays. It had been impossible at that stage to view it all, but it was realised that it could eventually trap the bomber, or, when he was arrested, provide evidence to tie him to the explosions.

*　　　*　　　*

On Friday morning, Copeland woke at about 10.00 am. He had a shower in the tiny cubicle in the room, packed the bomb, nails, other parts and tools into the black Nike bag, and put empty tubes of glue and other rubbish into a plastic bag. He left the hotel shortly before 11.00 am, dumped the rubbish bag next to others awaiting collection by dustmen, and started looking for another hotel where he could finish assembling his bomb. He found one just round the corner in Warwick Way, an Asian-owned bed and breakfast hotel, The Vegas. At the entrance was a cleaner, who told him the cost of a room was £40. Copeland thought it extortionate, and said he would think about it. When the cleaner's back was turned, Copeland gave her the 'finger', but he was seen by the manager, Ms Meena Clark. He went looking for another place to stay, but finding none nearby with vacancies he returned to The Vegas after a few minutes. Paying cash, he filled in the registration form, again using the name Hawkins. However, he was clearly confused. The subterfuge was useless because he gave his correct home address!

Allocated room No. 1, on the lower ground floor, he was told that it still had to be cleaned, so he could leave his bag in the safe area under the hotel stairs. Worried that someone could open the bag, or worse still, steal it, Copeland refused. He was eventually allowed to leave it in the room, returning to it after it had been cleaned. He started to assemble the bomb and asked the hotel receptionist where he could get some electrical equipment. He was directed to a shop in Churton Street where he bought some connectors. On the way back to The Vegas he bought some soft drinks. Constructing a bomb was thirsty work.

Ms Clark had not seen Copeland check into the hotel. She told us that if she had seen him, she would have turned him away because of his rude gesture to the cleaner and because she did not like the look of him. 'He looked like he was up to no good,' she said. 'He looked like a drugs dealer or something like that.' She took action against him after he had spent some time in his room, when he tried to make some phone calls. Calling from his room, he could not get an outside line. It was the hotel's policy not to let anyone who had paid cash run up big phone bills, as it was feared the person could disappear without paying. Copeland asked for a line, but Ms Clark refused the request. He was told there were three phone boxes in a nearby street, and he went to use one of them. Why he was so desperate to use the phone is not known, nor is it known who he called, or indeed how many calls he made. In mid-afternoon, he set off for Soho on foot, the bomb in the bag on his back.

*   *   *

At the Bermondsey café where Copeland regularly ate breakfast, the owner, Ben Panagiotou, had bought a newspaper and thought he recognised the picture of the suspect bomber on the front page. However, the photo showed him wearing a white baseball cap, whereas Copeland had always worn a dark one in the café. So Mr Panagiotou, known as Ben to everyone, was far from sure. Then, at lunchtime, one of Copeland's workmates came into the café. Paul Mifsud had been in a newsagents that morning and had seen the photograph on the front page of a newspaper, but had not given it a second thought. In the café, Ben approached him with a newspaper and said: 'Doesn't that look like your mate?', pointing out the likeness. Mr Mifsud saw the similarity. He showed the paper to Copeland's father who had also arrived at the café for lunch. Stephen Copeland agreed that it did look a bit like David, but said it could not be him as he did not have a white cap. Asked by Mr Mifsud what he would do if his son was the nailbomber, Mr Copeland replied: 'I would disown him if he did something like that. I've virtually done that anyway.' The conversation ended and the two men returned to work at the tube station.

During the afternoon, Mr Mifsud kept thinking that the disturbed young man he worked with could indeed be the bomber. He wondered why Copeland had not been at work that day. Although Copeland had increasingly been taking time off, he always telephoned to say he would not be turning up. There had been no such phone call that day. There were also all the conversations between the pair in which Copeland had expressed his hatred for various people. He had also dropped hints that he was up to something that had to remain secret.

The awful thoughts continued to nag at Mr Mifsud after

he finished work, growing in their intensity. He bought a newspaper and, driving home, kept glancing down at the front page photo that he had propped up on the passenger seat so he could look at it more closely. It really did look like Copeland, thought Mr Mifsud, but knowing that photos can be deceptive, he decided to look at other pictures. He stopped his car and bought five other national newspapers to check their photos of the suspect. Then the dreadful reality hit him. There was no doubt about it. Copeland was the bomber.

For the rest of Mr Mifsud's journey home, worrying thoughts raced through his head. He remembered that Copeland had said he was going to Soho the day before. He wondered whether Copeland was acting on his own. He did not seem to have any friends, but he also did not seem capable of making and planting bombs by himself. Copeland knew where Mr Mifsud lived, and if he had accomplices, Mr Mifsud thought he and his family could face reprisals if he contacted the police to inform on the young man. Copeland would know that he would be the one to contact the police. By the time he arrived home, he was in a terrible state, but after talking it through with his wife, he called the police freephone telephone number given in the newspapers.

Mr Mifsud's call was received at 5.25 pm, one hour before the devastating Soho bomb went off. He says he was put at ease by the officer taking the call who asked a series of prepared questions that included one asking how definite, on a scale of one to ten, was he that Copeland was the man. He answered that he graded the identification as eight out of ten. He apologised that he did not have Copeland's home address in Farnborough, but the police officer assured him they could trace it from the phone number Mr Mifsud provided.

There had been many phone calls to the police freephone number following the public appeal for information. While no useful information had been received prior to the appeal, no fewer than 572 calls were logged before the operation was wound down. The police were inundated and finding it difficult to cope. Forensic scientists had provided useful preliminary information about the make-up of the bombs, but the detailed examination of all the debris would take weeks. In addition, a tremendous amount of hate mail had been sent for examination along with various letters claiming responsibility for the actual bombings. But the senders of the vast majority of the letters had taken steps to avoid detection. They had left no fingerprints on the paper and the postage stamps had been stuck to the envelopes with water rather than saliva, from which DNA samples can be obtained. The operation turned out to have been a waste of forensic scientists' valuable time, resulting in the arrest of only one person, a seventeen-year-old youth who had no link to the bombing campaign. He was caught because his message of hate had been handwritten and he was known to the police as having written similar notes on a previous occasion.

Nevertheless, all the mail had to be checked and the same applied to all the phone calls from the public, which came in from all over the country. The response had been so overwhelming partly because the pictures were not very distinct and so could have fitted the description of any number of young men. In addition, the police appeal had not stressed or suggested that the bomber was a racist, possibly connected to an extremist group, nor had it said that he must live in the south-east of England. A few calls were deliberately misleading, but the great majority were from people doing their public duty, trying to be helpful in passing on their suspicions. Many, however, were virtually useless because they were so vague and following up the information would take far too long. One example involved a taxi driver who called in to say he had carried two men in the back of his cab who had been discussing bombs. It was some time before it became clear to the police operator who had taken the call that the conversation was not about how to make bombs, but rather a discussion about the bombings. Another person said they had seen someone resembling the suspect walking along their street. Asked whether she had seen the young man before or knew where he lived or worked, the caller replied negatively. However, all such callers had to be treated politely or phoned back and thanked for their help.

What officers manning the freephone number and the detectives sifting through the information were waiting for was more positive information from an acquaintance, relative or neighbour of someone looking very like the suspect. Better still if the caller knew that the person they were fingering held extreme right-wing views, or had not been around on the two previous Saturday afternoons.

While Mr Mifsud's call was the first naming of Copeland logged by the Anti-Terrorist Branch, it was not, in fact, the first to be made. Earlier that afternoon, Scotland Yard received information naming Copeland as a suspect. The tip came from *Searchlight*, who had received the information from a source within the far right. After a quick check through its files, the anti-fascist magazine came up with details of his employment and an address in Barking.

Although *Searchlight* is a widely respected and authoritive magazine about the extreme right, no one from the police had asked it for any help and one of its editors, Nick Lowles, had been one of the *Panorama* group who felt rebuffed the day before at Scotland Yard. Rather than suffer the same treatment, *Searchlight* decided to pass on the information via an intermediary who was known to be held in more esteem by Scotland Yard. Early on that Friday afternoon, a phone call was made to Special Branch who were told that someone from the far right had identified David Copeland from the CCTV images broadcast on TV. The intermediary reinforced the phone message with a fax to Special Branch spelling out his name, his last known address and that he worked as an engineer, possibly for British Rail.

This is understood to have been the first positive identification of Copeland, but it seems that this very important information did not reach the Anti-Terrorist Branch until after Copeland's arrest, because the intermediary was told later that his tip-off had played no part in events leading to Copeland's arrest. If this is the case, it represents a serious breakdown in communication. Although Mr Mifsud's information had reached the authorities too late to stop the Soho bomb, if the information held by Special Branch had been passed immediately to the Anti-Terrorist Branch, it could have been acted on much earlier. The tip-off had come from a respected authoritative source, which said Copeland had far-right political connections, something that Mr Mifsud did not know. If the two pieces of information had been put together, they would have provided devastating evidence that Copeland was a very serious suspect. At the very least, those police sent to visit him at his home would have made sure they were armed and protected against the threat he posed. But it was not be. The arrest operation came close to going disastrously wrong.

Even on its own, Paul Mifsud's call to the freephone number should have been taken seriously from the outset. He was fairly positive it was Copeland. He knew he was a racist and, although he had no idea of Copeland's movements at the time of the Brixton and Brick Lane explosions, he had not been at work since the police had issued their appeal. In addition, Mr Mifsud's information in one respect matched that from Rino, the taxi driver, who had picked him up from Waterloo. Mr Mifsud knew that Copeland lived in Hampshire and travelled by rail to and from Waterloo every weekday.

Meanwhile, London was rocked by Copeland's third bomb.

*   *   *

Once again, Copeland arrived at his target too early, but instead of walking around the area, as he had done at Brixton, he went for a drink. The first pub he tried was full of rugby fans and very noisy, so he went to another, bought a coke, and waited. The bomb carefully packed in his sports hold-all was timed to go off at 6.30 pm. At 5.40 pm he got up, left the pub, and walked to the Admiral Duncan, the gay pub he had chosen the day before. Like others in Soho, it had been visited by police who warned staff that a gay venue could be next on the bomber's list of targets. Special vigilance would be necessary on Saturday because, if the bomber stuck to his pattern, that would be when he would plant his third bomb. If Copeland had gone to the lavatory area at the back of the pub, he would have seen something that would probably have given him perverse pleasure. Pinned there prominently was a police poster warning of the nailbomber. He did not see it, however. The lavatory in a gay pub would have been a no-go area for him, as he was so scared about coming into close contact with those he called 'degenerate queers'. Copeland put his hold-all up against the bar, in the middle of the pub, where there were other bags on the floor. He positioned himself further along inside, where he could keep an eye on the bag, and again, he bought a coke.

At first there were about twenty people in the pub, but as it was the end of the working week and the start of a bank holiday weekend, it quickly started to fill up. He looked at them. 'I could see the people I was gonna maim and kill,' he said later. 'I didn't feel joy about it. I didn't feel sad. I just didn't feel anything.' Copeland's train of thought was disturbed by someone sitting on the stool next to him, someone he thought may have been trying to chat him up.

David, a businessman, saw Copeland enter the pub at about 5.50 pm, dressed in dark combat trousers and a Euro '96 T-shirt. With his close-cropped hair, he thought he looked a bit like the Sunderland footballer Kevin Philips. David thought the young man was 'straight', but that he could have been a rent boy. He noticed that Copeland seemed uneasy and kept looking at his watch, which had a blue luminous dial. David asked him the time. It was 6.00 pm. 'Are you waiting for someone?' he then asked. 'Yeah,' Copeland replied. 'A boyfriend?' queried David. 'Yeah,' said Copeland, 'He's late.' Five minutes later, Copeland asked the businessman if he knew of a cash machine nearby. Told there was one in Soho Square, he looked again at his watch and said he was going to withdraw some money. David offered to look after his drink while he was gone and Copeland accepted.

It was by then 6.10 pm and the pub was getting crowded. To get to the door, Copeland had to push his way past people, among them a group of four men and a woman standing close to his bag in the middle of the bar, happily chatting. Andrea Dykes was pregnant and she and her husband Julian had asked a gay friend, John Light, who had also been his best man, to be the child's godfather. Delighted to be asked, John had agreed and to celebrate had bought five tickets for the Abba-based musical *Mamma Mia!* at the Prince Edward Theatre. Also in the group were John's partner, Gary Partridge, and his former boyfriend, Nik Moore. As Copeland elbowed his way through them to get to the entrance, Gary and John exchanged glances, sharing the thought that the young man was very rude. Shortly afterwards, someone noticed the bag and alerted the bar staff. The manager, Mark Taylor, asked some of the customers whether the bag belonged to them, and when they all replied 'no', he became concerned. As he stood over the hold-all, beginning to move people away, the bomb exploded, causing death, devastation and appalling injuries.

Nik Moore and Andrea Dykes were killed outright, nails embedded in their bodies. John Light died in hospital the next day. Julian Dykes was seriously injured and unconscious for three weeks. Another victim had both legs amputated. Three other men also lost legs. Dozens of others suffered injuries and burns. All remembered a blinding flash of light, a huge bang, and then darkness.

Gary Partridge remembers finding himself in a crouched position, his arms covering his head. Dazed and unsure of what had happened, he reached out for his friends, but could not find them in the darkness, made worse by clouds of dust. There was a strong smell of singed, burned hair. He eventually saw light from the entrance, staggered towards it and got outside.

'I can remember looking at the reflection of myself in the window of a shop opposite the pub and seeing that my face and hair had all been burnt and my arms and one leg of my trousers had been ripped off, and my arm was bleeding, and only then did the horror really start to sink in. I spent a few minutes just wandering about the street outside looking for John, Andrea, Julia, Nik. I couldn't see anybody and I can remember going back to go into the pub. The closer I got I started screaming and I think a realisation sort of sunk in about what damage had been caused. There was so much carnage about. People were covered in blood and screaming and some looked like they had limbs missing. It was more like a scene from a war rather than what you'd expect to see on a London street.'

As he approached the pub, John Light was dragged out in a very bad condition. Gary stayed with him until the ambulances arrived and the pair were taken to University College Hospital. Gary had bad burns, shrapnel injuries, nails in his body and glass embedded in his head. He was told the following afternoon that John, Andrea and Nik had all died. 'I was totally shocked,' he said. 'I had been pumped full of drugs at that time, but even so, I just felt my whole world had been turned upside down. At that point I didn't want to go on living. I was consumed by guilt, the fact that I'd survived and they hadn't.' Gary Partridge was taken to the specialist burns unit at Broomfield Hospital in

Chelmsford, Essex, where he was joined by Andy Butcher, another bomb victim.

When the bomb went off, Andy Butcher, a nurse, was heading towards the entrance with his boyfriend, Darren, ahead of him. He remembers being thrown forward through the air before losing consciousness for what was probably less than a minute. 'I came to on the floor and it felt as though my whole body was on fire. I thought my clothes were on fire, so I rolled over and over to put the flames out. Then I just lay there. It seemed like minutes but it was probably only seconds, but then the realisation hit me that it was a bomb, because I remembered hearing the bang. Then a silly thing went through my head. I thought "but it's not Saturday", because obviously it immediately brought to mind the previous two bombs, which had both been on Saturdays. I just kept thinking, it's not Saturday.' In darkness, he eventually pulled himself up and started to walk towards where he thought the street was. But then, hearing muffled voices behind him, he looked round and seeing daylight, realised he had been walking the wrong way, further into the pub.

Outside, he saw he had been badly burned, with skin hanging off his arms and hands. His partner Darren and another man sat him down on some steps by the restaurant next door, and put his hands into a bowl of cold water. Others came with jugs of water which they poured over his head and body to relieve the pain of his burned flesh. 'They cut my clothes off, to see the extent of my injuries. My trousers were shredded anyway. My legs were burned. My head and my face were burned.' With others more badly injured, it took time for the paramedics to reach him. As he waited, he said he 'lost it' and started shouting for help, for someone to stop the unbearable pain. 'I started to go into shock. At that point, I just wanted to go to sleep, and I didn't care if I never woke up again. I just wanted out of there. I thought I've done my bit now, I can't deal with this situation any more. I'm switching off. I just vaguely remember hearing someone say that a paramedic was needed immediately, and that's when I was carted off to hospital.'

Mark Taylor is one of the luckiest to be alive, as he was standing over the bomb when it went off, landing him unconscious on top of it. His face, legs and an arm were badly damaged and he sustained seventy-five per cent burns. He was in hospital for seven weeks and nearly a year later had to go back in for more treatment.

* * *

The bomb went off just over an hour after the end of the hastily convened one-day course training 186 Metropolitan policemen and policewomen as family liaison officers. The session had been organised by a former Anti-Terrorist Branch officer, Detective Sergeant Dave Field, now with CO24. As he drove home he was telephoned with news of the Soho bomb and immediately went to Scotland Yard to help organise the after-care of victims. He contacted the police family liaison officers, including those who had just finished the course. Some of them literally went straight into action in Soho, having just completed the day-long training.

* * *

Meanwhile, Copeland, after leaving the pub, walked through the West End, past Green Park, back to the Vegas Hotel, arriving there at 7.00 pm. He switched on *Channel Four News*, which had just started. Copeland saw that news of his Soho bombing was coming in. The injuries were said to be much worse than in the previous two bombs and some were believed to have died. Asked later about his thoughts on the suffering he had caused, Copeland said: 'I feel nothing. I don't feel sadness but I don't feel joy. I did what I had to do. I think the woman was pregnant. I feel sorry for her, but I don't feel no guilt for the others.'

When the news finished, Copeland gathered together his tools, put them in a plastic bag and walked to Waterloo for a train home. His three bombs had hit West Indians in Brixton, Bangladeshis in Brick Lane and with his third, he had not only devastated the gay community, but, by advancing his plans, he had outwitted the police and all the authorities. He did not know what would happen to him now. If able to continue his campaign, he had already decided that his fourth bomb would be in Southall, Middlesex, which he believed to be the home of many Indians, particularly Punjabis. But even if he was arrested, he would still have accomplished his mission. It would be up to others to follow his lead, to take up the racist torch, to fight for a National Socialist Britain. He felt relief. At Waterloo, he stopped for a cup of tea at a stall. The variety he chose was English Breakfast.

The police were unlucky not to have caught him there or shortly after he had left the station for his home. Someone looking very like him had been seen heading for the platform area in the station, which was crowded with Bank Holiday travellers. Police at the station missed him, but the train he was thought to have caught was stopped at Guildford and searched from end to end by police, but Copeland was not on board. The train he had caught had left from the same platform and had travelled through many of the same stations as the other train, but it had branched off the line for Farnborough before reaching Guildford.

In his west London home, Mr Mifsud saw news of the blast on the BBC's *Nine O'Clock News*. He remembered that Copeland had told him the day before that he had been going to Soho to return the coprophilia video. 'After making the phone call to the police, I'd let it go out of my mind,' he said. 'But then seeing it on the news, I realised that things were stacking up, that Dave was responsible.'

Arriving back at Farnborough Station, Copeland unchained his bike, which was still punctured from the day before. He wheeled it home to 25 Sunnybank Road. As he opened the front door, Alison saw him come in and go upstairs to his room. She was watching *Frasier* on TV, so timed his return as a little after 10.00 pm. Copeland had half expected the police to be waiting for him. Although the net was closing, it would be another three hours before he was arrested, by officers from many miles away who, unknowingly, risked their lives to do so.

The Flying Squad officers based at the north London area headquarters at Finchley, were among those supplementing the strength of the Metropolitan Police's Anti-Terrorist Branch. By that stage, because of the volume of work, Scotland Yard had divided up the police effort, tasking different groups and calling on outside police help. Several Anti-Terrorist Branch detectives skilled in surveillance work had already been sent, before the Soho bomb, to watch the movements of other suspects during Friday evening and Saturday. It had also been agreed, prior to the public appeal, that any arrests necessary in the London area would be carried out by Metropolitan Police officers, and anyone outside London would be arrested by officers from the National Crime Squad. The arrangement had been followed prior to the Soho bomb with the arrests of four people, one from the Midlands. But that evening's bomb wrecked all the planning.

Why Metropolitan Police Flying Squad officers rather than those from the National Crime Squad were sent to Farnborough in Hampshire, why it was six or seven hours after Mr Mifsud's call, why they went unarmed, and why the tip given to Special Branch was not passed on, are questions that remain largely unanswered. It may be that Mr Mifsud's information was not going to be acted on until the next day. Certainly the police effort had been geared to the Saturday rather than the Friday, and there were cost implications in terms of overtime pay in sending police out on the Friday night of a Bank Holiday weekend, particularly those from non-Metropolitan forces. As for going without weapons, police rules dictate that when officers from one force go into another police area in an armed response vehicle, permission has to be obtained from a very senior officer in the area being visited. Alternatively, armed back-up can be requested from the other force. It is understood that no request was made and no permission was given by Hampshire. It would appear that, after the Soho bomb, there was no time to observe the rules. Scotland Yard was under the cosh from Downing Street, the Home Office and from MPs who stressed that the bomber had to be caught, and quickly.

The Flying Squad team at their base in north London were on stand-by, waiting for a possible call to visit someone identified by callers to the police freephone number. When the call came from Scotland Yard late on Friday night, there was surprise that it contained so little information. Amazingly, the police had difficulty in determining Copeland's address from the phone number provided by Mr Mifsud. The phone was at the bottom of the stairs at 25 Sunnybank Road and used by all the tenants. When detectives contacted British Telecom shortly after 6.00 pm to trace the address, they were told that the only person with access to the necessary equipment had gone home for the weekend. There was a delay of about two-and-a-half hours in obtaining the address while this special person was contacted and brought back into work.

It appeared to the Flying Squad detectives that Copeland was yet another possible suspect, and the officers were aware there had already been a number of arrests or visits since the pictures were issued and all of them had been negative. Before going to Farnborough, the officers went further into Hampshire, to the county's police headquarters at Winchester to check on what was known about Copeland. After finding out that his three previous convictions, although drink-related, did not involve serious violence, Scotland Yard has said a 'risk assessment' was made and it was decided that the officers should not be armed when they went to see whether he looked like the suspect. This was to be simply a visit. No warrant for his arrest had been issued.

The Flying Squad officers travelled in two cars and did not arrive at Sunnybank Road until after midnight. At least one local resident had seen them, thought it suspicious, and had wondered about reporting them to Farnborough Police. However, although the curtains were drawn at No. 25 in the front downstairs room, in what the officers rightly guessed was the living room, they could see through a chink that the lights were still on.

The decision was made to approach the front door. Unknown to the officers, Copeland had a crossbow, a Barnett Panzer. A fearsome weapon, he kept it by his bedside, loaded with a bolt. It was so powerful that if fired at the door, the bolt would have gone right through, hitting anyone on the other side. He was to boast afterwards that he planned to use it to kill anyone trying to arrest him. Also by his bed, between it and the bedside cabinet, was another lethal weapon, a gas-powered air pistol with the words Colt Government stamped on its side. There were also long-bladed hunting knives and a powerful catapult.

The officers got out of their car, rang the bell, and after a little wait, it was opened by a young dark-haired woman in a dressing gown. Alison was asked whether a David Copeland lived there. Not knowing Copeland's surname, she replied that there was someone called Dave in the back upstairs bedroom. Led by Detective Sergeant Peter Basnett, the officers went up the stairs. There was not enough space on the landing for all of them, so some remained on the stairs. An officer knocked on Copeland's door. 'Who's there?' was the response from inside. 'It's the police,' was the reply. After a delay, during which Copeland could be heard moving about, he opened the door, bare chested, the Nazi flag with its swastika pinned on the wall behind him. 'It's him,' exclaimed one of the officers. 'It's him, the bomber!' were the words passed down the stairs from one officer to the next. 'We've got him!'

Copeland was arrested on suspicion of causing the Brixton, Brick Lane and Soho explosions. When cautioned and warned that anything he said could be used against him, he said: 'Yeah, they're all down to me. I did them on my own.'

8

Confession

'I'm a fucking nut who goes round blowing things up.
I'm just totally shot away, a loner. You know, just weird
in the fucking head. I just had to do it. It was my destiny.'
David Copeland

THE OFFICERS WHO ARRESTED COPELAND had gone to his home
in Sunnybank Road in Farnborough to check out someone
who they had been told was simply a suspect. His confession
that he was the nailbomber, made within seconds of his
opening his door, shocked the officers crowded into the small
semi-detached house, but worse was to follow. They saw,
next to his bed, the crossbow ready to fire. They realised that
without body armour or protective vests, they had been in
great danger. Furthermore, after confessing, Copeland had
been asked by the arresting officers whether there were still

explosives in the room. He replied that there were two kilos of ammonium nitrate in the cupboard beside the door. He added that it was 'safe', which was correct, but the police could take no chances. These were Flying Squad detectives, more used to dealing with robbers and organised crime than explosives. They decided that the surrounding area had to be cleared in case of an explosion. Hampshire Police control room in Winchester was alerted, but it was about 45 minutes before local officers arrived in Sunnybank Road and by then some of the Flying Squad officers had started knocking on doors asking people to leave the area.

Hampshire had well-organised evacuation plans ready for such situations. Months later questions were still being asked about what had gone wrong. The local authority's chief executive should have been called, so that he could, in turn, alert staff to prepare a large hall in Farnborough, already earmarked for just such an eventuality. The Women's Royal Voluntary Service should also have been told so they could organise facilities. But the chief executive was not contacted until just before 4.00 am, nearly three hours after Copeland's arrest. In the meantime, a local community hall was opened, but it was totally unsuitable for a large influx of people in the middle of the night, with no bedding and no refreshments. However, those residents with nowhere else to go flocked to it, and were not allowed back to their homes until mid-morning. Among those in the hall was Graham, one of the other tenants of No. 25 Sunnybank Road. He told his neighbours gathered there that he was as amazed as them that Copeland had carried out the terrible nail-bombings. He said he and Copeland had rarely had more than brief chats. The other tenant, Alison, had been taken to Farnborough Police Station.

The arresting Flying Squad officers acted quickly on other fronts, too. They knew more was needed than Copeland's verbal confession that he alone had been responsible for all three bombings, as it was possible he could later deny ever saying that. They also knew that occasionally people for various reasons confess to crimes that they did not commit, or they can claim later that police tricked or forced them into making confessions. Hard evidence was needed.

Copeland had told them that he had assembled the Soho bomb at the Vegas Hotel in Victoria. The officers guessed that the room he had used there had probably been undisturbed since he had left it after viewing TV news coverage of the explosion at the Admiral Duncan. They contacted Scotland Yard with the information and within minutes of the call, police were at the hotel in Victoria gathering hard evidence linking him to the Soho bomb. But that came after a strange coincidence.

Although Copeland had told the arresting officers that he alone had done the bombings, it was too early for Scotland Yard to know whether this was true. The officers sent to The Vegas in Warwick Way had no idea what they would find. There could still be explosives there, or even an accomplice, so they took no chances and blocked off the street. Inside the hotel, a startled night porter let the police in. The arresting officers had passed on information that Copeland had stayed in Room 1, using the name Hawkins. But when the officers at the hotel looked at the hotel register, they thought there had been a mix-up. Despite being an unusual name, registered in Room 2, next door to Room 1, were a Mr and Mrs Copeland. It looked to the police that Copeland either did have accomplices, or that he had been staying in room 2. They were undecided about what to do. If they used the hotel's duplicate keys to get into one of the rooms, anyone inside could raise the alarm, alerting occupants next door. Nor could they smash their way inside.

Their dilemma was solved by the manager, Ms Meena Clark, who had been roused from her bed. She remembered Copeland from the day before. She had been suspicious of him, not because he looked like the bomb suspect, but because he had been rude to one of the cleaning staff and looked a bit scruffy. She assured the officers that Copeland had indeed stayed in Room 1 and that he had checked out. Asked about the Copelands in Room 2, Mrs Clark replied that they were a middle-aged couple from Australia visiting London and they had no connection at all with the single man she knew as Hawkins.

Assured by Ms Clark that no one had been in Room 1 since Copeland had left and it was not due for cleaning until later in the day, the police entered to find it just as Copeland had left it, with some small pieces of wiring in the waste basket constituting hard evidence. The room was sealed to await the arrival of forensic scientists and fingerprint specialists. As there were no explosives in the room, evacuation of the hotel was unnecessary.

Meanwhile, Copeland had been dressed by police in a white, hooded overall and gloves, so that any microscopic traces of explosives on his body, or under his nails, would not be lost, and he would also remain uncontaminated by any substances lingering in the police vehicle in which he was to travel. Copeland was taken to central London, arriving at 2.43 am at Charing Cross Police Station, just a few hundred yards from where his third bomb had exploded only hours earlier.

In the immediate aftermath of the arrest, Scotland Yard was determined to see that every procedure was done properly. So far, Copeland had been more than co-operative. Not only had he confessed, but he had also revealed the ammonium nitrate in his room and confirmed his stays in hotels. Whether this co-operation would continue was uncertain, but first there were a number of hurdles to cross before he could be charged with the three bombings. The arresting officers' notes of their conversation with him at Farnborough had to be read to Copeland at Charing Cross Police Station. When that was done he was asked to sign it as 'a true and accurate record of what was said and what

occurred'. Without hesitation, he scrawled his signature, 'D Copeland'. It was 6.03 am.

News of the arrest was spreading, but confusion still remained when police appeared not to know that his family home was just a few miles away, let alone that he had lived there until a few weeks before. Although police at that stage were officially saying only that an arrested man was helping them with their enquiries, sufficient details were being given in background briefings for the news media to be left in no doubt that the bomber had been caught. Copeland's brother Jon heard of the arrest on the radio news that Saturday morning. The previous day he had seen the photographs of the Brixton bomb suspect in the morning newspapers and thought that they bore a remarkable likeness to his brother. Perhaps understandably, rather than contact the police, he tried to telephone his father and his brother, without any success. Eventually, after hearing the radio news, he managed to speak to his father and put his concerns to him. Mr Copeland repeated what he had told Paul Mifsud, that although it did look like David, it could not be him as he did not have a white baseball cap. Later that morning, on learning that the suspect had been arrested in Farnborough, Jon went to his brother's home to get to the bottom of what was happening. The area round 25 Sunnybank Road was cordoned off, so Jon approached a police officer, told him who he was, and was asked to go to Farnborough Police Station. Learning there that it was indeed his brother who had been arrested, Jon telephoned his father from the police station at about midday. Even then, so many hours after the arrest, no police officer had contacted Stephen Copeland, the man who worked with Copeland every day and who also often saw him at weekends when Copeland visited the family home. If the police had had time to research the tip-offs they had been given that Copeland was the bomber, then they would have visited his father at an early stage to gather background information that could have been used as evidence.

Paul Mifsud went to work normally that morning, but Anti-Terrorist Branch police telephoned him, saying they wanted to see him again. He agreed to travel home, but on the way, overcome with emotion, he had to stop his car. When he eventually reached his home, he spent six hours making a full statement, telling the detectives everything he could remember about Copeland and his attitudes. When he finished, the officers told him that they were now completely certain that they had the right man.

Copeland himself was allowed to rest in his cell at Charing Cross Police Station during the day. Although he had confessed, police wanted to question him more thoroughly to obtain more information and evidence before charging him. The officers briefed for the questioning, both skilled interrogators from the Anti-Terrorist Branch, knew that to get the whole picture, the full truth, they had a lot of area to cover and time was limited. They had to get it right because after someone is charged, no further questioning is usually possible.

As they prepared for what was to be a series of interviews, a lawyer had to be contacted to represent Copeland's interests. Peter Silver was the 'duty solicitor' on call that Saturday at Charing Cross Police Station. He was asked to go there and told briefly by telephone who he would be representing. Mr Silver's firm in north London is small, fairly new, and had never handled anything as big as this case. There was another worry for him. He is Jewish and did not know if his client, an alleged racist, was also anti-Semitic. Mr Silver arrived at the police station determined to receive a full briefing from detectives before questioning started. Without having to ask, Mr Silver was given that briefing, as was a young woman, Laura Gifford, who, like Mr Silver, was also on call to act as 'an appropriate adult'. Each police station has such independent people attached to them, ready to sit in on interviews with people judged for various reasons to be at risk or vulnerable. In Copeland's case, he was young and facing the most serious charges possible and he had also shown signs of mental instability. Ms Gifford works with Westminster Council's West End Community Mental Health Team, based in Soho offices a couple of hundred yards from the Admiral Duncan pub. She had been on duty and had heard the bomb go off.

Questioning of Copeland started shortly after 6.00 pm, almost exactly twenty-four hours after the last of his three bombs had exploded. There were two sessions of questioning, lasting altogether for just over four hours, the second ending in the early afternoon of the following day. We have obtained a copy of the full transcript of these interviews, 274 pages in all, and it is devastating material, providing a remarkable insight into the motives and mind of this angry young man.

Switching on a tape recorder, Detective Sergeant Terence Boland and Detective Constable Philip Johnstone introduced themselves to Copeland, and Ms Garrod explained she was there to ensure the interview was conducted properly and fairly and that Copeland understood what was happening. He was then read a formal caution: 'You do not have to say anything, but it may harm your defence if you do not mention when questioned, something which you later rely on in court. Anything you do say may be given in evidence. Do you understand that, David?' Copeland replied that he did, but Mr Silver, wanting to make sure, spelled out in greater detail what the caution meant. Again, Copeland said he was happy. There was an interruption as another officer entered with refreshments. The transcript shows how this broke the formality of the occasion, allowing those in the room to relax a bit for what could turn out to be a harrowing and difficult interview.

Any doubts the police harboured that Copeland's co-operative attitude might end were dispelled within minutes. There was no need for the two officers to use the hard-man, soft-man tactic still frequently employed to get a suspect to open up during questioning. Copeland was eager to help. He again agreed that the notes made by the arresting Flying Squad detectives were accurate, a 'spot-on' record. The Anti-Terrorist Branch officers then summarised the three bombings. Boland's next question to Copeland got straight to the heart of the matter.

'Did you plant these devices?'

Copeland replied: 'Yes, I did.'

'David, could you tell me, please, why?'

'Terrorism, fear. To terrorise people.'

The police, still seeking hard evidence, had structured their interviews in advance so that they would start with the freshest outrage, the Soho bombing, then go back to deal chronologically with Copeland's background, then the Brixton and Brick Lane bombs, with more, if necessary, on the Soho bomb and, finally, the key questions relating to his motives. It did not go entirely to plan, largely because Copeland jumped from one subject to another, sometimes introducing new aspects not known to his questioners. He was eager to explain how and why he had done the bombings, and the officers were prepared to let him expand, occasionally bringing him back to the point.

Talking about the Admiral Duncan explosion, Copeland said he had been in Soho on the Thursday afternoon deciding where to leave his bomb. That particular pub had been pointed out to him as 'a queer one' by someone in a sex shop, but while there he heard on the radio that police had issued photographs taken from CCTV of the Brixton bomb. He had bought a newspaper, saw his picture, thought 'flip', and realised the game was up, that it was only a question of time before he was arrested. He had bombed the black and Asian communities and was determined to kill gays, too, before police caught him. Copeland said he then dashed home to 25 Sunnybank Road in Farnborough. He had thought police might have been waiting for him there, but as there was no one, he grabbed parts and explosives for his third bomb, stuffed them into a hold-all and dashed back to London by train, staying in a bed and breakfast hotel in Victoria where he assembled his bomb. He moved round the corner to a second hotel the next morning, put the finishing touches to the device and set off for Soho, arriving there far too early. To pass time he went into another pub, and then at 5.50 pm, he went into the Admiral Duncan. In a matter-of-fact way, he described how he'd bought a drink and put his bomb bag down halfway along the bar, where he could keep an eye on it. He stayed for about 25 minutes, walked back to his hotel, and watched news of the pub bomb on Channel Four. He then went to Waterloo, took a train back to Farnborough, and wheeled his bike home from the station, as he had got a puncture cycling to the station with the bomb on his back.

Each of the tapes used by the police lasted only thirty minutes, and with the first recording about to finish, Detective Sergeant Boland again returned to motives.

'David, can I ask you, what made you decide that you wanted to put some bombs down?'

Copeland replied: 'I had a thought once, it was at the time of that Centenniel Park bombing [the Atlanta Olympics bomb in 1996]. The Notting Hill Carnival was on at the same time, and I just thought in my head — why can't someone blow that place up? That'll be a good 'un, you know. That will piss everyone off. And after a few years, the thoughts were getting stronger and stronger.'

Just as Copeland appeared to be getting into his stride, the recording machine's buzzer sounded a warning that the tape was about to finish. The discussion had to end, but then, with a fresh tape inserted, Copeland, still eager to tell all, picked up from where he had left off, explaining that the thoughts of carrying out a bombing kept returning to him:

'It kept going round, floating round my head, day after day, after day. And then, after a while, do you know what I mean, I became that thought. You know I was gonna do it. I was gonna get it out of my head, and the only way to get rid of it, was to do it.'

'How long ago was this, David?' Boland asked.

'Just gone three years, I've been planning this.'

'How many bombs did you plan, or intend to plant?'

'As many as I could, one a week.'

'Can I ask, how did you pick your targets?'

'I knew that Brixton was the focal point for the black community. I knew that Brick Lane was the focal point for the Asian community. I knew that Soho was a focal point for the gay community. I knew it would just piss everyone off. Mr Blair, Mandelson, whoever.'

The questioning then turned to Copeland's first attempts at making a high-performance bomb in 1997, which had ended in failure. He gave up the idea, but then said that early in 1999, while alone in his room in Farnborough, he again turned to *The Terrorist's Handbook* which he had printed from the Internet two years before.

'I was just bored one night and I thought I'll read through that manual. There's nothing else to do. I didn't really read through much of it, and I found a bit that said how to make a real pipe bomb. And then, it was easy after that. The idea started floating round me head again.'

'The Brixton and Brick Lane devices, there was a lot of nails, perhaps screws?'

'All nails.'

'Were there any nails in the device last night [in Soho]?'

'Yeah, I'd say the same quantity. They were carbon copies of each other.'

He then went into considerable detail about how he had made the bombs and where he had bought the explosives and other parts, most of them from shops in or near Farnborough. Asked to describe what he did on the day of the Brixton bomb, Copeland replied in a staccato way, as though he was being debriefed.

'The night before, I built the bomb. Let it dry overnight.

Made the device in the morning, and wired it all up. Set the time. Took the bike to the station. Got the train. Train to Clapham Junction. Got off there. Messed up my time a bit. I was about an hour and a half too early. Sat in a pub for ten minutes, twenty minutes. Had a drink. Decided then to look round Brixton. I got a taxi from Clapham Junction to Brixton. A black cab. Just parked up in the middle of the road outside the station. I was about an hour too early. Done a bit of window shopping. Marked where I was gonna put the device. Needed a piss. Went in the library. That was just to see if they had a toilet.'

Copeland said that he was surprised to find Brixton so multiracial. He had expected that, as a white, he would 'stick out like a sore thumb'. If he had known in advance that a fair proportion of people in Brixton were white, then he would have bombed another area of south London, Peckham, which he knew had more blacks. But his mind was set on Brixton. He decided that, although he had arrived too early, he was not going to attempt to re-set the timer on the bomb. On the other hand, he did not want to put the bomb down too early. So it was a question of filling in time. Amazingly, he appears to have experienced no tension. He repeatedly told police that wandering round the area was 'boring'. At one stage he went to a small park in the heart of Brixton. While sitting on a wall, there occurred, once again, another bizarre coincidence, the black humour of which escaped Copeland. He was approached by two people asking questions about what he thought of the police. The pair were carrying out a survey and Copeland was happy to answer their questions, which included one about whether he thought there were enough Bobbies on the beat.

DS Boland and DC Johnstone then asked Copeland exactly where he had placed the bomb. They explained to him that they knew where the bomb had exploded, but it had been moved to that position and they were not sure exactly where it had first been. Shown a detailed map of the area, Copeland pointed out the Iceland shop entrance next to a busy bus stop, marked it with a little x, and, chillingly, said he had left it there 'to get the people walking by and the people at the bus stop'. Even though they were experienced officers, some of Copeland's responses took them aback, so, just to make sure that they had heard correctly, DC Johnstone asked, 'You were hoping to hurt the people at the bus stop?'

'That's correct,' replied Copeland.

Later in the interview, Copeland said he had got so bored that he put the bomb down about half an hour before it was set to explode. He stayed at the scene for a few minutes, taking off the gloves he had been wearing to avoid leaving fingerprints, then he casually wandered off, walking south along Brixton High Road. He turned into Acre Lane, walked along to a mini-cab office, and took a cab from there back to Clapham Junction Station. He had something to eat in a burger restaurant and then returned by train to Farnborough, cycling from the station back to his room.

That evening, Copeland watched TV to see the results of his bomb. Next day, he bought the Sunday newspapers, and cut out the pictures and descriptions of the injuries and devastation he had caused. He pinned the cuttings up on the wall in his small bedsit, alongside photos of other atrocities. Asked why he kept the Brixton bomb cuttings, and added Brick Lane material, Copeland gave another chilling response, suggesting that he was a craftsman who liked to admire his work: 'I get off on them, I think.'

'You get off on them?' repeated an intrigued, DC Johnstone. 'Tell me a bit more about that?'

Copeland replied: 'I don't know. I just like them, to see me handiwork. I just think most people would do.'

The two detectives then asked Copeland about the Brick Lane bomb. Again, the young man, eager to help, dealt with his second bomb in the same matter-of-fact way. He had assembled it on the Friday night and the next day had set the timer and then cycled off towards Farnborough Station. But half-way there he realised that he had forgotten his rail pass, so he returned home, re-set the bomb for a little later than originally planned, and then took a taxi to Farnborough Station. He went by train to Waterloo and then took a black London taxi to Shoreditch Station, next to Brick Lane. But on arrival, he again realised his planning had gone wrong. He was a day early. The famous Brick Lane market, where he intended leaving the bomb among the crowds, is held on Sundays, not Saturdays. He said he decided 'to abort the mission'.

'I presumed the market was on a Saturday, but I asked someone when I got up there, and they said, no, it was on a Sunday,' said Copeland. 'So then I was in two minds whether to disassemble the device, and go back on Sunday. Then I just dumped it.' He abandoned it in Hanbury Street, off Brick Lane, between two vans, hoping they would be blown up and 'make a bit of smoke, a bit of fire, a bit of damage'. But he also said he chose the spot for another reason. There were few people about and he did not want to be seen planting the device, and reckoned the vehicles would mask his escape. However, that explanation was immediately contradicted when police asked him whether he had been looking around for CCTV cameras or police on patrol. 'Not really, no,' responded Copeland. 'Personally, I wanted to get caught.'

Asked why he hoped he would be arrested, Copeland's reply and the exchange that followed were most revealing.

'I wanted to be famous. I believe in what I believe in, and I took that belief to the extreme. That's the only way I can put it.'

'But I mean you're a young man, aren't you?' Boland asked.

'Yeah, I'm 23.'

'And you know the consequences of this?'

'Well, I don't care. I had no life anyway. I'd say this is freedom to me.'

Johnstone asked: 'What do you mean, you had no life?'

'Well, I'm a fucking nut who goes round blowing things up. I'm just totally shot away, a loner. You know, just weird in the fucking head.'

'Why?'

'I had a horrible, bad childhood.'

He explained more about the motives behind his bombing campaign and his plans if he had not been caught by police. Referring first to Brixton, he said: 'First of all it was gonna be the blacks, then the Asians, then queers.' Copeland said that his next target would have been Southall, but he would have had to leave his attack for several weeks, as he had run out of bomb equipment and fireworks.

He explained that he did not like ethnic minorities.

'I want them out of this country. I'm a National Socialist. Nazi, whatever you want to call me. I believe in a master race.'

Boland asked: 'But you're saying to us that you're a loner. You're not part of any organisation?'

'No, I wouldn't trust any of those idiots. They're just a bunch of yobs, that's all they are.'

Johnstone then asked: 'How would you obtain this state as an individual then?'

'Well, I'd just be the spark, that's all I would plan to be — the spark that would set fire to this country. 'Cos every nutter out there now, if he wants to get on the news, he's gonna have to blow something up. They're all thinking about it. If you've ever read *The Turner Diaries*, you'd know, [in] the Year 2000 there'll be the uprising and all that racial violence on the street.'

'So, your aim was more than just to plant bombs and hurt people?'

'That's right. My aim was political. It was to cause a racial war in this country. There'd be a backlash from the ethnic communities, then all the white people would go out and vote BNP. Do you know what I mean? It'll be obvious.'

'That's how you understand it.'

'If I was a white person with kids in London and they had all these blacks and Asians coming after you with knives and what have you, what are you gonna do? Put up with it? No, you're not. You'll vote them out.'

The two officers then moved on to Copeland's third target. They asked him more about the Soho bomb and probed his attitude towards homosexuals, making an observation about his demeanour that Copeland appeared to think meant that they were suggesting that he was homosexual.

'I chose the gays 'cos I hate them. I mean that was personal. [The Soho bomb] I'm sorry to say it was, but it was.'

Johnstone queried: 'The tape can't pick this up, but whenever we speak to you about the gays, you have to close your eyes and you seem to be quite intense there, David.'

'Yeah, I just don't like them. I just don't like them. Yeah. I'm completely straight, yeah, don't worry about that.'

'No, no, no. It's not a problem, but it upsets you. Now I don't know why it upsets you. It's upset you enough to plant a bomb, I don't know why.'

Boland continued: 'I can see you've explained your political interest but you say that's purely a personal thing, the gays?'

'They're a minority. I knew it would piss everyone off, especially like Blair and Mandelson and all them lot [and] Mr Boateng [the junior Home Office minister].'

At that stage, just before 8.00 pm, that day's series of interviews finished. A lot had been covered in one and a half hours, and although Copeland had clearly said enough to be charged, that would have meant there could be no more questioning. When talking through his confession at the end of the day's interviews, the Anti-Terrorist Branch detectives decided to continue questioning him the next day. They wanted more information from him about each of the bombs, the kind of detail that only the bomber would know. They wanted more about his motives and his mental state, whether he fully comprehended what he had done. And they sought to find out more about his connections with the extreme right, as they were not accepting his assurances that the three bombings were entirely his own work.

Meanwhile, another of the Soho bomb victims died in University College Hospital. John Light had fought bravely to survive his awful injuries, but he finally succumbed on the Saturday night. Copeland was told the news and his short response, a question, probably summed up his state of mind. 'Does that make me a serial killer?' he asked.

Sunday's questioning was to last, excluding a lunch break, for nearly three hours. It started at 10.16 am with the same people present, Copeland, DS Boland, DC Johnstone, Copeland's solicitor, Peter Silver, and Laura Garrod. The police quickly got to the point, with Boland questioning Copeland.

'David, could you please explain to me, when you made these devices, what your intent was?'

'Murder, mayhem, chaos, damage, to get on the news. It's a top story really.'

'So you're saying to me, your intent was to really harm as many people as you can or could?'

'My main aim was to spread fear, resentment and hatred throughout this country.'

'And were you aware that the content of these explosive devices would possibly kill somebody?'

'I had calculated there would be casualties.'

'Had you calculated for the possibility of fatality?'

'Yes.'

'As you're aware, three people have died as a result of the device on Friday night. Can you tell me how you feel about that now?'

'I feel nothing. I don't feel sadness, but I don't feel joy. I did what I had to do.'

'Are you sorry?'

'I'm sorry for the woman and the child. I think the woman was pregnant. I feel sorry for her. But I don't feel no guilt for the others.'

Copeland was referring to the baby injured in the Brixton explosion, the eighteen-month-old girl who had a nail stuck in her skull.

'I'm sorry for the baby as well. But no one else. You know, that's it. I knew there'd be casualties and I'm very glad that the child will make a full recovery. I was prepared to take casualties, yeah, but the thought of killing someone, I don't enjoy the thought. I knew it could happen. I don't feel sad about it. I was just like a robot at the time. I had to do it.'

Johnstone continued the questioning: 'You had to do it, yeah. When you put it down, did you think of the consequences or of other people?'

'No. Not at all. No.'

'No. And Brick Lane?'

'The same again. I just didn't feel anything.'

'And Soho?'

'The same again. When I was in there I saw the people I was gonna maim and kill. I didn't feel joy about it. I didn't feel sad. I just didn't feel anything.'

By this stage, if not long before, the police questioners and those sitting in on the interview must have realised that they were dealing with a classic psychopath, someone who usually appeared quite normal but was also devoid of feeling and capable of inflicting severe violence. The police, however, wanted to make sure there was enough to sustain murder charges. If these were later dropped to manslaughter due to the balance of his mind being disturbed, then that would be decided by lawyers and the Crown Prosecution Service. To be insane under the law, a person must be unable to distinguish between right and wrong. What the police needed to know was that Copeland knew the difference and intended to injure and kill people, that he knew that was the logical outcome of exploding bombs loaded with nails. The detectives pressed on, asking Copeland how people caught by his bombs would get hurt.

'I knew people would get hurt. Maimed. Killed. I didn't fantasise about killing people. I never have done, I don't get off on that. I fantasise about the chaos and disruption that's caused.'

Johnstone said: 'Right. So you knew that when you put that bomb out that people would get killed?'

'I was just like a robot. I knew that.'

'You knew they'd be killed?'

'I thought they would be.'

'You knew that people would be seriously injured?'

'Yeah.'

'So has that anything to do with the make-up of your bombs then? These bombs are pretty lethal, it would appear.'

'Yeah, they were lethal bombs. It's the only sort of bombs I could make at the time.'

'Right. Why did you put nails in them. What did that mean to you by putting nails in the bombs?'

'It means they'd smash windows, stick into people and maim people and kill people.'

Boland asked: 'Roughly what sort of poundage weight of nails would you say was in each device?'

'About 10 lbs.'

Johnstone continued: 'Could you estimate how many nails there would have been in each bomb?'

'Hundreds, from small ones up to big ones, all brand new, bought from B&Q.'

The detectives then asked him specifically about his state of mind when he planted the Brick Lane and Soho bombs. Again, his responses were revealing, suggesting that he knew he was bordering on insanity. Laura Garrod, who was sitting in to see fairness was done, had hardly said a word during two hours of interviews, but she was to ask a telling question. Once more, Copeland describes himself as being like a robot, compelled to bomb. First, Brick Lane: 'I didn't want to kill anyone, but if anyone did die, it wouldn't have bothered me. I was like a robot. I just done it, I had to do it.'

Johnstone asked: 'What about Soho?'

'I knew that people would be killed, but I had to do it. It just wouldn't leave my mind'.

Garrod then asked: 'You keep saying you had to do it. Why? What would have happened if you didn't do it?'

'I'd have probably gone insane, ended up as a tramp or something. I don't know if that would have been a bad thing or a good thing. It was just something that wouldn't leave my mind. I had this thought for years.'

Boland continued: 'How do you feel about it now? We're a few days past, you know the consequences.'

'I don't feel nothing. I don't feel sadness or sorrow. I don't feel joy in killing anyone. I do feel sorrow about that woman as she had a child, a baby. I do feel sick about that, I just had to do it. It was my destiny.'

At that crucial stage, the discussion had to stop because the recording machine again buzzed, warning that the tape was about to run out. After a fresh one had been inserted, any worries that Copeland would be reluctant to continue were dispelled. Copeland was more than happy to continue with his confession. Over the previous weeks he had had to keep his thoughts and actions secret. Now he was with people who were interested in him and his innermost feelings. He was unburdening himself.

Johnstone began: 'You said you had to do it, otherwise you may have gone insane and become a tramp.'

'I might not have gone insane, but I just couldn't get it out of my mind. I had to do it.'

'What sort of thoughts did you have on that front? I don't want to labour the point, but when you say you had to do it, what sort of things were you thinking about?'

'On the train, I just kept imagining it exploding. Walking through the High Street, and I just imagined it exploding. I just saw the flash.'

Garrod asked: 'Were you looking forward to it exploding?'

'In a way I think I was hoping it would explode, killing me.'

Boland wondered: 'Why, David?'

'Because I'm a coward. I've had suicidal tendencies for a long time. But I can't end my own life.'

'You can't what?'

'End my own life.'

'Did you have any fear at any time that it might explode on your back?'

'No, not at all. I didn't think of it.'

'You were confident in your own sort of mechanics, were you?'

'It's not that I was confident. It wasn't that I was confident. I just didn't care. If it did [explode], it did. I just didn't care.'

Copeland went on to tell the officers that he had not stayed behind after planting his bombs, preferring to watch what had happened later on TV news programmes. Boland, probing into Copeland's warped mind, said he found that strange as Copeland had told them a minute before that he had imagined seeing the flash.

'Clearly you would have an opportunity to stand, as quite often people do, to stand across the road and watch your deeds. You never thought about doing that?'

'I thought about hanging around, coming back afterwards. Helping out afterwards. But I just never did it. I thought a lot of times about phoning, trying to torment you lot.'

The police then went on to ask him about his personal life. Copeland said he did not drink. He was teetotal and had not been in a pub for years. He said his only vice was cigarettes, on which he spent about £4 a day. Asked about girlfriends, Copeland said he had not had one for about three years. He used prostitutes, travelling to Soho on some Fridays. He would watch strippers and then, about once a month, would look for a prostitute, a different one each time. As for his family, Copeland said he never saw either of his brothers and had not seen his mother for two years. He did not want to speak to her. There had not been an argument. He simply did not like going to see his mother and her parents, with whom she was staying. He did not get on with any other relatives, and as for his father, with whom he worked, Copeland said: 'I don't like him, but you know I can get on with him. I have the odd conversation at work. Nothing about this, though. I think he knew I was a National Socialist. I've never denied that to him.'

Taking that as their cue, the officers then probed more about his terrorist links. But Copeland repeated what he had said earlier, that although a member of the fascist Nationalist Socialist Movement, he had carried out the bombings by himself. He said he did not know anyone in either of the two groups that had claimed responsibility for the bombings, C18 or the White Wolves, and indeed, he had never heard of the latter group until a few weeks before. Their claims were 'fictional'. They were trying to 'take my glory'. He did say, however, that after planting the Brick Lane bomb, he had tried to claim responsibility on behalf of C18. He had dialled 999 from a phone box near Brick Lane and on the push-button dial, had pressed the digits 218, the two representing the letter C. He had intended to speak, but instead had put the receiver down. Curiously, the detectives did not follow up this apparent contradiction in Copeland's account. Here he was saying that he had no connection with C18, calling them at one stage 'drunken yobs, football hooligans', but he made a phone call on their behalf.

For the next half hour, Copeland was shown maps and CCTV taken at Brixton and at Waterloo when he had arrived by train on his way to bomb Brick Lane. The officers asked him to point himself out in the crowds of people at Brixton and he willingly co-operated, marking Xs on the maps as well. It was a tedious business, but something that had to be done by the police to ensure that they could tie him in to each scene. Certainly, Copeland was impressed with all the work they had put into discovering the CCTV footage of him. With the interrogation almost over, after all the talk of death and maiming, Copeland's observation that the detectives 'must have spent hours watching all these videos', allowed a joke, a bit of light relief:

Johnstone said: 'Look at my eyes, mate. Look at these eyes.'

(Everyone laughed.)

Silver (the solicitor) remarked: 'You've only had your glasses for a week.'

Boland continued the joke: 'No, he never used to wear them till the 18th [the day after the Brixton bomb].'

'I didn't have this squint either,' Johnstone shot back.

The last ten minutes of the interview largely summarised what had been covered earlier. The detectives made sure that they had not made any mistakes in their understanding of what the bomber had said. Satisfied, they then allowed him free rein to expand on his views, occasionally interrupting with provocative, almost teasing, questions, showing up his naïve, racist, half-baked political views for what they were — ridiculous.

Copeland began: 'I chose political targets. I am political.'

'What's political about Brixton?' Johnstone wondered.

'I presumed it was at the heart of the black community. I am a National Socialist.'

'What does that mean?'

'It means I am a socialist who believes in my race and my country.'

'Go on, then, tell me a bit more.'

'I put that before anything else. My race and my country.'

'Go on. What's the difference between a white person and a black person then, apart from the colour?'

'There's ... er ... certain races are better at certain things. I admit the black race are predominantly better athletes at certain things, [like] the power events, sprinting, and I'm not too sure about that 'cos I reckon there's a lot of drugs going around in those events. The white race is the best mentally. When it comes to Japanese, they're very good mentally, maybe on the same level as the white race. The Asian people seem quite clever, good at business. But I do predominantly say that the white race is the master race. Over the whole thing, it's best at more or less everything. I mean, if you look over history, the white race has invented every venture [sic] ever created. You look at every white country, they're now in disarray, falling apart, but they are still a hundred times more advanced than the Asian or black country.'

The interview then turned to Copeland's other great hate, homosexuals. Once again, a question from Laura Garrod was to show that Copeland had not thought through his ideas. He had described gay people as 'degenerates', without any place in society.

Copeland began: 'The whole point of animals is to breed. These people can't breed. They're just taking up space.'

Boland queried: 'Yeah, but we're not animals, David, are we? We're human.'

'Yeah, we're still animals though, intelligent animals.'

Garrod interjected: 'Can I ask, you're focusing on the homosexual. Is that directed at homosexual men or homosexual women as well?'

'I probably think just men. I've got nothing against lesbians.'

'Why not? If you hate the men, why not the women?'

'I don't know.'

'It's the same thing, isn't it?' Boland pushed him.

'Same thing, yeah. But being a straight man, yeah, I can see women would do that, but I can't see why a man would want to do that.'

Johnstone kept up the pressure: 'So how do the gay

people fit in with your political beliefs then?'

'I don't know. They're different. They're wrong, they're perverted, they're degenerates.'

'So, a white gay man, how does he fit into the scheme of things?'

'Well, he don't. He's unnatural. I mean if you look at any religious book ever written, The Bible to The Koran, they all pronounce them as degenerates that should be put to death.'

'And is that what you think?'

'Personally, yes.'

It then emerged in the interview that Copeland's hatred of homosexuals could have been greater than his hatred of ethnic minorities. Asked how he would compare a gay white man to a heterosexual black or Asian, he replied that he would prefer the black or the Asian. The detectives then turned the discussion back to the bombings, reintroducing the subject by way of ethnic cleansing. They referred to the cuttings and photos of Kosovo that Copeland had stuck up on his wall. Copeland said he thought ethnic cleansing was good: 'I think the Serbians have a right to ethnically cleanse.'

Johnstone asked him: 'What about you as an individual then, in these acts you've committed, does it fit in with that?'

'I think perfectly British people have a right to ethnically cleanse. You know the British people didn't ask these people over. They were brought over for the main reason as cheap labour, and every white man and woman now has to work for cheap labour so, it's totally wrong. You know we've got so many poor white people in this country. It wasn't so bad thirty years ago, 'cos the councils were still white and they looked after their own. But now you get all this bullshit, everything has to be equal. It demeans the white man in this country. People like me, I'm looked on as a second-class citizen.'

'And how do you feel now that all these things have happened?'

'I don't feel any different. I don't feel joy. I don't feel

sadness.'

Boland pushed him: 'Got any remorse, David?'

Copeland, referring to Andrea Dykes, who was killed in the Soho bomb, said: 'Yeah, I do a bit for the woman, because she was heavily pregnant, 'cos I didn't even see any women there. I feel very sorry for that woman and for the child, even if it's a black one, the one that got the nail in the head [the baby injured in the Brixton bomb].'

'How about the three people that are dead?'

'I couldn't help it. I had to do it. You know what I mean. I'm not gonna sit here and lie to you, but they're dead. I feel nothing about it.'

'And the people that are injured?'

'Nothing.'

'The property that was damaged?'

'Chaos, damage, fire, it's OK.'

'And the mayhem that you've caused throughout the country? Fear?'

'I like that.'

'You've terrorised the UK basically. Do you like that?'

'Yes, I do. That was the plan at the start.'

DC Johnstone then asked whether there was anything else he wanted to say, and Copeland replied 'nothing'. But Johnstone's police colleague had not quite finished.

Boland asked: 'You know, you said you wanted to be famous.'

'That's part of it, yeah, that's part of my fantasy.'

'Who's your main hero then?'

'Adolf Hitler.'

'Any others?'

'Stalin and Saddam Hussein'

'Why?'

'They're just real dictators. They're strong. Strong people.'

He repeated that another of his role models was Henry Lee Lucas, a Chicago serial killer. His story *Henry: Portrait of a Serial Killer* was Copeland's favourite film. DC Johnstone then drew the interview to a close, with a short summing up.

'David, you've murdered three people.'

'Yeah, I understand that.'

'You've injured countless people.'

'I understand that.'

'You've caused a lot of damage.'

'Yeah.'

'And you've caused a lot of fear within the United Kingdom. Do you accept all that?'

'Yes, I do.'

'And were they your intentions when you started this thing?'

'Yeah, I'm not gonna lie to you. Yes, it was.'

DC Johnstone then asked Copeland's solicitor, Peter Silver, whether he had anything to say. Mr Silver said he had not, but Laura Garrod had a question for Copeland. The resulting exchange lasted only about a minute, ending the series of interviews with this disturbed young man. We reproduce that last minute almost in its entirety as it is a further demonstration of just how unbalanced Copeland had become.

Garrod asked him: 'How do you see your future now?'

'I believe [they will] give me five years [then] I'll be released.'

'Why?'

'I can't see that Mr Blair will be running this country in five years.'

'On what grounds will you be released, David?'

'I believe that I'll be released by the Home Secretary, whoever that is. He'll release me and by that time, the BNP, the National Front will be in charge. Give it five, ten years.'

'In this country?'

'Or even the National Socialists, 'cos every right-winger now must be thinking to themselves they've got to blow something up now. Especially these White Wolves or whatever they call themselves.'

'Why have they?'

'They're saying in the Press [that] all these bombings are theirs, but they're not, they're mine.'

'So?'

'So they have to carry it on.'

Boland ended the conversation: 'It is now six minutes past two and I conclude the interview, David.'

9

Gathering Evidence

'I just want to look him in the eye and ask him — is it true?'
David Copeland's father

COPELAND'S FAMILY, AND THOSE WHO KNEW HIM, reacted to his arrest with a mixture of amazement, disbelief and shock, none more dramatically than his workmate Paul Mifsud, the man who had given the key information to the police. On Saturday, the day after telephoning the police, Mr Mifsud made a long statement to detectives, telling them all he knew about Copeland. Afterwards, he was beset with doubts. He could not believe that the young man with whom he had been so close could really be the same person responsible for such horrific bombings, or that Copeland was capable of keeping up such a deception with him. He worried that he could have landed an innocent man in the worst kind of trouble. Agonising that he had done wrong and unable to sleep, he left his home in the early hours and went walking, trying to resolve the turmoil in his mind. He remembers ending up in a park at 2.00 am, shouting and screaming that it could not have been Copeland. Then he recalls the truth suddenly hitting him. The young man he had tried to befriend was indeed the nailbomber.

From that moment on, Mr Mifsud started to feel better, but he stayed off work for some weeks, and even months later he was still clearly affected and under medication. His main concern was the continued guilt he felt about the Soho bomb, that it could have been prevented if he had contacted the police earlier. That was not the case, officers had told him, but they had given no further explanation. He was relieved and grateful when told months later that Copeland had left his home for Soho the day before Mr Mifsud had seen his photo in newspapers.

Copeland's father was devastated. With the family home besieged by reporters, he stayed inside, wandering around in his pyjamas. Eventually he prepared a statement with help from his son Jon. On the Tuesday, four days after the arrest, Mr Copeland went outside, dressed in motorcycle gear and helmet, so he could not be properly seen. 'What has happened is absolutely horrendous,' he said. 'It doesn't make any sense. I keep cracking up, so do all the family. We are in terrible shock. We are all extremely upset and our thoughts are with those innocent people who have been killed or maimed. We are praying for those on the critical list to pull through. It is terrible. Our whole family's best wishes go out to the families of those who have been injured and killed. I can't imagine how they must feel.'

He said his son was no different from any other youngster and when growing up had not been more trouble than anyone else. 'If I'd had an inkling that my son may have been involved, as a responsible dad, I would have questioned him for my own peace of mind. I have to see him face to face. I just want to look him in the eye and ask him – is it true? I'm praying he doesn't refuse to see me.'

Mr Copeland went a few days later with Jon to the high security Belmarsh Prison in south-east London. David Copeland's first words shocked them both. Instead of any expression of emotion, whether of defiance or remorse, or an inquiry about how his family had been affected, his main concern was for his dear pet rat. 'How's Whizzer?' he asked.

Copeland's mother was even more devastated. She had seen the TV news broadcasts of the CCTV footage of the Brixton bomb suspect and it had never crossed her mind that the pictures even looked a little like her son David. Although he had not spoken to her for some time, even after his arrest, she simply could not believe he was capable of such dreadful acts.

By a strange twist of fate, she had been very close to one of the bomb explosions. On 30 April, the day of the Soho bomb, she went to central London with some younger friends from the Berkshire hospital where she works to celebrate one of their birthdays. They got to Covent Garden, where Mrs Copeland had not been since she was eighteen years old. The group set off on foot to have a look at the nearby Soho sex shops and gay bars, but halfway there they decided to go into a bar at Leicester Square, where they stayed for the rest of the evening, meeting some Americans and having a lively time. It was only on the way home in a cab that she and her friends heard the news on the radio, and realised that they could have been caught up in the blast if they had continued into Soho.

She already knew that her sister-in-law Jane's daughter Sally could have been caught by the Brixton explosion. Sally lives near Brixton and usually went shopping with her partner, who's black, every Saturday afternoon at Brixton market where the first bomb went off. However, that day she had decided not to go as she was heavily pregnant and tired. By the time Mrs Copeland went to Belmarsh Prison to visit her son, she had been seen by the police but she was still grappling with the awful reality and under medication. An emotional person normally, she knew she would find the visit shocking and upsetting, but she was determined that David be told of the personal devastation he had caused.

Mrs Copeland had never been in a high-security environment before and she told us that, as she passed through one security check after another in Belmarsh, her insides got tighter and tighter until she felt she was going to have a seizure. She said seeing him was terrible. He looked so thin and gaunt that she wanted to touch him, but there was security glass between them. Weeping and close to breaking down, she told him the Soho bomb could have killed her. He hardly responded, and afterwards complained she had upset him by winding him up.

The police were jubilant at the arrest. True, three people had died and more than a hundred had been maimed or injured, but, given the circumstances, it could have been much worse. The belief was that if it had not been for their excellent, methodical investigation, Copeland could still have been at large. The police had triumphed. That was the prevailing mood when senior Scotland Yard detectives gave a news conference after the bomber's capture. Police released more information than is usual after someone has been charged, but, even so, there were major omissions in what reporters were told by Assistant Commissioner David Veness, and head of the Anti-Terrorist Branch, Deputy Assistant Commissioner Alan Fry.

What journalists wanted was background material on the bomber, and the triumphant police at that stage were more than happy to oblige. Their position was understandable. They knew they had the right man. Copeland had made detailed confessions during two days of police interviews. There was no question of him having been subjected to any kind of oppression or trickery. Not only had a defence solicitor been present, but also sitting in the interview room had been a trained psychiatric social worker.

The case was cut and dried. The police were proud of the job they had done and they wanted credit for it. But no matter how heinous the crime legal safeguards apply, aimed at ensuring that a charged person gets a fair trial in front of a jury which has been untainted by prejudicial comments. The police knew Copeland's rights had to be respected, but what about the rights of his victims and their friends and families? Did they not have a right to know of the police's success? And what about the wider public, in particular, the minorities who had been in such fear that they were to be the next targets on the bomber's list? Should they not be told in the clearest possible terms that the bomber had been caught, that he had been acting alone, and that there was no need for further panic?

At the time of the news conference, police knew that Copeland had confessed that he was in the far-right National Socialist Movement. A membership card had been found in his room. He had also expressed sympathy in his police interview for the BNP. The police also knew he had received literature from neo-Nazi groups in the USA. Furthermore, he had told police that he had telephoned to claim one of the bombings as the responsibility of C18. This was one of the groups that the police and public knew had claimed responsibility for the attacks.

But none of this information was passed to journalists or the outside world relying on their reports. Assistant Commissioner Veness and Deputy Assistant Commissioner Fry made no mention of Copeland having declared himself on arrest as a Nazi, or that he was an NSM member. Copeland was portrayed as a lone bomber with no connections with the extreme right.

Mr Veness said: 'There is no suggestion at this stage that the arrest is linked in any way to the extreme right-wing groups which have been reportedly claiming responsibility for these attacks on innocent people. The man is not a member of any of the groups which made claims of responsibility for the bombings, nor did he make any of the claims using their names. It is understood he was working alone for his own motives.'

While Mr Veness was correct — the National Socialist Movement had never claimed responsibility for any of the bombings — newspapers the next day predictably seized on Copeland's apparent lack of connections with the extreme right. The *Daily Telegraph* said 'Neo-Nazi links ruled out as "loner" charged'. *The Guardian*'s headline read: 'Police say man on bomb charge was acting alone'. The paper's introductory paragraph said he was 'not linked to any extreme right-wing organisation'. *The Times* headline read 'Nail bombs: loner charged'. The *Daily Mail* said: 'Police suspected the bomber "was not a member of any neo-Nazi group"'. After Copeland's first court appearance, the *Independent* reported that Scotland Yard had said 'the bombings were not linked to any Right-Wing or neo-Nazi group'.

To be fair, it has to be said that Scotland Yard never made such claims. But anyone who knows how the media operates, including the police, might have expected such headlines to follow what had been said at the news conference. Only a very thorough reading later of the full police statement demonstrates that it could have been misleading and that there were omissions. There was overwhelming relief that the police had got their man and deserved their success.

Immediately after the news conference, however, the police were concentrating on gathering more evidence against Copeland. It was decided that he should not be put on any identification parades. Although by that stage the police knew there were witnesses who had seen him at Brick Lane and at Soho, the legal advice was that, given the circumstances, any evidence resulting from ID parades would not stand up in court. It could be argued by defence lawyers that anyone picking out Copeland in a line-up could have been mistaken because their memories had been tainted by the pictures that had appeared of the suspect in newspapers and on TV. Anyway, his confession had been very comprehensive, and detailed. But there was still a problem with it — Copeland could have obtained details of the bombings from the extensive media coverage and he could have made up the other points. As much as possible of what he had said and admitted to in the police interviews had to be proven as fact.

A mass of evidence supporting his confession and linking him to the three bombs was found in his room in Sunnybank Road. From the amount of material recovered, it is clear that he kept virtually everything left over from making the devices. The police found Internet print-outs of *The Terrorist's Handbook* which gave detailed instructions for making pipe-bombs, clockwork timer delays, the use of nails for anti-personnel effect, and guidance on using flash powder-based explosive obtained from fireworks. Among the literature in the room were posters and newspaper material concerning the Brixton and Brick Lane bomb victims, and a copy of the *Sun* from 30 April which carried the photos of the bomb suspect taken from CCTV footage. Clothing included a National Socialist T-shirt, black combat style trousers and a white polo shirt with a UEFA Euro '96 England logo, which he had worn when planting the Soho bomb. There were also lengths of plastic pipe, some of which were capped and glued at the ends; electrically initiated 'match head' igniters with plastic sleeves that matched fragments found at Brixton; electrical wires, connectors and insulating tape; plastic seal-tight sandwich-type box containers similar to those used in all three bombs; batteries; parts from the alarm clocks used as timers in the bombs; and large quantities of nails as well as tools and glue.

Littering the room were large numbers of fireworks, including 140 Air Thunders from which explosive powder amounting to several kilos had been removed. One kilo would have been enough to cause just one of the explosions. Other empty casings included fireworks called 'Wicked Demon' and 'God of Thunder'. Copeland had told detectives that he had bought 'Air Thunders' and 'Flash and Thunders' from local shops, spending about £1,500 over a 4–6-week period. It appears that none of the shops involved thought there was anything unusual about such large purchases, even when some of the fireworks were bought at the height of the bombing campaign. Even after the release of the CCTV footage of the Brixton bomb suspect, no one from the area contacted the police.

Detectives visited the main shop involved, Raison Brothers, in Park Road, Farnborough. Staff there remember selling a mixture of fireworks and other items over a few months to a young man fitting Copeland's description who always paid in cash. The purchases included large numbers of '56-shot' Roman candles and 'Air Thunder' rockets. He also bought a Barnett Panzer crossbow, crossbow bolts and a telescopic sight. On one occasion, 30 March, because he had bought so much and he had his bike with him, staff phoned for a taxi from A-Line Taxis. Police traced the driver, Timmy Rossiter, who remembers taking Copeland to 25 Sunnybank Road. He also recalls his passenger praising the police for recovering his bike which had been stolen. There had been some bureaucratic difficulty in handing the bike back to Copeland that had necessitated him going to meet police to sort out the problem. Anti-Terrorist Branch detectives later obtained Hampshire Police records relating to Copeland's reporting of the theft of the bike and its return to him. Even the Hampshire Police who dealt with Copeland appear to have failed to have recognised the pictures of the Brixton bomb suspect issued just a month later.

Copeland also bought fireworks from the Joke Shop, a hundred yards further up Park Road from Raison Brothers. Two days after the Brixton bomb, Copeland purchased forty

'Air Thunder' rockets there, taking them away in another A-Line taxi. He returned a week later, two days after the Brick Lane explosion, and bought twenty more 'Air Thunders', presumably for the Soho bomb. Both transactions were recorded on the shop's CCTV.

Also found in Copeland's room were two receipts for the hold-alls used in the Brick Lane and Soho bombs. The first was a receipt for a £11.99 Reebok sports bag bought at the Littlewoods Index store in Farnborough's Prince's Mead shopping centre. Detectives looked through CCTV from the centre and saw Copeland at the doorway of the Index store at the time the sale was made, 1.46 pm on 21 April, three days before the Brick Lane explosion. The second receipt was for a Nike hold-all, bought with cash two days before the Soho bomb at 3.24 pm from the Argos store in the adjacent King's Mead shopping centre. Again, CCTV linked Copeland to the purchase. Although no receipt was found for the Head bag used in the Brixton explosion, Copeland had told police that he had bought it from the same Index shop from which he had bought the Brick Lane bag. The records show a Head bag being bought for cash at 3.31 pm on 13 April, four days before the first explosion. Once again, video was found showing him at the Index doorway at the precise time the sale was made.

Another receipt, for £4.99, was for one of the old-fashioned Acctim brand alarm clocks, used in the bombs. This, too, had been bought at Littlewoods Index store in Farnborough shortly after he had bought the Nike hold-all used for the Soho bomb. A search of records at the store showed the same model clock had been sold on two other occasions that month, on 12 April and 22 April. CCTV again showed him at the store at the relevant times.

Other receipts for April found in Copeland's room were from the Farnborough B&Q DIY store for a hammer, nails and epoxy resin glue that he had used to seal up the end of each bomb. There were receipts for batteries bought at the

Tandy store in the King's Mead shopping centre, and video footage taken there linked him to the purchase.

Empty nail packets were found, which would have contained well over 10 kilos of assorted nails. They had been bought at two other DIY stores, Homebase and Wickes, as well as from B&Q.

Copeland had told police that the Reebok baseball cap he had worn at the Brixton and Brick Lane bombs had been bought a few days before the first explosion from the JB sports shop in Queen's Mead. A search of the records there showed only one such Reebok cap sold in the week before the Brixton bomb.

Two other items linking him to the Soho bomb were also found in the room. The first was a wristwatch with a face that, when illuminated, shines blue. David, the businessman who had been at the Admiral Duncan, remembers speaking to a young man wearing just such a watch shortly before the explosion ripped through the pub. The final evidence was the receipt for the cup of tea Copeland had bought at Waterloo, on his way home from blowing up the Admiral Duncan.

Interestingly, a list prepared by the prosecution of what had been found in the room did not include the crossbow that had been beside his bed. The initial notes of the officers who arrested him also appear to make no mention of the fearsome weapon either. Why both sets of people, lawyers and police, made the same omission remains unclear.

Anti-Terrorist Branch detectives set about finding even more evidence linking him with the three blasts. At Brixton, there was plenty of CCTV footage showing the bomber in the immediate vicinity. Copeland himself had been played some of the footage during his police interviews and had confirmed that the man in the light-coloured baseball cap had indeed been him. After planting the bomb, he said he had walked along Acre Lane, from where he took a mini-cab back to Clapham Junction. Police found video footage of him

leaving and returning to Clapham Junction Station, and of
him turning into Acre Lane.

The police picture of Copeland's movements that
Saturday afternoon would have been complete if they had
managed at an early stage to trace the cab driver who had
taken him from Brixton to the railway station. For some
inexplicable reason he was not contacted until months later
by which time he had forgotten all about his passenger. The
cab office used by Copeland is very easy to find. It is the first
cab office reached by anyone walking along Acre Lane from
the centre of Brixton. The office records there show someone
walking in and asking to be taken to Clapham Junction. The
timing is consistent with when Copeland left Brixton and
when he was seen back at Clapham Junction, about half an
hour before his bomb went off.

More CCTV evidence was found linking Copeland to the
Brick Lane explosion, and the two taxi drivers who had
carried him during his journey there remembered him
clearly. Colin Elson, from A-Line taxis, had taken him to
Farnborough railway station, having picked him up from 25
Sunnybank Road. He told us that as Copeland got into the
cab, he hit the door with the bag he was carrying, which was
obviously a heavy one. Mr Elson recalled saying: 'Steady on,
mate, mind the paint,' and Copeland apologised. Mr Elson
also apologised: 'I was late for his booking. He wasn't
worried at all. He said it was no problem. He just relaxed
and sank back in the back seat and off we went.' Had he
seemed nervous? 'Not at all. I might as well have been taking
him for a night out on the town. He looked like he could
have done with a shave. Other than that the thing that drew
my attention was that it was a hot sunny day and the
windows on the taxi were closed at the back. He had a winter
coat on, a black quilted jacket, done up to the neck. That
seemed to me to be strange. But his actual manner was very
relaxed, happy, cheerful. I had been late on the job and he
could have missed his train. He didn't, but he wasn't worried

at all. I dropped him at the approach to the station. He gave me £5, which was slightly over the fare, and said, "Keep the change, mate, see you later," and he took his bag and walked off.'

Mr Elson contacted the police after hearing of Copeland's arrest at Sunnybank Road. Reflecting on the episode now, Mr Elson said: 'I've come so close to somebody who's done something so horrific, and he just seemed a normal young lad — 22 or 23, the same age as my stepson and all his friends. It's just disbelief. You expect someone who commits an act like a bombing not to be the same as the rest of us. He just appeared to be another happy-go-lucky lad, and there he is, sat in the back behind me with a bomb not two feet away from me. That's quite a sobering thought.'

Copeland caught the 3.30 pm train from Farnborough to Waterloo where detectives found CCTV of him taken by different cameras around the station. He is first seen coming from the entrance to platforms five and six, then walking across the concourse, passing telephones, the gents lavatory and a ticket office, and then leaving the station, walking along the pavement to the taxi rank. He approached the head of queue and got in a taxi that took him to Brick Lane.

The driver, Rino, contacted the police after the CCTV footage of the bomb suspect was issued. He told us what he remembered of his fare and the journey: 'My first impression was that I didn't like the look of him. He stood out like a sore thumb, because it was a very hot day and he was over-dressed. He had a shirt buttoned up right to the neck and a baseball cap covering his head. You could just see his eyes and his eyebrows. As I was on the rank, I had no choice but to take him to the destination. Had it been on the street, and he waved me down, I wouldn't have stopped. He asked for Shoreditch, which is a bit unusual. Then he straight away asked how long would it take, not how much it would cost. When he said that, I thought he was aggravation because most people would ask how much first, rather than how long it would take. He looked at my face. He saw I didn't like it, and he said straight away that he wasn't in a rush. But now I know why he asked.'

During the journey, Rino occasionally looked at his passenger in his rear view mirror. 'Halfway through the journey, as we got to St Paul's Cathedral, he made a silly remark, asking whether it was Trafalgar Square. I thought it was a bit stupid really, considering that it's a well-known landmark. I ignored it. I thought he was just winding me up. Looking back now, I'd say he was very nervous. He sat rigid in the middle of the cab when a customer on his own normally sits in the corner. He had a bag with him, which he was holding on to for dear life. He did not let it go. It was between his legs, so it didn't move. Normally someone puts a bag on the floor and you can hear it sliding across the floor as you fly around the corners, but it didn't move and he didn't move. He pulled me over rather sharply when we got to Brick Lane. It was about 200 yards from Shoreditch Station. Considering he'd said that he didn't know London, I was a bit taken aback really. Obviously, he just wanted to get out. He'd sort of panicked. He had the £5 note in his hand to pay the fare, and it was saturated with sweat — obviously, thinking back now, you can understand why. I pointed out the way to the station, and I just stopped there for a second. I watched him walk up this side road. He stopped, turned round, and looked at me. I was a bit surprised at him looking like that, and then I just drove off.'

Police obtained CCTV film of Rino's cab on its way to Brick Lane from three separate cameras, and from another on its way back through the City of London, empty. After planting the bomb, Copeland said he caught another cab back to Tottenham Court Road in central London. There has been no response to police appeals in newspapers and magazines for whoever may have picked him up in the Brick Lane area to contact Scotland Yard.

Police were to find more video evidence against

Copeland tying him in with the Soho bomb. Copeland was picked up by a camera walking past a shop in Old Compton Street, heading in the direction of the Admiral Duncan pub. He was carrying a bag and the time was 5.47 pm. He is also seen on video from another camera in the same street, again carrying a bag. Eighteen minutes later video from that same camera shows him walking in the opposite direction, away from the pub, without the bag.

During his police interviews, Copeland had described where in the pub he had left the bomb bag, where he had sat, how someone had talked to him and how he had left in a hurry. Detectives were able to confirm all these points of detail from interviewing the survivors, and on examination of medical notes of injuries. Copeland had said he sat at the end of the bar, bought a Coke, and left after a few minutes, during which time a man had chatted to him. That man was the businessman, David, and he told police that he remembered talking to the young man, who had been uneasy, looking frequently at his watch, which had a blue face. Copeland had also described pushing his way through a group of people to get outside. His rudeness is remembered by Gary Partridge, another of the victims.

The pub's staff told detectives that they had seen the suspicious bag, lying against the bottom of the bar. They were about to raise the alarm when the device went off, sending out a hail of nails that sliced through people's legs. Some of the wounds sustained in the pub bomb later became infected, unlike those caused by the first two bombings. This led to suggestions that the Admiral Duncan bomb may have been deliberately contaminated. Copeland denied the claim, but did say that his pet rat Whizzer could have urinated or left droppings on some of the bomb parts.

After leaving the pub, Copeland returned to the Vegas Hotel in Warwick Way, Victoria, where he had assembled the bomb that morning. Asked by police after his arrest, whether he could have left anything at The Vegas, Copeland replied that there may have been some wires left behind there. When police went to his room at the hotel, they found small pieces of wire in the wastebasket. By the time police learned that he had also stayed round the corner at the Airways Hotel, in St George's Drive, his room there had already been cleaned and was being occupied by someone else.

Copeland's confession in his initial interviews with police had been full and detailed. His disclosures about how he had carried out the bombings were consistent with the facts. But over the following weeks, as detectives checked out what the bomber had said about his background, there was a growing realisation that it was not the whole truth. Not only did some minor points given as fact fail to stand up to examination, but there were also distortions and omissions. Some of the latter probably occurred because his police interrogators had not explored his motivation in great detail. No blame, however, should be attached to them. They had been looking for a full confession and they had got it. It is not known how much they had been told of Copeland's background and of what had been found in his room before their two long interviews with him. But if he had been asked about some of what had been discovered at 25 Sunnybank Road, it could have proved very embarrassing for Scotland Yard.

Copeland had bought a crossbow, bolts and a sight from Raison Brothers in Farnborough. He had boasted about it to his workmate, Paul Mifsud, who had passed the information on to police. We have learned that the crossbow and a gas pistol were found in his room. Curiously, neither weapon is mentioned in the list of the room contents prepared by the prosecution for a preliminary court hearing. Only the crossbow bolts appear. The police who questioned Copeland asked him nothing about either the crossbow or a gas gun. If they had done, Copeland may well have given the same response as he gave to someone in prison — he had the crossbow in anticipation of a siege situation at No. 25 and that if police came through his door, he would shoot them with crossbow bolts. He went on to explain why he had not carried out his plan when he was arrested. Although the police version of events is that they knocked on his room door and announced who they were, Copeland denied hearing them and claimed he opened the door because he thought one of the other tenants, Graham or Alison, had knocked.

Whether Copeland was fantasising or not misses the point. The Flying Squad officers sent to Farnborough at short notice went into the house, we are told, without guns. Copeland had a crossbow. If he had used it, one or more of the arresting officers could have been killed or badly injured. Whether the officers involved knew before or afterwards of the danger in which they had been placed, is a point Scotland Yard has refused to discuss.

Some of the inaccuracies in Copeland's account to police of his background could be attributed to poor memory. He said, for example, that his second address in London had been 47 Bective Avenue, Forest Gate. There is no Bective Avenue anywhere in London, but there is a Bective Road in east London. When we knocked at No. 47 there, a couple answered who said they had been living there by themselves. They said the police had also visited the address, and they gave us, as they had given the police, the name and telephone number of the landlord. When contacted, he said he had never heard of a David Copeland. It later emerged that he had stayed at No. 45 next door, a house divided into several bed-sits.

There were also straightforward lies, particularly when he was asked by police about his contacts and connections with the extreme right. What did he have to hide? Were there others involved in his bombing campaign? Why did he lie when asked whether he had made any telephone calls on the day of the Soho bomb? Staff at The Vegas said Copeland had tried to use the phone in his room to make calls but he had been directed around the corner to three phone boxes.

Knowing this sequence of events, the police asked him about the phone calls, but Copeland denied making any and the police did not pursue him on the matter.

A mass of literature and correspondence involving Nazi and other far-right groups had been found in his room, as well as the names of individuals with whom Copeland had been in contact. His police interrogators barely touched on these links, apparently accepting Copeland's assurances that he had carried out the bombings alone. He claimed he did not know anyone in the Nazi group C18 as the racist right could not be trusted as they were either 'idiots' or 'a bunch of yobs'.

If that had been the case, why, after the Brick Lane bomb, had he tried to telephone a claim of responsibility on behalf of C18? Unfortunately, the question was not put to him.

The significance of the book *The Turner Diaries* appears also to have been missed by the two detectives. A copy of this immensely influential book, which had inspired, among others, the Oklahoma bomber, Timothy McVeigh, had been found in Copeland's room. Copeland himself introduced it into the police interview, but he was not questioned further about it.

The detectives unwittingly missed another opportunity to get Copeland to open up about one of his main motivating forces — religion. They were not to know how important the ideas of the Christian right were to him. Although some Christian Identity literature had been found in his room, its significance appears not to have been recognised, and police had yet to visit Kirk Barker, the rabid right-winger who had met Copeland six months before and had been put off by his spouting Christian 'rubbish'.

Other literature found in his room included Hitler's *Mein Kampf*, and correspondence from the American Nazi group Aryan Nations. More importantly, there was a volume of material from the UK National Socialist Movement, which included a colourful calendar, newsletters and a membership card. Copeland played down the connection. He said correspondence was sent to his father's address. Curiously, the detectives asked him whether he had a PO Box numbered 3335 in London WC1. This is the box number used by the secretive NSM. Copeland replied that it was not his and, when he was asked whether he had ever heard of it, replied that he had not. Why the detectives did not probe further, pointing out that he must have known it belonged to the NSM, is unclear. He was also not questioned about who he knew in the organisation. If he had been asked, would he have answered that he had been in contact with the movement's leader, Tony Williams? Would he have given the names of those NSM members he may have sounded out about forming a cell of activists?

There were also no questions to Copeland about the address book which had also been found in his room. It contained contact details for a number of people, not only NSM members and supporters, but also some from the British Movement. In the 1970s, the BM had been very active as an extra-Parliamentary racist organisation with about 3,000 members. Now relatively inactive, a shadow of its former self, its two remaining areas of operation are in south London and the East Midlands.

Also during the interview, Copeland had praised the BNP, saying that he believed they would be forming a Government within five years. What did not emerge was that Copeland's introduction to the far right had been via the BNP in east London, that he had been to several of their meetings, and that he had met and talked with one of its leaders, Tony Lecomber, who is believed to be the only other right-wing extremist imprisoned for a nail-bomb attack. Unfortunately, not a single question about the BNP was put to Copeland.

After Copeland had been charged, investigators realised that there were still many unanswered questions. They wanted to visit him in Belmarsh to ask him about his crossbow, and they also recognised that his background links required further exploration. However, it was too late. Copeland's solicitor, Peter Silver, refused permission, believing that his client had already spent enough time with the police.

When the bomb suspect's picture was shown and Copeland was named, anti-fascist campaigners recognised him. They were angry that the police were not revealing his Nazi connections and were portraying him simply as 'a lone wolf'. So information about Copeland's BNP membership was given to the *Daily Mirror*, along with photographs of him standing next to the BNP leader, John Tyndall, who had himself been jailed earlier for possessing offensive weapons and incitement to racial hatred. The *Mirror* decided to publish the story and on 25 May, shortly before the European elections in which the BNP was standing, the paper splashed it across the front page. Under the big headline 'The Link' was a 1997 photograph of Tyndall with Copeland, over whose eyes, for legal reasons, the newspaper had put a black block. Pointing at Copeland was an arrowed caption that read 'HE is the nail bomb suspect' while the caption pointing at Tyndall said ' ... and HE is the leader of the BNP.'

The then Metropolitan Police Commissioner, Sir Paul Condon, was furious. The paper had made the police look foolish by suggesting the police had known nothing of Copeland's BNP connections. In fact, the *Daily Mirror* had told the police in advance that it was about to run the story. On the morning of publication, Scotland Yard announced that it had just raided the addresses of several people connected with the National Socialist Movement or other extreme racist or nationalist groups. Whether it was a chance coincidence that the raids took place on the same day as the *Mirror* story is a matter for speculation.

We have been told by one of the BNP leaders who was raided that some of the police information about Copeland's connections with the party were at best sketchy.

Tony Lecomber became the BNP's national organiser, but

in 1997 he was one of the party's two east London organisers. He explained why he thought he had been subjected to a 7.00 am raid on the day after Special Branch officers had visited Ken Francis, the other east London organiser. Asked about Copeland, Francis had told the officers that Lecomber had said the man arrested for the nailbombings was not the same Copeland who had been a BNP member. Lecomber told us: 'The Special Branch must have thought, what's Lecomber got to hide, denying Copeland's involvement with the BNP? I didn't know what Ken had said at that stage. But while the Special Branch were in my flat, Ken phoned to tell me that he'd had a visit.' By another strange coincidence, the barrister who defended Lecomber on the nail bombing charge, Michael Wolkind, came to represent Copeland on the bomb charges.

In all, eleven houses were raided by police, who are understood to have found some of the addresses in Copeland's room. Among those visited was the heavily tattooed Kirk Barker, who had served three years in jail in the early 1990s for a racial assault.

Barker claims to have met Copeland only once, a few months before the nailbombings. This was at a time Copeland was contacting extreme racists, probably sizing them up on whether they wanted to join him in a secret cell that would carry out violent acts. Barker says the NSM leader, Tony Williams, contacted him, asking him to meet and check out Copeland, someone who Williams said had just moved into the area near Barker, in Basingstoke, Hampshire. Barker took a dislike to his 'going on about Jesus', and reported back to Williams that 'he was a normal sort of lad, but was a Christian'. Barker told us that the detectives who questioned him did not seem surprised when told about Copeland going on about The Bible. He has some experience of police interviewing techniques and agrees that the officers may not have wanted to let on that they had not known of Copeland's religious side.

The NSM's leader, Tony Williams, was also raided. Copeland had joined the NSM after moving from the BNP because it was not violent enough. He became the NSM's Surrey and Hampshire organiser. As soon as Copeland was arrested, Williams knew he was in trouble. His contacts with the bomber would come under scrutiny and it would be suggested that he had encouraged Copeland, if not directly, then with hateful NSM literature. He was also worried about reprisals as he lives in an Essex village close to Colchester, the home of relatives and friends of those who died in the Soho bomb. Williams took immediate action, by closing down the NSM. Without mentioning his famous member by name, or anything at all about the nailbombings, Williams announced his decision in an NSM-headed newsletter carrying three slogans in gothic script — 'Blood is our loyalty. Honour is our duty. Nature is our struggle'. It was dated 4 May, three days after Copeland's arrest:

'It is with regret that I have to inform you that I have taken the decision to disband the National Socialist Movement with immediate effect. Pressures of work and other commitments ... plus an escalating number of extremely difficult circumstances, which cannot be detailed, but which place an insuperable barrier to further progress have combined to make it apparent that it is impossible to continue. Obviously this will be a shock and disappointment to you, but it is sometimes necessary to alter course if this is quite clearly in the best interests of the movement's comrades and fellow members. It only remains for me to thank you for all the comradely messages of encouragement and support and to reassure you that our blood spirit lives on and our flame of struggle burns as bright as ever, regardless of names and times.'

Williams' calm words hid mental turmoil, according to another Nazi, Steve Sargent, brother of Charlie Sargent, the former leader of Combat 18, now serving a life sentence for murder. Williams had also written that NSM money and subscription details to the magazine *Column 88* were to be handed over to another Nazi publication, *White Dragon*, run by Steve Sargent. This came as news to Sargent who claimed not to have been consulted by Williams beforehand. In a newsletter dated 13 May to NSM members and supporters, Sargent, writing on White Dragon headed notepaper under the pseudonym Albion Wolf, explained that the first he knew of Williams' decision was when he received the NSM newsletter of 4 May:

'There was no excuse for not telling me. It was all done in a totally sneaky un-Aryan fashion. It later transpired he had booked into a mental institution after suffering a nervous breakdown. Oh, the pressures of being a Nazi. On 11 June I made another visit to his home and caught him in. Williams was in a total shambles talking gibberish and stinking of cheap whisky, claiming he was setting off to Egypt to seek harmony at the Pyramids! He has effectively destroyed what many of you had worked so hard for, and I offer no excuses or explanations for his behaviour, which was cowardice, pure and simple.'

Sargent, too, avoided mentioning either the nailbombings or Copeland's name. The closest he got was to sign off with the words 'Together we can Cope the Land'. In a later newsletter, Sargent returned to the attack on Williams: 'For a "madman" he certainly had his wits about him when he dissolved everything behind everyone's backs. Mental health problems are a tried and trusted method used by those looking for sympathy for their cowardly actions. When they get captured, they scream about voices in their heads and look for a "nutty ticket" to get a soft sentence, yet they were able enough mentally to hide the body, get rid of the weapon and avoid detection as best they can, so think on! Williams has a long track record of being involved in the movement. He used to speak at meetings and to all intents and purposes seemed a fanatic, but sadly one without a backbone, which nobody can see until a bit of heat comes down.'

Ten weeks after Copeland's arrest, when we saw Williams at his home, he was extremely guarded about his connection with the bomber and with Kirk Barker. He would not confirm or deny that he had talked with either of them. As for what Barker had said to the police and us, that it had been the NSM leader who had introduced him to Copeland, Williams admitted that Barker had been a NSM member who could now be making such claims for a number of reasons. He could have been quite close to Copeland and been the one who tipped off the police or could be trying to distance himself from the bomber by blaming others for what had happened.

Clearly Williams had thought deeply about Copeland and the nailbombings. He described them as having been totally counter-productive and done the wrong way. In a pre-war situation, he said such bombings and violence could be justified, but if embarked on, a bombing campaign should be carried out in a more organised way than Copeland's. Threats should be made first, accompanied by a list of demands, before the carrying out of any violent or terrorist actions.

Much of what is now known of Copeland's Nazi background and of what had motivated him, would never have come to light if he had behaved in the way expected by the authorities. What appeared to be a full and frank confession had been made and that had been supported by a massive amount of independent evidence. Confronted by this, the expectation was that Copeland would have to plead guilty to the three bombings and the three murders. But even with a guilty plea, it would still take time for the Crown Prosecution Service to prepare the legal case against him, and summer holidays had to be taken. A date in September, four months after the arrest, was pencilled in for a hearing at the Old Bailey. The proceedings should be finished in a day, or, at most, a day and a half. The charges would be read out, and Copeland's plea of guilty would be followed by the prosecution giving a brief outline of the case against him. Copeland would then be given three life sentences, with a recommendation that he serve a specified number of years, and the judge would congratulate the Metropolitan Police for having done a wonderful job in bringing the perpetrator of such heinous crimes so quickly to justice.

Such an outcome at that stage would have satisfied virtually everyone. There would probably have been little or no mention in court of Copeland's Nazi links. The role of the BNP and the NSM and other race-hate groups in shaping his beliefs and actions would have gone unrecorded. The failings of the intelligence services would have gone unremarked. The picture presented in court would have been one of success. The authorities had triumphed over a lone, twisted bomber.

But it was not to be. Much to everyone's dismay, a few weeks after the arrest it emerged that Copeland was not going to play ball and roll over. He was fighting on.

10

Awaiting Trial

'*David Copeland suffers from a serious mental illness,
the nature of which is psychotic and the diagnosis, schizophrenia.*'
Broadmoor psychiatric report

'*They can't believe that a sane person could carry out such acts of
violence. I do not suffer from any mental illness whatsoever.*'
David Copeland

AFTER HIS ARREST, COPELAND'S FIRST SIX MONTHS in custody was
spent in Belmarsh Prison in south-east London. At first he
was held in solitary confinement as the prison authorities did
not know how he would react to other prisoners and, more
importantly, how they would react to him. Feelings about the
nailbombings were still strong in the black, Asian and gay
communities and it was feared he could be the target of a

revenge attack. However, it was recognised that solitary confinement could not continue indefinitely, especially as Copeland himself wanted to mix with others on the high-security wing. Questions were also being asked about his mental state, which would inevitably suffer the longer he was kept out of circulation. After a couple of weeks, he was allowed to mix with others in the special secure unit, Double Category A prisoners, the highest security category.

From them, Copeland learned how to deal with the prison regime, and more specifically, about his legal rights. He had also received some letters and other messages of support from people inside and out of the prison system. Typical of these was a ranting message posted on an extreme right-wing website a few days after Copeland's arrest: 'I'd like to say thanks to the London bomber he's actually got off his arse and done something useful we need more people like him with proper guts to do something. In basingstoke not far from Cove [where Copeland had been arrested] the support is growing for this action. We need more bombers to sort out the paki's and niggers to send them back to their own countries and fear OUR WHITE country and not think they are above us like they do in certain areas of our country over-run by these parasites ,and whites that are anti-racist (most whom are probably queer or just sheep led by big brother (THE GOVERMENT) who can't think for themselves and follow the leader like lambs to the slaughter ...'

By the following month, stickers supporting Copeland were being produced by C18. Alongside a drawing of a man with a gun were the words: 'Stand by Dave Copeland - Leaderless Resistance Works! COMBAT 18'.

Another anonymous missive sent months later to the Anti-Nazi League included a well-drawn cartoon set in a supposed sewage treatment works. It depicts a lavatory bowl filled with caricatures of blacks, Asians and gays. Beside the bowl are two young men wearing jackets with the words 'English Patriots' on the backs. Next to them on the floor is a hold-all containing a bomb with a clock timer. On the wall is a poster reading 'Hero. English Patriot. David Copeland. First Treatment Worker.'

The text accompanying the cartoon refers to immigrants and asylum seekers 'pouring in' to England, and goes on to lament that legal restrictions on media coverage of Copeland and his arrest means that no encouragement is being given to 'any other young English patriots to let more bombs off under our immigrants and perverts ... Do you like what's happening to you, the English people, in your own country? David didn't! And like St.George reacted like the good patriot he is ...'

Strengthened by such messages, he started to cause problems, bucking the system, breaking the rules. For example, he knew that prisoners such as him are not allowed to change their appearance without prior permission from prison staff. Copeland defied this regulation by shaving both sides of his head and starting to grow a Mohican hairstyle.

During his bombing campaign he had been in charge, creating terror, giving the police the run around. He had made powerful bombs, deciding where and when to explode them. He had been calling the shots and pulling the strings. He wanted to stay in control in prison, to keep people guessing. He had nothing to lose.

He became more vocal with his racist views, upsetting prison and security staff. When escorted to Bow Street magistrates court for his second remand hearing, he ranted about blacks and 'Pakis' to the security men inside the prison van, even though one of them was black. The bravado extended into court. The hearings were very short, but Copeland would fidget and yawn loudly. On one occasion he kept the court waiting, refusing to leave the cell for the court room, word eventually filtering through that he was suffering from a panic attack. After hurried consultations, it was decided not to force him into the court room. Instead, the court went to him. The Deputy Chief Metropolitan

Magistrate, Ronald Bartle, along with prosecution and defence lawyers, and a token reporter filed out of court to the cell area. Copeland appeared at his cell window and was told he was being remanded in custody for a further two weeks.

In Belmarsh he also set about getting himself fit again. He would try to spend hours every day working out in the gym and running several miles a day. He also desperately wanted to know how he was regarded by the extreme right. In fact, some thought him a hero, believing that he had had the guts to do what many of them had dreamed of doing. Congratulatory messages appeared on websites. NSM members boasted to those in other Nazi groups that he had been 'one of ours'. The BNP officially attempted to distance itself from Copeland, claiming wrongly that he had been at only two of their meetings. But grassroot members who had known him were pleased.

Once again the question of whether he acted alone was raised. While in prison, Copeland said he had been 'acting under orders'. It was a direct contradiction of what he had said in his confession to police, when he had insisted that he had carried out the bombings on his own. He had also denied knowing anyone in C18 or of ever having heard of the White Wolves, one of the organisations that had claimed responsibility for the bombings. In prison, however, Copeland changed his story. He said he was, indeed, a member of the White Wolves. He disclosed that he had been recruited to form a cell of four or five people. He had not wanted to do this because he was a loner. He said he had been ordered not to take any action until the year 2000, but he could not wait and had decided to advance the bombings. Asked why he was now saying this, Copeland replied that he had received a coded White Wolves message while in prison telling him that he could now reveal he was part of the organisation and had been acting under orders. To what extent this was true or a product of Copeland's warped mind is impossible to determine.

Since childhood, Copeland had wanted to go one better than his contemporaries, and in that way gain the recognition he felt he deserved. He had become disillusioned with the BNP, believing it had become too moderate. He joined the more extreme NSM, founded by the man believed responsible for the initial White Wolves propaganda. Hate mail prior to the bombings on White Wolves-headed paper had warned ethnic groups to leave the country by the turn of the year because it would be then that the 'wolves would howl'. However, Copeland could have picked up a lot of information about the White Wolves from newspaper speculation about who was responsible for the bombs. He is known to have been an avid reader of reports on the bombings, even sticking some on his bedroom walls. More credence could have been given to his claim that he was one of the White Wolves if he had kept the coded message he claimed to have received. But Copeland said that because of the note's nature, he had destroyed it. Months later he would again suggest a connection with the White Wolves.

In an attempt to get to the bottom of his connections with the extreme right, the BBC's Home Affairs correspondent, and one of the authors of this book, Graeme McLagan, wrote to Copeland, asking him to set out his political views and when they had been formed. Copeland's reply was brief: 'I cannot express my innercense or guilt in any letters I write due to a bullshit law, which I find extremily hypocritical coming from a DEMOCRATIC government [sic].' He went on, however, to say that he did want to communicate. His note's closing words were very sad, given the devastation and suffering he had caused: 'Sorry about any spelling mistakes.'

Unwilling or incapable of writing more, he filled in an official form requesting a visit from McLagan, but the Home Office blocked it. An official wrote that while the case was of significant public interest there were other factors involved in refusing permission, including the feelings of victims and their families. In a second letter the official turned the request full circle by suggesting that the BBC write to Copeland so that he could divulge information via correspondence.

In other letters and statements written after his arrest, Copeland suggests that 'religion' was his motivating force and that Jews were to have been his next target: 'I am David Copeland and I am a profit sent by God, to show Gods chosen people the Aryans what must be done to save us from Damnation. The Jew (Devils Deciples) and people of mud must be driven out of our lands. It is Gods law and we must obey. I bombed the blacks, Pakis, Degenerates. I would of bombed the Jews as well if I got a chance. An innocent was killed which I am deeply sorry for, but God is cruel and it is his way of showing us that not just the guilty will suffer. Yours sincerely, D J Copeland (Diciple of the Lord)'

In a later letter, he gives a list of biblical references and says he is studying the bible: 'Strangely, it makes very good reading. All the things which the Government run church say is the total oppersite off what God supposedly says. He says that slavery is good, mixed racing is bad, queers deserve to die, black people are of mud and have no sole and are not of his creation ... No wonder he plans to wipe us out soon.'

In another letter, he explains what the NSM stands for: 'NSM stands for the National Socilaist Movement. It's the political wing of C18. I was a recruitment officer for the North Hampshire area, as I new a lot of people there. I would be able to find out if someone who wants to join is genuine. Sometimes it would get very violent....'

The question of other people's involvement in the bombings was to continue to be asked, but of growing concern in those first weeks in prison was whether he would plead guilty. Copeland craved fame and notoriety. The bombings and his arrest had received enormous publicity, but he was disppointed that so little had been written about him personally in newspapers. This had been because contempt laws restrict what can be said about a case, in order that when a defendant stands trial he is in front of a jury that has been untainted by prejudicial comments. Copeland wanted his day in court. He wanted a platform to promote his evil beliefs, and to hit back at all those who over the years had thought him useless.

Other prisoners told him, however, that he was less likely to achieve a place in history if he chose to plead guilty, because the court proceedings would be over in a day and he would probably be denied an opportunity to make a speech. If he pleaded not guilty, however, he could go into the witness box and say whatever he wanted. As for all the evidence against him, the fellow prisoners pointed out that nearly all of it was circumstantial. No one had actually picked him out at an identification parade. His confession represented a major problem, but he could explain it away with a number of different claims — that he had been in a state of shock when arrested, he did not know what he was saying, his police questioners had suggested things to him, he told them what had already been in the public domain in media reports, or that he had made it up as a joke.

Copeland told his solicitor that he wanted to plead not guilty. This placed Peter Silver in a difficult position. It was clear to any lawyer that the evidence against Copeland was overwhelming. A coherent defence to the charges was impossible. At that stage it looked as though the best that could be offered to the bomber was a very full speech of mitigation from his QC, attempting to explain how factors such as his unhappy childhood and adolescence, homophobia and his involvement with Nazi groups had made him an unbalanced person. But the end result would be the same for Copeland — he would be locked away for many, many years, maybe for ever.

It became clear at Copeland's various pre-trial court appearances at the Old Bailey that he was unhappy with his legal team. He tried to change solicitors but was blocked because the court would not allow a switch of legal aid. Frustrated at not getting his own way and not being in control, he spoke out at one hearing declaring that he would defend himself. At one stage he even demanded to be released from prison on bail. His agitation in court was matched by increasingly erratic and contradictory behaviour in prison.

Originally he had denied being mentally ill. He did not want to go down in history as a madman. However, in prison he co-operated with doctors and psychiatrists, having long discussions with them, during which his religious obsessions became apparent. He had been receiving neo-Nazi religious material while in prison. Among the literature was a leaflet listing biblical references to, among other things, homosexuality, race and the Apocalypse. At the same time, Copeland began to discuss the other legal options open to him, including the possibility of being 'nutted off', the prison term for being declared insane, or unfit to plead. He was not legally insane as he could tell the difference between right and wrong, but it could be argued that he was suffering from a personality disorder. His panic attacks could have been a sign of schizophrenia. If he was found to be mentally unfit to plead, he would be sent to a secure mental hospital, probably Broadmoor. It was just a few miles from his family home, so visits from his father and brother would be easy, and his mother also lived close by. Copeland was told he would find life more comfortable there than in prison, and there would always be the chance in the future that he could recover and be freed.

Broadmoor must have been tempting for him, especially as in prison he was visibly becoming more tense and irritable. His sleep was being disrupted. Each day he woke at 4.00 am and was unable to get back to sleep. He was startled by sudden noises and for the first time he was tearful. This was not out of any apparent remorse. It was because he was becoming increasingly depressed about his own condition.

He commented that he had even messed up the Soho bombing. He had set out to kill gays, but while two gay men had died, he had never intended to murder a woman, especially one who was pregnant.

Prosecution and defence lawyers decided at a hearing on 8 October to set in motion a proper assessment of his mental condition. A psychiatric report had been prepared by Copeland's defence team, which had been handed in advance to the Crown's barristers, the highly respected Nigel Sweeney and his junior, Mark Ellison, the same team who had prosecuted in the Mardi Gra case just a few months before. The report by Dr P Gilluley of the Maudsley Hospital in south-east London gave the first startling insight into Copeland's very disturbed mind.

It said Copeland initially co-operated with the chats, but had then become increasingly suspicious. 'At times he has appeared distracted and easily startled by sudden noise,' the report read. 'More recently, he has described having a "bad head" which makes him unable to think clearly. Mr Copeland denies any ideas or plans of self-harm or suicide. He reports, however, that he has little to live for and that death may come as the ultimate answer. Mr Copeland describes a complex delusional system, which includes religious, grandiose and persecutory components. He told me in my last interview that he was "a prophet". He describes his life as "a mission", where everything has been predestined for him. He told me that the outcome of his case did not matter as it would start "the first domino" to fall which would result in others rising to herald the Apocalypse. He believed he would thus be "free" and assume "a powerful position" in the world. This would end with the arrival of Jesus who would take the just to heaven before the world ended. Mr Copeland was unable to give any time for this. At times, he described himself like Jesus and how he is "special". He had only started to read The Bible in the past eighteen months. Through this he had suddenly become aware of his mission in life. On occasions he would quote scriptures to explain his actions.'

The report said Copeland had accused his solicitor of collaborating with Scotland Yard and claimed he had become the victim of a Zionist conspiracy that involved the Home Office, the legal establishment and the police who were all co-operating to cause his downfall.

Dr Gilluley continued: 'On my last interview he told me that the interview room was "bugged" so the authorities could gain more information. He also reported his cell was "bugged". He told me he knew this, but he was unable to get any tools to allow him to dig out the bugs to prove his claim. Prior to being remanded, Mr Copeland described two occasions where he would hear people speaking but no one was in the room. He told me he searched to find the source of these voices, but was unable to. He denies any present hallucinatory experiences. Mr Copeland does not believe he is mentally ill. He described at times a fear that he is "losing my mind". He told me he is unable to concentrate and does silly things like putting on two odd socks, without realising it. He does not believe he requires treatment in hospital.'

The report concludes that Copeland requires urgent assessment and treatment in a hospital setting such as Broadmoor. 'He is suffering from a psychotic illness,' said Dr Gilluley. 'This is characterised by a complex delusional system with religious, grandiose and persecutory components. He has an associated perplexed affect and exhibits a delusional mood (a first rank symptom of schizophrenia). I believe he has partial insight into his illness. It is my opinion he is likely to be suffering from a schizophrenic illness. Due to his underlying mental illness, Mr Copeland is presently unfit to plead. I believe he is unable to instruct counsel or conduct his own defence due to his persecutory delusions. I would also suggest that he is unable to fully understand the consequences of entering a plea due to his religious delusions. Mr Copeland believes that no matter what happens, he will be "freed" and that his case will start the Apocalypse.'

Although it is not in the report, Copeland told the doctor that divine intervention would occur at his trial. He suggested that he would be swept up to heaven from the court room.

At a hearing in the Old Bailey on 8 October, Dr Gilluley's report was given to the judge who was told that both prosecution and defence lawyers had agreed that he should go to Broadmoor for an assessment of whether he was fit to plead and stand trial. There was no immediate place for him there and he would have to join a queue. It seemed that he was third in the waiting list, so would probably be admitted within two weeks. Copeland was not asked for his views on the move, but at his next appearance in court, after being in Broadmoor for a few days, he caused a commotion protesting that he was being held illegally, shouting that he wanted to plead not guilty there and then. The judge ordered him to be taken away, and he was led out of court, each of his arms held by security guards.

In Broadmoor, he again wrote to Graeme McLagan, saying he was trying to arrange a visit. His letter was less coherent than the first, and echoed the psychiatric report by referring to a political conspiracy against him organised by ZOG, an acronym for what those on the extreme right call the Zionist Occupation Government. This term, according to C18, is used to describe 'the assortment of traitors and Zionist lackeys who control most of the White nations. A typical example is the Blair Government and their willing collaborators in the police, media, civil service and local councils, who enforce their anti-White laws on the British people.' The phrase ZOG had first been coined by William Pierce, the author of *The Turner Diaries*, a book cherished by Copeland.

Copeland wrote: 'I'm trying to get you to visit me hear at broadmore, try from your end as well. You are being prevented from visiting me for political reasons only, the Zog are trying to cover up, sweep me under the carpet, as you are a media person and there for part of the Zog maybe unintensionally, you could pull some strings with your Jewish masters. I think you want to find out the truth [sic].' Copeland then highlighted his possible connections to the White Wolves by writing the two letters 'ww' after his signature, which can only be interpreted in the context of the letter, and in light of what he was telling people in prison and Broadmoor, that he was, indeed, a White Wolf.

C18's definition of ZOG appeared on its Blood and Honour website after Copeland's arrest, demonstrating the level of support that exists for violent, including homophobic, action. A cartoon on the site's main page shows a heavy boot coming down hard on a gay man's face. The caption reads: 'Make sure you stamp out your fag properly.' The piece defining ZOG goes on to attack groups such as the BNP and National Front, and calls on National Socialists to adopt a change in tactics to defeat ZOG:

'Are you going to carry on marching up and down whingeing about Blacks coming here, etc., forever, waving your little Union flags to an apathetic public who stop and stare at you as though you were a travelling circus, while the real enemy count their shekels and drink their vintage champagne? Wake up, White man — you're shutting the stable door after the horse has bolted — that stage of the battle is over and we've lost. Those who appreciate the gravity of the situation and can look past ZOG's coloured cannon fodder and see the Capitalist dogs who pull the strings, the unscrupulous one-worlder race-traitors who play the Jews' game to satisfy their greed and lust for power, will realise that NOW IS THE TIME TO REGROUP! GO UNDERGROUND AND TRAIN FOR THE COUNTER-OFFENSIVE! WHATEVER IT TAKES! COMBAT 18.'

Back in the real world, the authorities blocked McLagan's visit to Copeland, saying that only his parents and brother

Mr Evil

Jon would be allowed visits during the three months he was being assessed in the secure hospital. Copeland's father, Stephen, had taken the major role in trying to handle his son's affairs. He went to every court appearance, offering him silent support from the public gallery. His presence was barely acknowledged by Copeland, even though he knew his father was trying to help. While in prison, Copeland was short of money for the little extras that made the tough regime more tolerable. He asked his father to sell his £300 mountain bike and anything else of value. Mr Copeland failed, but it was not for want of trying. The police said they were keeping the bike as evidence for any trial. When David Copeland learned of the decision, he asked his father to try to retrieve £800 in cash, which Copeland claimed had been in his room when he was arrested. The police told his father there had been no such amount of money. Mr Copeland did not know what to think. He knew his son was careless with money, but on the other hand, he knew his son could simply be making trouble and may have thought that an allegation of corruption would cause problems for the authorities. Dutifully, Mr Copeland made an official complaint on his son's behalf.

Mr Copeland was himself doing battle with the authorities over his treasured shotgun. He had been worried at the end of 1998 when his son had returned home from London that he might lose his gun licence because of his son's criminal convictions. Mr Copeland thought the problem was solved when Copeland moved out to Farnborough, but after the arrest, police had seized the shotgun from Mr Copeland. Months later, he wanted it back. The police refused to hand it over, and Mr Copeland started a campaign to get it back, writing to Hampshire's chief constable, his local MP, the Tory Gerald Howarth, the Home Secretary, Jack Straw, and even contacting the media. He explained that he wanted the shotgun back out of principle. It was not him who had criminal convictions. Why should he have to suffer because of what someone else had done? It was totally wrong, he argued.

On visits to Broadmoor, Mr Copeland noticed changes in his son. He had seemed quite relaxed at first, his father noting that he was playing table tennis with another patient while waiting for his visit. But Copeland disclosed that he feared his food was being drugged. He insisted that he was not mad. He said he had lied to doctors in Belmarsh and he was lying now to doctors in Broadmoor. They had been giving him a series of tests that included some bizarre questions to study him for his reactions. Typical of these, said Copeland, was one relating to the six long-bladed knives found in his room. These included a brown sheath embossed with an eagle and swastika, with an elastic leg strap. In the sheath was a brown-handled knife with 'Alles Fur Deutschland' engraved on its nine-inch blade. There was a 5-inch black-handled sheath knife with a swastika on its handle and also a green-handled knife embossed 'Old Timer', with a four-inch blade stamped 'Schrade USA 1420T'. The last of these had a nylon webbing sheath and an elastic leg strap. Asking him about the knives, he said a doctor had asked him if he masturbated over them.

Diagnosed schizophrenic, doctors wanted to start him on a course of treatment that involved injections, but he refused to co-operate. Nurses had to hold him down when he struggled against being injected. He vowed to continue resisting.

When he arrived at Broadmoor, Copeland had been given a standard leaflet by the hospital management that explained his rights, or lack of them, regarding medical treatment: 'Your doctor will talk to you about any treatment that you need for your mental disorder. You can be given medicine or drug treatment for your mental disorder *for up to three months without your consent.*' [Our italics] It said if treatment continued beyond three months and 'you do not or cannot consent', an independent doctor can be called in and other medication recommended. Other patients told Copeland that resistance was pointless because the regulations meant that authorities could do what they wanted, using force every time if necessary.

Copeland did not give up so easily. He began a hunger strike and telephoned his father complaining that Broadmoor was turning him into a zombie. He told his father: 'I am now on hunger strike due to being forced to take drugs for no reason. I was quiet and kept myself to myself when I arrived here at Broadmoor, and several nurses have expressed a view that I am fit to plead, but the doctors are trying so hard to make me unfit to plead. I am 100 per cent worse now than I was before being placed here. If this continues, I will be forced to hold up the trial well into 2001. When I came here I was fit and healthy in body and mind, but in two months I am much worse, and I'm planning to sue the authorities for malpractice for allowing my condition to worsen.'

Copeland called off his hunger strike after only a few days. Once again, other patients had told him it was pointless, that no notice would be taken of him and he would lose some privileges in the meantime.

As 1999 drew to a close, Copeland's defiance appeared to have ended. He had lost control of his situation. His father had visited him in Broadmoor on five or six occasions, noting that each time he seemed more withdrawn and unwilling to talk. His mother had visited, too, but he walked out on her after a few minutes. Shortly before Christmas, he phoned his father and said that he did not want any more visits from him or any other family member. Copeland withdrew. This was probably because he was depressed at getting nowhere in his fight against the authorities he believed were conspiring against him, but there could have been another reason.

Like many others with Nazi or religious leanings, he believed the dawn of the new Millennium would herald either an uprising or Apocalypse or both. He may have been preparing for the cataclysmic event.

While Copeland was in Broadmoor, and said to be suffering from schizophrenia, parallels were drawn with another famous case — that of the Yorkshire Ripper, Peter Sutcliffe, who killed thirteen women and attempted to murder seven others. Prior to his trial in 1981, doctors had diagnosed Sutcliffe as a schizophrenic. Accepting this, the then Attorney-General, Sir Michael Havers, told the judge who was about to start the trial that he did not think Sutcliffe was guilty of murder. Because of his mental condition, it was a case of manslaughter due to diminished responsibility. But the judge refused to accept the argument and a trial took place ending with the jury finding Sutcliffe guilty of murder. The judge gave him twenty life sentences and said he hoped he would never be freed and should not even be considered for release until he had served at least thirty years. Relatives of the dead and survivors of some of his attacks packed the court. All said they were happy with the murder verdict, and would have been angry if the verdict had been one of diminished responsibility.

In dealing with Copeland, the authorities seemed to be hoping that the Broadmoor specialists would find him, like Sutcliffe, unfit to stand trial. The original hope had been that he would have pleaded guilty in the autumn and that there would have been only a short hearing, denying him his platform but allowing praise to be heaped on the police for a successful operation. Such a course, it was argued, would also have spared the victims and their relatives from further pain and suffering. Their ordeal would be prolonged if there was a full-blown Old Bailey trial and they had to give evidence against him or endure weeks of detailed reporting of the trial in the media. These hopes were dashed by Copeland's insistence that he wanted to plead not guilty. A few months later, however, hope was rekindled. If Copeland was declared unfit, all that was then necessary was for the Crown to prove that he had carried out one of the bombings. The prosecution would then outline its strongest case against

Copeland, in this case Brixton where he had been caught on CCTV. None of the victims would need to be called, and Copeland would be found guilty and be consigned to Broadmoor. In this scenario, he would not have an opportunity to give a speech.

However, most of Copeland's victims who have spoken to us said they wanted everything out in the open. They shared the view of those who suffered at the hands of the Yorkshire Ripper. Although Copeland was clearly disturbed, they believe he knew exactly what he was doing when he set out on each of his three bombings. They wanted him punished and some said they thought Broadmoor would be too easy. They wanted him to know the depth of the suffering he had caused, how their lives had been devastated. That, at least, would be some compensation for them.

'Life is never going to be the same again,' said Gary Partridge, who spent weeks in hospital recovering from dreadful burns received in the Soho blast. He had been in the Admiral Duncan with his partner, John Light, and two friends who died, the pregnant Andrea Dykes and the best man at her wedding, Nick Moore. 'John has left a big gap as well as Andrea and Nick,' Mr Partridge said, months after the bombs. 'I still have vivid pictures of what happened. I didn't have nightmares at first, but now they're starting. Never one day passes without me thinking of what happened. It affects your decisions. You live more for today. You value people more. I try not to think of the bomber too much. I don't feel real anger. He probably doesn't know what he's done.'

Colin Moore, Nick Moore's brother, should have been with the group in the pub, but it had proved impossible to get a ticket for the *Mama Mia* show, which the group was going on to see. 'If the police hadn't released the bomber's photo on the Thursday, he would probably have done his third bombing on the Saturday, and then none of this would have happened to my family and friends. But then, I know that's selfish as someone else would have got it, and I wouldn't wish what's happened to us on anyone. Every day when I wake up, I think of my brother and my friends. I'm so angry, but it's diminishing with time. I don't want to lower myself to the bomber's level with hate, but does he know what he's done? Does he feel any remorse at all at destroying people's lives?'

'At first I felt like killing the bomber,' said Andy Butcher, treated in the same severe burns unit as Gary Partridge. 'Then there was hate. Now I can't say that I hate him, but I'm very angry, and obviously he should be punished for what he's done.' Mr Butcher wants Copeland's evil remembered, and hopes that the mood of public outrage at what happened is not forgotten, so that it puts off other like-minded people. Like many other gay people caught in the Soho blast, he felt guilty about the 'straights' there who had been killed or injured. Mr Butcher is also aware that some of the people in the pub had not 'come out', so that after being injured, it was doubly difficult for them, dealing with their injuries and having to explain their sexuality to their parents and families. David, the man who talked to Copeland in the Admiral Duncan, also did not want the charge reduced to manslaughter. 'He knew exactly what he was doing and what would happen when his bomb went off. He wasn't mad.'

'I would like him to be locked in a dark room for ever,' said Mark Taylor, the Admiral Duncan's manager. 'Death would be too easy for him.'

Paul Maskill, the Iceland manager hit by eight nails in the Brixton bomb, said race had not been an issue in the area, which had a tremendous community spirit. He had never viewed the shop customers as black or white. Now, he is embarrassed to be white. The bomb had changed his life. What does he feel about the bomber? 'Nothing,' he replied. 'I've got no thoughts about him whatsoever. I just hope he realises what he's done.'

Copeland's withdrawal lasted until mid-January 2000,

when any hopes that he had been tamed by his treatment were shattered. Doctors had finished their assessment of him and Copeland believed they had concluded that, although he was schizophrenic, he was fit to plead. Copeland was very upset as it looked as though he would not be allowed to plead not guilty and state his case at the Old Bailey. Meanwhile, he had resumed contact with his father and asked him to issue a statement. Mr Copeland, still fighting over his shotgun licence, had set up an Internet website, Citizens' Rights Action Group. Its stated aims were to campaign for innocent people who were suffering, as in Mr Copeland's case, because of guilt by association. The website included a section headed 'Statements from David Copeland', which explained that his father would use it to get his son's views across to the public.

Copeland's first statement, posted on 20 January 2000, protested about being diagnosed as schizophrenic, and came close to admitting that he had been responsible for the bombings: 'Since being here at Broadmoor, I have not shown signs that I have a mental illness, and several nurses have expressed this to me. They say that I have some odd beliefs, but doesn't everyone, and that is the only evidence they have to back up their diagnosis. They have come to this conclusion *as they can't believe that a sane person could carry out acts of such violence, but people like this do surface now and again* [our italics]. I want to say now that I do not suffer from any mental illness whatsoever, and I do not have any of the symptoms that would suggest I am suffering from a psychotic illness.'

Broadmoor's psychiatric report on Copeland after his assessment went further than the earlier report prepared on him in Belmarsh Prison for the defence lawyers. Dated 26 January 2000, and prepared by Dr John V. Basson, Broadmoor's medical director, it provided more interesting information on his childhood, his youth and his religious and political ideas.

'He has reported that he was bullied at school and in his early teenage years his family became concerned about his height and it seems that he became concerned about possible delay in onset of puberty. His consequent low esteem and concern about his self image and sexuality became linked to the development of a psychotic illness. It is possible that his use of alcohol and illegal drugs in his late teenage years was in part an attempt to self-medicate his illness as well as part of an adolescent experimentation in minor delinquent behaviour. As his illness was developed, he has developed delusional beliefs which are connected to his low self-esteem and concern about his sexuality and he took an interest in extreme right-wing and fundamentalist Christian ideology. His attitude to others and more recent offending behaviour shows evidence of arrogance and a lack of empathy and there are significant sadistic elements to his thoughts and behaviour and it is not clear how much these aspects of his personality would alter with treatment of his mental illness.'

The report says Copeland claimed he had begun having right-wing political ideas during his childhood and that at the age of twenty he had joined the BNP. He went to some of its meetings but did not like their adherence to democracy. He had then 'plodded along on my own', before joining the National Socialist Movement. The report also says he implied he had contact with other organisations.

'He said he had begun reading The Bible about two years ago and believed that white people or Germanic people were special and superior to others. He described other people as "people of mud who have no souls. They are not His creation". He felt he was one of the chosen and that he was in "the seed line". Asked about his mission, he said he did not want to talk about it. He said he hated the outside world which he said was "controlled by the Devil and his disciples" and which was full of "degenerates and people who needed to be put out of their fucking misery".

Copeland's paranoia continued as Dr Basson reported

that he was generally suspicious and guarded during interviews: 'He felt there might be cameras in Broadmoor monitoring him and when asked about his interviews being tape recorded, he pointed to a switch on the wall and said it could be a microphone. In fact, there was no machine in the room and certainly no taping was done. He said he did not want to discuss his beliefs or offending in any detail and said he did not wish to be assessed at Broadmoor.'

Returning to Copeland's religious obsessions, the report continued: 'He said that he believed he was alive where others were dead and "soulless". He said he lived his life by The Bible and that his only sin was smoking which he described as "gluttony" and said that he was "desecrating, not polluting" himself. He believed that he was different from most other people and believed he was on a mission chosen by God and that the Government would like him to be diagnosed as mad and "swept under the carpet". He believed he was an artist who had used "streets, glass and blood" to show people and teach them what the future would bring. He believed that the future would bring Armageddon and the end of the world and this would begin on the first day of the new year and end soon afterwards. He wanted people to see the truth and said "the Creator is displeased, we are not what he intended". He described himself as a prophet, "a simple man", not like Jesus, but more like "Moses or Ben Hur". He laughed inappropriately when he talked about these issues. He said that his role had been to "awaken people". When asked about events, he said one needed to read The Bible, but "not the one re-written by Jews, homosexuals or blacks". He said that whilst at school he had been a Devil worshipper and someone had suggested he should read The Bible. He talked further about the end of the world in the Year 2000 and added "the nuclear holocaust will come". He was worried about being diagnosed as mentally ill and kept stating "I expect you think I am a psychopath".'

The Broadmoor report ends with four conclusions, the first of which seems surprising, given what preceded it:

1. 'David Copeland is fit to plead. He understands the charges against him. I think he could, if he wished, instruct his lawyers and he can understand the proceedings of the court.'

2. 'David Copeland suffers from a serious mental illness, the nature of which is psychotic and the diagnosis, schizophrenia.'

3. 'The mental illness from which he is suffering is possibly responsive to treatment and he has been started on treatment, but it is early days, although already there have been signs of some improvement. The full impact of treatment on his psychosis has yet to be seen.'

4. 'The patient is appropriately placed in a mental hospital and, given the circumstances, a high security hospital such as Broadmoor is the best choice.'

At another preliminary hearing at the Old Bailey on 28 January, both sides agreed that further assessments were needed of Copeland's state of mind. The Broadmoor report had been for the court. The prosecution decided it wanted its own psychiatrist to carry out an assessment, and Judge Neal Denison, the Common Sergeant of London, gave permission for one to be done in February while Copeland was still in Broadmoor. Approval for a further defence assessment was also given to Copeland's QC, Michael Wolkind, who wanted it conducted under different circumstances. He told the court about Copeland's objection to forced medication. One of the side-effects of the drugs he was being given was to reduce his concentration to only a few minutes, making it impossible for him to give meaningful instructions to his solicitor, Peter Silver. Mr Wolkind said the new defence assessment should be done when Copeland was not on drugs. If that was not possible in Broadmoor, he wanted his client transferred back to prison, where drugs could not be forced on him.

Copeland's parents also noticed a change in him on visits. They saw that his eyes were distant and that he did not seem to be interested in conversing. Copeland himself complained about ill-treatment in another letter to Graeme McLagan. Once again he insisted he was not mad, but said the authorities were trying to 'nut him off' to save themselves from embarrassment: 'Even though I do not act like a schizo, I have been diagnosed one. I believe it is political as they couldn't get me in here fast enough and get me drugged up to the eyeballs shortly before my trial. People come in here normal and are turned into vegetables. Some of them are petty crooks. I have seen this with my own eyes. This is what they are trying to do to me. The drugs have slowed me down so much it's taken an hour to write this short letter. The powers that be are trying to nut me off without giving me a trial as it will be embarrassing to them.'

Further letters to Copeland asking questions about his beliefs were blocked by Dr A Payne, Copeland's forensic psychiatrist at Broadmoor, who wrote that he had stopped two letters 'in the interests of the patient's safety'. Dr Payne refused to explain his decision, which appeared to conflict with the Broadmoor assessment that Copeland was mentally fit to stand trial. McLagan complained about this inexplicable high-handed action to the Mental Health Act Commission, which has similar policing powers in mental institutions to those of prison visitors. After reviewing the correspondence, Copeland's situation and asking Dr Payne for an explanation, the Commission ruled in McLagan's favour and ordered Broadmoor to let the letters through to Copeland. By then, however, Copeland had changed his plea.

A few days before he was next due to appear at the Old Bailey to enter pleas to the charges he faced, he surprised everyone by switching from his declared position of not guilty to one of pleading guilty. The only explanation put forward to explain the change has been that the drugs he was being forced to take at Broadmoor had at last had an effect, and that he realised there was no point in contesting such a massive amount of evidence against him. However, his guilt came with a condition, as a crowded Old Bailey court learned on 24 February.

News of the changed plea spread beforehand. Reporters understood that Copeland was going to plead guilty to causing the three explosions at Brixton, Brick Lane and Soho and plead not guilty to the murders of Andrea Dykes, John Light and Nik Moore, but guilty to the manslaughter of the three due to diminished responsibility, a plea meaning that he was seriously mentally ill at the time he planted the Admiral Duncan bomb. Manslaughter pleas have to be agreed by the prosecution and the judge and, if successful, would mean the defendant being sent off to a special mental hospital. However, preliminary indications were that the prosecution would not accept such pleas at that stage, partly because their own psychiatric assessment of Copeland had not been completed, but no one knew for certain that that would be the stance taken.

As Copeland was led into the dock, flanked by five guards, the court was packed with lawyers, police and journalists, standing in the aisles and at the back of the court. In the public gallery were many friends and relatives of those who had died as well as some who had themselves been injured. Copeland's workmate, Paul Mifsud, the man who had tipped off the police was at the back of public gallery. Sitting in front of him, but ignoring him were Mr Copeland and his eldest son, Jon.

Copeland was asked to stand and, as expected, pleaded guilty to the first three charges relating to the explosions. As he then pleaded not guilty to the first murder, but guilty to manslaughter, there were outbursts from the relatives in the public gallery. In the front row, Andrea Dykes' sister began shouting and sobbing and had to be restrained. There were shouts of 'shame' and 'send him down' when Copeland pleaded guilty to the manslaughter of the second and third of his victims. As the protests continued, Copeland's father stood up in the public gallery. Most people in his situation would have sat quietly, taking in the enormity of what they had heard their son just admit to, but not Mr Copeland. Showing insensitivity to the feelings of those who had lost loved ones at the hands of his son, Mr Copeland turned on the relatives and began shouting and gesticulating at them to keep quiet.

Down below in the well of the court, Copeland's barrister, Michael Wolkind, explained to the judge that his client was suffering from serious schizophrenia, delusions and emotional disorders that made the appropriate pleas manslaughter on the grounds of diminished responsibility. Nigel Sweeney, for the prosecution, responded by saying that the Crown's preliminary view was that the pleas were not acceptable and if that position changed, he would tell the court on 29 March. A trial date in June was then set by the judge, the Recorder of London, Michael Hyams.

Although Copeland's family had previously been told of the huge amount of evidence against him, his guilty pleas at that stage still came as a surprise. Just a couple of days before, he had been continuing to insist on his innocence to his brother Jon who was visiting him in Broadmoor. After the hearing, Stephen Copeland said he had still been shocked to hear his son admit his guilt to such terrible acts. He recognised that it must have been a nightmare for the relatives of those killed and maimed, but when they had started shouting in the public gallery, he had remonstrated with them because he could not hear what was being said by his son and the lawyers.

One of those in the public seats with strong feelings was Colin Moore, brother of Nik Moore who had died in the Soho bombing. 'It's coming up for a year since the horrific bombing,' he said, with tears in his eyes. 'If somebody had said a year ago that I'd get to where I am now, I'd have said "no way". I mean me and my brother Nik and John [Light], all of us were very good friends. I spoke to my brother every single day. We were like best buddies. And suddenly, that's gone and it's been very difficult ... it was very difficult when I went to court, to see such a little ... just such a pathetic looking person, standing there, with no remorse on his face or anything. Does he really realise how much damage he's done and how many people's lives he's ruined? I'm sure he doesn't. It wasn't a very nice thing I had to do, going to the court, but I did it, and it almost gave me strength because I looked at that guy in court and thought you have messed up my life, you have messed up a lot of people's lives, and you're not going to get to me. I mean he does get to me, but I try not to let him ruin any more of my life. I need to live my life the way Nik, John and Andrea would have wanted it. They wouldn't want us to be miserable and unhappy. So, I'm going to fight him.'

11

The Trial – Mad or Bad

'I have been evil from my early teens...
I'm just a Nazi who likes killing people'
David Copeland.

'Nothing can excuse or justify the evil you have done and
certainly not the abhorrent views you embraced'
Judge Michael Hyam.

DAY 1 - Monday 5 June.

WHEN THE TRIAL OPENED IN THE grand court no.1 at the Old
Bailey, it was a very different David Copeland who stood in
the dock. He still looked young, but he had put on weight
and was now pasty-faced. Gone was the very short, almost
skinhead hairstyle. Replacing it was a mop of dark brown
hair which throughout the trial looked uncombed and

untidy. But it was his manner which had most changed. The aggression and swagger had disappeared. Instead, his walk was a mechanical shuffle, and his face a blank. He had told police in his confession interview that when planting his bombs, he had felt like a robot. Now he looked like one.

Behind him in the dock, packing the benches at the back of the court were some of his many victims with their friends and relatives. Separated from them, sitting behind the defence lawyers, were Copeland's father Stephen and his brother Jon who both went to court every day. There were forty reporters and up above, the public gallery was packed as the jury filed in. Concerns that it could take time to achieve a jury of twelve unbiased people proved unfounded. The eight men and four women chosen were asked if any support they had for race equality or gay rights groups would prevent them giving the defendant a fair trial. None of the twelve, who included four clearly belonging to ethnic minorities, said their duties would be hampered, so they were sworn in and told that this was a murder trial. Copeland had admitted the bombings, and pleaded guilty to manslaughter, due to diminished responsibility, a plea that was not acceptable to the Crown. Nigel Sweeney, Treasury Counsel, then opened the prosecution case, outlining the evidence and attempting to convince the jury that Copeland was guilty of murder rather than manslaughter. In short, that he was bad, not mad.

Many prosecutors begin their opening speeches with a flow of dramatic, flowery words. But not, on this occasion, Mr Sweeney. He let the facts speak for themselves as they were dramatic enough without any additional comment. He detailed the devastation caused by Copeland's three bombs, each of which had contained about 1,500 nails, up to six inches long, acting as shrapnel. Copeland had said the Brixton and Brick Lane outrages were political. He hated blacks and Asians and wanted them out of the UK. He was a Nazi, a National Socialist, who believed in a white master race. He wanted to be the spark that would set fire to the country, to cause murder, mayhem and chaos. Spreading fear, resentment and hatred would start a race war, resulting in white people voting for the BNP, the British National Party. Continuing to deal with Copeland's confession, Mr Sweeney said the young man's third bomb, which killed three people at the Admiral Duncan in Soho had been 'personal'. Because of the way he had been treated by his 'strange parents', he hated homosexuals, saying they were perverted degenerates who were no good to society and who should be put to death.

Mr Sweeney described how Copeland had learned how to make bombs from the internet, from a manual called the *Terrorists' Handbook*. He had used flash powder from fireworks bought at shops in Farnborough. After being identified from CCTV at Brixton, police had gone to his room and arrested him. The jury then looked at photographs taken of the inside of his room. They showed two large Nazi flags, a crossbow at the end of his bed, and a wall of photographs of atrocities from around the world, including some from his own bombings at Brixton and Brick Lane.

CCTV of the bomb scenes and of Copeland's movements were then played on the television screens dotted round the court. Film of Copeland walking around Brixton and his bomb there going off brought gasps from his victims at the back. It was too much for one white middle-aged man, who fainted and slumped from his seat to the floor. The court stopped for a few minutes as he was helped out, ashen faced.

DAY 2 - Tuesday 6 June

The prosecution outline of Copeland's bombing campaign continued on the second day of the trial. By explaining in detail how and where Copeland had bought parts for his bombs and how he knew that people would be killed and maimed, Mr Sweeney was getting across that the degree of planning and knowledge involved made it a clear case of cold-blooded murder, not simply manslaughter.

More video was shown. Copeland was picked up by CCTV arriving at Waterloo on the day of his Brick Lane bomb. He was seen strolling across the station concourse with his bomb bag on his back, heading to an exit. Other cameras outside showed him walking up the taxi rank, and getting into a cab driven by Rino, who took him to Brick Lane. There was no video taken there of the nailbomber, but there was of the car exploding outside the police station. Very few people were nearby, when the bomb went off followed by a sheet of flame as the vehicle caught fire. Mr Sweeney explained how Copeland had thought the famous Sunday Brick Lane market was on Saturdays and how he had been in two minds whether to dismantle his bomb and return the next day, but he had eventually decided to dump it in a side street.

Immediately afterwards, he visited Soho, looking for a suitable target for his 'personal' bomb. Two days later, on the Monday he bought another load of Air Thunders and on the Wednesday a Nike hold-all and another alarm clock to act as a timer. Mr Sweeney said Copeland had used the name Hawkins at the two Victoria Hotels he used to assemble the Soho bomb, and had then walked across central London to arrive at the Admiral Duncan at about 5.50 pm. As the deaths and terrible injuries were detailed, some in court amongst the victims and relatives started crying. When the bomb went off, Nik Moore had been at the bar buying drinks for Andrea and Julian Dykes and their friends, amongst them John Light, the best man at their wedding. Mr Moore had extensive burns and shrapnel wounds, a fractured skull and lung damage. He died instantly as did Andrea, who had substantial burns and shrapnel over her body, a fractured skull and a nail in her brain. John Light had 40% burns, internal bleeding and terrible injuries to his right leg. He had four operations.

His leg was amputated. But he continued to deteriorate and died the next day. The three who died were closest to the bomb and to an extent shielded the other two in the group from the very worst of the blast. Even so, Julian Dykes had extensive burns, a nail in his lung, shrapnel wounds to his stomach and was unconscious for three weeks. Mr Light's boyfriend Gary Partridge also had a long stay in hospital with bad burns. Seventy others were injured, some losing legs and eyes.

Copeland told police afterwards that he had felt neither joy nor sadness for the bombing, but he did feel 'something' for Andrea Dykes because she had been expecting a baby. The bombings were for political and religious reasons and were something he had to do. It was his destiny. He wanted to be famous and wanted to get caught. 'If no one remembers who you were, you never existed.'

DAY 3 - Wednesday 7 June

Survivors from the Admiral Duncan pub bomb were expected to go into the witness box on the third day, but Copeland did not appear in the dock to hear them describe how they had suffered from what he has called his 'handiwork'. He was said to have been sick several times, starting early that morning in Broadmoor and continuing while at the Old Bailey.

The first witness was businessman David Williams, who had talked to Copeland at the bar. He remembered Copeland as looking uncomfortable. He fidgeted, twitched and kept looking around. He said he was waiting for a boyfriend. After Copeland said he was going to a cash dispenser, Mr Williams offered to look after his drink, a Coke. The next witness was the pub manager, Mark Taylor, who said the bomb went off as he was raising the alarm after the barmaid Veronica Sande had alerted him to the unattended bag by the bar. He said he was still receiving hospital treatment for his injuries.

Mr Sweeney's junior barrister, Mark Ellison, read out statements from other wtinesses in an unemotional monotone. A Frenchman, Sebastian Loret, had seen Copeland come into the pub carrying a large sports bag. He had seen publicity warning about bombs and thought to himself: 'I hope it's not a bomb. I dismissed it as I didn't want to be paranoid.' Thomas Satiropolis was another who saw the bag. He kicked it with his foot and found it was heavy. Shortly after telling the barmaid, he headed for the door and then the blast blew him through it into the middle of Old Compton Street. Mauro Mazzon also saw the bag and 'felt frightened by it'. He was blown to the floor when the bomb went off. With great difficulty, he managed to get back up and only then noticed that he no longer had his left foot. Thomas Douglas saw everything moving towards him, like a scene from the film *Titanic*. He found himself on the floor, his legs pinned down by debris. Unable to move, he heard his partner David Hayes shouting. Someone walked over him, then firemen came and slapped him round the face to get him to talk, to stay conscious. He woke up weeks later in hospital, without his legs. He also had severe internal injuries and nail puncture wounds all over his body. One of the last statements to be read was from Gary Reid. He had been in court every day, sitting in a wheelchair, his left leg having been amputated after the blast. He described how he had still been standing after the bomb went off. He remembered turning, and then, as he started to fall, being held by a woman. He woke up in hospital five weeks later.

When the Soho evidence was finished, Copeland returned to court to hear evidence about his membership of the National Socialist Movement and the letters from its leader, Tony Williams, ending 'Heil Hitler'.

DAY 4 - Thursday 8 June

The day's first witness was an explosives expert, Martin Sime, who had constructed a dummy bomb, exactly like Copeland's devices. He explained that the blast wave from such a device could rupture eardrums and damage lungs. Parts of the alarm clock timer and bits of pipe would act as shrapnel, along with the nails which would be projected outwards at two hundred metres a second.

Much of the day, however, was taken up by the playing of the tape-recording made by police of the first day's questioning of Copeland. The nailbomber's voice and manner was a surprise. He answered all police questions, replying in a flat, matter-of-fact way. There was no emotion or remorse, instead almost pride as he detailed his bombing campaign which he knew would 'piss off' the Prime Minister, Peter Mandelson and others. He said if he had not been caught, his next bomb would have been at Southall, a largely Asian area in West London. Asked if he knew of the consequences of his arrest, he replied: 'I had no life anyway. I'd say this was freedom for me. I'm shot-away — a loner — just weird in the fucking head.'

In the dock, Copeland listened to his confession to the awful bombings, staring straight ahead, showing no kind of emotion.

DAY 5 - Friday 9 June

By the end of the first week, interest in the trial had fallen off. Copeland's victims and their friends and relatives took up only half the seats allocated to them. There were fewer than half the reporters present compared to the number at the beginning of the trial, and there were even spaces in the public gallery.

The tape of Copeland's second day of police questioning was played, but after an hour the defendant again left the dock, having told his lawyers that he was suffering from a panic attack. After the tape was finished and with the jury out of the court, the judge, the Recorder of London, Michael Hyam, expressed concern, asking if there was any evidence that the defendant was, indeed, subject to panic attacks. Copeland's QC, Michael Wolkind, replied there was a history of such attacks, adding that he did not want evidence by doctors to be given that afternoon without Copeland present.

Frustrated that valuable court time was being lost, the judge offered to see Copeland himself to determine whether he was fit to sit in court. The offer was rejected by the defence, so the judge, with the approval of both sets of lawyers, summoned Matron to court. She was briefed on the problem, saw Copeland and then, half an hour later reported back to the judge that he was showing none of the usual signs of panic attacks. His pulse, temperature and blood pressure were normal. He was lucid and there was no sweating or hyperventilation. The judge then suggested that Copeland could be trying to manipulate the court by feigning illness, but because of the time of day, by then 3.00 pm, he said he would adjourn the trial until Monday, adding a warning that he would not necessarily allow the trial to be held up again by Copeland.

DAY 6 - Monday 12 June

Copeland was back in the dock at the start of the trial's second week, looking even paler and more mechanical with his hair more dishevelled. His mental state had barely been touched on during the first week. But that was to change suddenly with the next days taken up with nothing other than consideration of the crucial issue at the trial: was he mad or was he simply bad?

During the day, the court heard three medical experts give evidence of how they had examined Copeland before and during his police questioning and had found no mental illness. The first of these witnesses was Dr Peter Dean who had to assess Copeland's fitness for police interviewing at Charing Cross police station after his arrest. He said he found him lucid, understanding what was going on. Copeland told him that he had been a nervous wreck months before, but the doctor told the court how he was surprised at how the prisoner had been exceptionally calm and composed. He told Dr Dean that he had been dreaming about the bombings for ages. He was exhilarated by media coverage of his devastation but when others claimed responsibility, he began to feel cheated that they were getting the credit due to him. However, once in police custody and in the media spotlight, he seemed to be enjoying himself.

Next in the witness box testifying that he had seen no evidence of mental illness was Dr. Subrahim Yogadeva who had seen Copeland shortly before the police interview started. He was followed by Laura Garrod, the 'appropriate adult' who had sat in on the police interviews. A social worker with training as a psychiatric nurse, she had also seen Copeland before the police questioning. She said she found him cold, detached and unemotional but was also adamant that he was sane, emphasising that he had carried out the bombings logically and rationally. He told her that from his early teens his only ambition had been to be a serial killer or mass murderer. This had been the sole driving force to his existence in recent years. She said that although what he had done was 'beyond normal behaviour' it did not mean he was mentally ill.

DAY 7 - Wednesday 14 June

With the court not sitting on Tuesday, Wednesday opened with the last of the prosecution witnesses, Detective Constable Paul Webber, called to undermine the anticipated defence case that Copeland was mentally ill, and driven by God and the bible to carry out devastation. The officer was asked only one question by Mr Sweeney. Had he found a bible in Copeland's room or at his father's house? After he replied negatively, Michael Wolkind, Copeland's QC rose for cross examination and asked him if he was familiar with the bible. When DC Webber replied yes, Mr Wolkind asked if he knew what was in Matthew 7. When the officer answered 'no', Mr Wolkind handed him a sheet of paper that the officer himself had found in Copeland's room. It was headed 'Aryan Nations' and was the front page of a document outlining the organisation's racist beliefs, giving various biblical references which Copeland had used to justify his bombings against blacks, Asians and gays. The lawyer then told the officer that Matthew 7 said: 'Seek and you shall find.'

Pleased to have scored a point over the prosecution, Mr Wolkind opened the defence with a speech outlining the case that Copeland was, indeed, mentally ill and had been so, not only at the time of the bombings, but for some time before. He was also unfit to give evidence. Mr Wolkind said a series of psychiatrists would say the nailbomber was a paranoid schizophrenic who believed he was a messenger from God. He had religious, grandiose and persecutory delusions. Mr Wolkind said that under the law someone who killed should not be convicted of murder if he was suffering from an abnormality of mind arising from inherent causes which had substantially impaired his actions. In Copeland's case, his mental illness led to an obsession so strong that he *had* to bomb, kill and cause mayhem and chaos. He was not guilty of murder.

Mr Wolkind criticised the prosecution's medical witnesses. They had spent only a short time with Copeland before concluding he was not showing any signs of being mentally ill. Against that, the defence psychiatrists had spent many hours with him. The first of these, Dr Paul Gilluley, then gave evidence and said he had eight sessions of two hours each with the nailbomber. He said Copeland blamed his parents for his homophobia. When he was thirteen, he claimed they had started suggesting he was homosexual. His mother asked him: 'Is there anything you want to tell us?' He described how on one occasion, he had arrived back at the family home to hear his parents singing along to the *Flintstones* TV cartoon, emphasising the words 'have a gay old time', directing them at him. Dr Gilluley believed Copeland's religious and grandiose delusions started in 1996 when he saw television pictures of the Atlanta Olympics bombing and thought he had been chosen by God who gave him a mission in life. Thoughts of killing then occupied him for 90% of the time, and he had been disappointed when no one had died in his Brixton bomb.

During one interview, Copeland said he had been evil from his early days, and had become fascinated with Naziism from the age of thirteen. At sixteen, he started dreaming of being a tall, blond powerful S.S. commander with female sex slaves. He would torture and kill men, but not women or children. With his bombings, he believed he was like an artist, using the streets, glass and blood to show people what the future would bring. Seeing himself more like Moses or Ben Hur, rather than Christ, he predicted that in twenty years time, there would be no planet Earth as it would have fallen into pieces. Jesus would come down and take the righteous to heaven, including himself, as he had carried out the bombings.

DAY 8 - Thursday 15 June

Cross-examining Dr Gilluley, Nigel Sweeney pointed out that during hours of questioning by police, Copeland had been asked on no fewer than sixteen occasions why he had launched his devastating attacks, and had never told police that he had been compelled to do them by God. Mr Sweeney suggested that Copeland may have had a severe personality disorder but that did not mean he was mentally ill at the time of the bombs. Could it be that Copeland was making up that God was driving him? Dr Gilluley agreed that Copeland had admitted to doctors that he was a compulsive liar; that he liked tricking and confusing people; that he had made up symptoms and on one occasion, with his guard apparently down, had said he had first got the idea of claiming that he was on a mission from God after his arrest, while in prison. Despite all this Dr Gilluley continued to maintain his belief that Copeland was a paranoid schizophrenic, adding that such types could still lie.

DAY 9 - Friday 16 June

More of Copeland's fantasies were outlined by the next psychiatrist appearing for the defence, Dr Ian Cumming, in

charge of mental health at Belmarsh prison in south east
London to which the nailbomber was sent after being
charged. In interviews, Copeland told the doctor that when
aged thirteen or fourteen, he had dreamed of butchering,
strangling and torturing people, including his classmates at
Yateley School. He would use hooks as in the film *Hellraiser*.
His homophobia developed after he thought his parents
believed him gay, and from late in 1996 he had carried a knife
to use against anyone making homosexual advances. Then
he thought of going to a gay bar, picking up a man and then
killing him. On one occasion he had gone out with his knife,
targeted a man and had come close to stabbing him.

By then, Copeland had become involved with the
extreme right, but thought the various groups had been
penetrated by the security services. He himself thought that
MI5 was following him. Leaving the BNP because it was 'too
democratic', he favoured the dictatorship espoused by the
National Socialist Movement. He had also contacted the
Christian Identity movement in America. In other interviews
Copeland said God had made him evil and he talked of
being immortal.

Dr Cumming agreed that Copeland had been misleading
to psychiatrists about his symptoms, but this was after he
had been sent to Broadmoor and at a time he wanted a
transfer back to Belmarsh because being in the special
hospital was 'a living death'.

The doctor said that after being in Broadmoor Copeland
had shown improvement in his mental state, but in a visit
just a few days before the start of the trial, the doctor noted
that he still had the same grandiose views of having been
chosen by God and of still being on a mission. More
worryingly, Copeland said that if released from prison or
hospital, he would still feel the need to do more bombings.

(The authors learned during the trial that while in
Belmarsh, Copeland had been suspected of trying to make an
explosive mixture using milk powder. One of the prison staff
there had seen that he was hoarding it and passed the

information to doctors. Copeland admitted to one of the medical staff that he would have liked to have made more devices but could not find the constituent parts.)

DAY 10 - Monday 19 June

In his cross-examination of Dr Cumming, Mr Sweeney continued to argue that Copeland was not mentally ill at the time of the bombings and may have been fooling psychiatrists. He elicited from the doctor that security staff at Belmarsh had mixed views about the bomber. Some thought him odd but vulnerable, while others believed fellow prisoners were coaching him on how to conduct a defence, advising that he should play the mental illness card. Dr Cumming replied that he had always been cautious in diagnosing that Copeland was schizophrenic, and that was one of the reasons he had been sent to Broadmoor for a proper assessment. The doctor told Mr Sweeney he was unaware that while in the special hospital, Copeland had told someone that a fellow prisoner in Belmarsh had put him up to running a diminished responsibility defence.

In a roundabout way, Mr Sweeney pursued the same line with the next defence witness, Dr Andrew Payne, the consultant psychiatrist in charge of Copeland's ward at Broadmoor. Copeland had given him a litany of problems, now becoming very familiar to the jury. His parents had thought him a 'raving poofter'. He wanted to be notorious and described as a psychopath rather than mad. To avoid being branded insane, he had done no more than simply answer questions in his police interview, but he knew he was a 'special person' and had been so from the day he was born.

Mr Sweeney then referred Dr Payne to a bundle of correspondence between Copeland and a Ms Patricia Scanlon with whom he had fallen in love since being in prison. The problem was that the woman who had been writing to him was not a woman at all. 'She' was a man with a criminal record and other aliases who had given the letters to the *Daily Mirror*. Although this was described by the judge as shabby and Mr Sweeney as 'a low trick', it did not stop the prosecuting counsel outlining all the correspondence with the occasional reference to Copeland having been completely fooled by Scanlon's deception.

The first letter expressing sympathy was written on May 2, the day Copeland was charged. Scanlon wrote that she could not believe that Copeland was as evil or such a monster as the press was making him out. This first letter ended Patsy X. By the end of the month her letters ended 'Lots of love, Patsy XXXXXX.' Later letters called him 'my little soldier', and ended 'all my love and lust'. Copeland could not believe his luck. He fantasised over a photograph she sent purporting to be of herself. Here was someone who had never been able to form a proper relationship with a girl receiving loving letters from a woman who said she understood how he was feeling. Scanlon wrote that there was not much chance of them having a relationship if he was sent to prison. She advised him to think through the options. If he pleaded manslaughter due to diminished responsibility, he could go to hospital and then 'get better…you'll get through and I'll be at your side'. Later, in Broadmoor, and wanting a visit from 'Patsy', Copeland wrote: 'I cannot believe that I have fooled all the doctors.' Two months before the trial, the bomber forecast that it would just be 'a bunch of quacks' giving their opinions. In a later letter, he wrote that 'things were not looking bad' because if his plea of diminished responsibility was accepted by the jury, it would be up to the doctors to decide when he was released.

DAY 11 - Tuesday 20 July

Eventually the next day, having read out large extracts from the correspondence, Mr Sweeney got to the point: 'Where, in all these letters, is there any sign of mental illness?' Dr Payne replied that there was none and went on to give a simple explanation. It could be that Copeland did not want to appear mad to his 'girlfriend'.

Mr Sweeney then read out notes from another Broadmoor doctor whom Copeland had asked to be taken off the medication he was being given because it was making him a 'mental and physical wreck'. The doctor noted that he said: 'I don't need medication. I am just a Nazi who likes killing people. I'm a psychopath because I don't feel remorse.' He told the doctor that he had made up previous statements in Belmarsh because fellow prisoners had encouraged him to go to Broadmoor. 'I didn't realise what it was like,' he continued. 'Now I think it is a hundred times worse than in prison. If I had been told to do the bombings by Jesus Christ, I would have said so in the original police interview. There are two reports saying that there is no mental illness. If you take me off the medication, I will tell the truth about everything. I'll tell you about the real me.'

Re-examined by Mr Wolkind, Dr Payne said he did not think Copeland had been faking illness and fooling doctors. He had protested that he was not mad because he had wanted to get back to Belmarsh. This view was supported by the next witness, Dr Payne's boss, Dr John Basson, medical director at Broadmoor for four years. He spoke with authority, it was noticeable that more jurors started taking notes. Points that had probably puzzled them were being cleared up.

Dr Basson said Copeland was a schizophrenic and the illness must have affected him for some time before the bombing campaign. His belief that he was on a mission from God drove him to commit his crimes. But why, asked Mr Wolkind, was there little mention of God or Jesus in his interviews with the police? Dr Basson replied that this was because police interviewing techniques were different. The officers were after evidence. Psychiatrists would have drawn out the information relating to his motives. Dr Basson said

Copeland's religious beliefs probably interfered with the discipline required to do the bombings well. He had been precipitated into them. If he had been more cold and calculating, he would have realised that he should have had a better disguise and should have carried out proper reconnoitering of Brixton and Brick Lane beforehand. What was the difference between Copeland and a straightforward extreme right-wing terrorist? The doctor replied that from early on Copeland had grandiose delusions, arrogance and a certainty that he was right, whereas the ordinary right wing activist would recognise that there was another viewpoint.

Dr Basson said he believed that Copeland had still not told doctors everything that lay behind his bombing campaign. Sometimes in interviews he appeared to be opening up and then he would suddenly stop and refuse to elaborate further. This was a sign of religious grandiosity, said the doctor. Copeland had some additional secret that he was not going to impart to the likes of him. 'The quacks are not going to learn the last secrets?' asked Mr Wolkind. 'Yes,' replied Dr Basson, 'he believes we're not on the same level of intelligence.'

DAY 12 - Wednesday 21 June

Mr Sweeney found flaws in Dr Basson's assertion that Copeland's beliefs had prevented him from carrying out adequate planning for the bombings. He reminded the doctor that Copeland had visited Soho on at least two occasions before targeting the Admiral Duncan. As for Brixton and Brick Lane, Copeland had shown pre-planning and concern for his own safety because he told police that the most important thing for him was to plant the bomb bags without being seen. He had worked out that he should leave them close to people who might be expected to have bags with them, such as those waiting at a bus stop. Copeland had also said that he thought he would stand out like a sore thumb in Brixton. Because of that, asked Mr Sweeney, could he not have reasoned that it would have been risky for him to visit the area twice? Dr Basson accepted that there could be an alternative view.

Turning to Copeland's defence that he was driven by God to carry out bombings, Mr Sweeney again questioned why no mention had been made of this during his long police interviews. Dr Basson replied by saying that Copeland probably wanted that motivation kept secret. In response, and ending his cross examination, Mr Sweeney said that maybe Copeland was simply not deluded and not compelled by God at all.

However, the next defence witness, another psychiatrist, caused surprise by saying that Copeland had talked freely of being motivated by God, just two days after the end of his questioning by police. Dr Sarah Isherwood, as a consultant psychiatrist at Belmarsh, had examined the bomber immediately after his arrival at the top security prison. It was unclear why she had not been called to give her important evidence earlier. She told the court that it was only the night before that she had been asked to attend.

Dr Isherwood said Copeland told her on May 4 that he saw himself as Christ, programmed to carrying out bombings. He was controlled by someone who could turn out to be God or the Devil. He said he had acted righteously and claimed that God did not talk to anyone else. During questioning the next day, he repeated that he had been carrying out God's work. Asked why she thought Copeland had opened up to her about his religious motivation, Dr Isherwood replied that she, unlike the police, had been trained to look for psychiatric symptoms in defendants.

More evidence that the nailbomber was obsessed with religious thoughts *before* his outrages came from three people connected to the far right who had talked to him. Statements were read to the court from Tony Williams, leader of the National Socialist Movement, Kirk Barker, a member, and Howard Lyne, a disillusioned BNP member who had been thinking of joining the organisation. Copeland had talked to

Williams about Christian Identity. He 'went on about the bible' to the racist Barker to such an extent that Barker made excuses to avoid meeting him again, and Lyne said religion and the religious right had been the main topic of Copeland's conversation with him.

The defence team had been hoping that their last witness would make a big impression on the jury. Prof. John Gunn, CBE, is one of the country's most respected psychiatrists, sitting on many committees here and abroad and also advising the Home Office, the Foreign Office and numerous other organisations. Unfortunately, he was seriously injured in a road accident earlier in the week in the United States and his evidence also had to be read by Mr Wolkind. The professor had seen Copeland with Dr Gilluley but had met him on his own too. At the first of these examinations, Copeland told him: 'I have been put on this planet to prove myself…to show myself worthy to rule. I have passed that test.' He knew he was breaking the law but the bombings were justified and he was pleading not guilty because he believed he had done nothing wrong. 'He said he was under instruction,' said the professor, 'carrying out God's will in cleansing the world.' Later, after months in Broadmoor, Copeland continued to talk of the bombings as having been 'good' and the 'work of God'. Professor Gunn's conclusion matched that of all the other psychiatrists from Belmarsh and Broadmoor who had appeared for the defence. Copeland was a paranoid schizophrenic.

That conclusion was then disputed by the next witness, the only psychiatrist to be called by the prosecution. Dr.Philip Joseph, a consultant forensic psychiatrist at St. Mary's Hospital in Paddington, west London, immediately acknowledged that he had been a pupil of Professor Gunn, who had taught him all he knew. However, Dr Joseph then said he believed Copeland had been suffering from a personality disorder from the age of thirteen, but it did not amount to mental illness at the time of the bombings. After his arrest, his personality structure broke down and mental illness probably emerged. Following medication, he still maintained his beliefs in white supremacy, but these were related to his underlying personality disorder, and were not a product of mental illness.

As a child, watching war films, Copeland had wanted the Germans to win and, in westerns, for the Indians to beat the cowboys. At thirteen, said the doctor, Copeland started to feel a sense of isolation and developed fears about his sexual orientation. He had been very embarrassed when taken to a growth clinic where his genitalia were examined. His elder brother had matured earlier, while Copeland preferred to play with toys. He believed everyone thought him 'a faggot'. His mother asked him: 'Is there anything you want to tell us?' At school, other children would 'take the piss' by branding someone as gay. When such jibes were directed at him, he took it personally but kept it to himself. He turned into a loner.

At the same time, said Dr Joseph, he became interested in Naziism, because it made him feel powerful. His feelings of 'extreme rage towards others' led to 'his drive to destroy'. He was an extreme fantasist who dreamt of being powerful because he was fundamentally so small and insignificant. His personality disorder stemmed from overwhelming weakness, insignificance and fear of sexuality. Dr Joseph said Copeland's fears became objects of his hate. To make life more bearable, he took large quantities of drugs and alcohol, but he decided to stop using them in 1996, coinciding with his decision to embark on his own bombing campaign, after viewing TV coverage of the Atlanta Olympics bombing. Planning and building bombs gave his life new meaning, but what he was suffering from remained a personality disorder rather than mental illness, because he retained sufficient choice, will-power and ability to decide whether to carry out the bombings or not. In other words, whatever compulsion he was feeling was not strong enough to impair his judgement. His was not a case of diminished responsibility.

DAY 13 - Thursday 22 June

Dr Joseph was in the witness box for the whole day, enlarging on what he had said the day before. But there were also new revelations about what Copeland had wanted to do, which emerged during the doctor's interviews with the bomber while in Broadmoor. Copeland revealed that as a child he had liked setting things on fire and had tried to send his old school, Yateley Comprehensive, up in flames. He had later thought of getting a gun and going on a shooting spree as Michael Ryan had done in Hungerford. He decided not to go ahead as it would have resulted in his own death. Instead, he bought a gun to assassinate the Prime Minister, Tony Blair. (A gas powered pistol was found in his room. Lethal itself at close quarters, such a gun can be made more powerful following instructions detailed in the *Terrorists Handbook*, which Copeland had downloaded from the internet.)

The doctor said the photos of atrocities and suffering found on Copeland's wall were consistent with him suffering from a personality disorder. What was also important in his case was what was not amongst his collection. There was nothing there about God, who Copeland had later claimed had driven him to carry out the bombings. The doctor said people with severe mental illnesses often covered their walls with drawings or photos, but these would be of a bizarre nature, showing, for example, aliens, or they would be religious, or show large eyes. The correspondence with 'Patsy Scanlon' also showed no sign of mental illness, said the doctor. Someone suffering from schizophrenia would be expected to jumble up letters, and sometimes refer to themselves in the third person.

Dr Joseph was in conflict with all five of the psychiatrists called by the defence who had concluded that Copeland was a paranoid schizophrenic. He suggested that one reason why they were wrong and he was right was possibly because they had not appreciated the significance of the racist material read by Copeland. This included the strongly racist and homophobic NSM material, the Aryan Nations literature and the *Turner Diaries*. When Copeland was talking to the police and psychiatrists, he was simply repeating ideas expressed in that extreme right wing literature. Any psychiatrist unfamiliar with such ideas might think that what Copeland was saying was delusional, but it was not, as such views, although very extreme, were put forward by some intelligent people in all seriousness.

In mid-afternoon, Copeland was allowed to leave the dock and a little later he was said to be quite ill and a nurse advised that he should return to Broadmoor. Because of the defendant's absence, the court adjourned about an hour earlier than usual.

DAY 14 - Friday 23 June

Dr Joseph was again critical of the defence psychiatrists. He said they had relied almost entirely on what Copeland had told them for their conclusions that he was mentally ill. According to the doctor, in other cases where a patient is describing psychotic symptoms, there are other objective features to support mental illness, but he suggested that these did not emerge until Copeland was in Broadmoor. He added that having read the 'Patsy Scanlon' letters he was now sceptical about anything that Copeland was saying at that time, because he had referred to having fooled the doctors.

Dr Joseph went on to complain that he thought opportunities to understand Copeland more fully had been lost while he was in Broadmoor. There should have been many more tests on him. Even at this stage, an assessment of his personality was incomplete. The judge then sprang to the defence of the psychiatrists being criticised, and said that they had taken the view that it was not possible to examine his personality because it was so overlaid by mental illness. It was difficult to disentangle the two. But Dr Joseph replied that even if that had been the case, there had been a number of months when a detailed assessment of his personality could have been carried out.

Michael Wolkind's cross-examination was laced with clever sarcasm and the occasional jibe that Dr Joseph had been talking 'psycho babble'. Pressed as to why he was right and the other psychiatrists wrong, Dr Joseph replied that this had not been the first time he had been on his own, and on each of the previous occasions he had been right. He added: 'I don't want the jury to think it's like a football match — 5 to 1, so the five must be right.' The doctor gave as good as he got and by the end of the day, the judge declared that he and the jury had probably reached saturation point. Battle could resume on Monday.

DAY 15 – Monday 26 June

With the court not sitting in the morning, Michael Wolkind continued his cross-examination in the afternoon in the same abrasive and confrontational style, but it seemed that the jury were losing patience. Even the judge was getting tired, pulling the defence counsel up on two occasions, questioning the validity and purpose of his line of argument. Dr Joseph's long spell in the witness box finally ended in late afternoon.

DAY 16 - Tuesday 27 June

With so much information having been given about Copeland and his motives, it was surprising that the trial's final witness managed to provide fresh insights into his mind. Dr Jackie Craissati, a consultant psychologist at Belmarsh, only saw Copeland once, shortly after he was charged, but she managed to get him to open up, so much so that he was occasionally tearful when recalling events in his adolescence.

In addition to believing that his parents thought him homosexual, he felt that his parents had wanted a girl. They would talk about having had three boys and look at him, the slightest of the three, during their discussion. As for relations with girls, Copeland said his elder brother had been sexually active from an early age and that he himself was sexually inadequate because of his small genitalia. He said he had sexual intercourse with a girl but she had not enjoyed it. He had been 'no great shakes' and 'not up to scratch'. Probing further, Dr.Craissati asked if he thought the problem was because his penis was too small. 'Yes,' he replied. 'I'm not well endowed.' Copeland related that from late adolescence he had visited prostitutes, adding that had he not been embarrassed he would have asked them to tie him up. As he described his feelings, he became agitated and tearful, closing his eyes and leaning forward, saying, 'It's so humiliating…distressing.' Then, suggesting that even at that stage he desired revenge against his family, he said: 'It makes me want to hurt someone.' He then went on to talk about his violent sexual fantasies which usually involved drugging girls so they would comply with his demands. He sometimes thought of himself as a god, who could pick and choose the prettiest women. On other occasions, he would be in the Nazi SS, picking a victim, raping her and then shooting her dead.

Dr Craissati said Copeland realised that his desire to maim and kill people was related to his adolescent failures. He said it was at at that time 'that the true me died, and the real me was born. I have so much hatred in me. I have no soul. I wanted revenge for my shit life.' He told her that he had made a list of potential targets for his bombs. Gays in Soho had been on the list, but they were low down it. However, when he realised that the ethnic minorities were banding together after his first two bombs, he moved Soho to the top of the list. His Brixton and Brick Lane bombs had been political, but when they went off he realised he was more excited by the chaos caused rather than by the injuries. It emerged that when the Brixton bomb exploded, he had been on Clapham Common, excited by seeing smoke from the explosion and hearing fire, ambulance and police sirens.

Copeland also told her that he wanted to be caught, to be

a notorious, ruthless killer. He was 'pretty phlegmatic' about the years he would be spending in custody. His life was going nowhere, anyway. He was a failure and he would be no worse off in prison than in the community.' The doctor said Copeland's social withdrawal over the last few years was compatible with having a personality disorder. She believed that he was not mentally ill, although he was a depressed and despondent individual, conveying hope-lessness, self denigration and contempt for himself and others. These feelings underpinned his pre-occupation with revenge. She said his hatred, his pre-occupation with making bombs and his ideas of revenge, enabled him to manage his anxieties and stress.

The results of IQ tests on Copeland caused some surprise to those in court. Dr Craissati said she had given him a test which resulted in him being given an IQ of 106, slightly above average. But that test had been based on him having a reasonably good reading ability. When he was in Broadmoor, he was found to be dyslexic, so he was given another more sophisticated test, one not based on reading ability. His result was an IQ of 126, putting him in the top ten per cent of the population.

DAY 17 - Wednesday 28 June

With all the witnesses having been heard, it was time for the closing speeches to the jury from the opposing counsel. First came Nigel Sweeney for the prosecution, who said that Copeland was 'bad, and not mentally ill.' Far from being compelled to carry out bombings, Copeland had exercised free choice when trying to deal with his personality difficulties. He had chosen the bombing route. When his first attempts at bomb-making ended in failure, he chose to give up and resumed a fairly normal life.

Later, when his personal problems were mounting, he chose to to go back to trying to build bombs. He chose to abort the Brick Lane bomb. He chose gays as a target, not because he was compelled by God, but because they were an easier target. The ethnic communities had banded together and he believed that the gay community had not and would not be expecting that they would be bombed.

Mr Sweeney told the jury that Copeland had not been deluded by mental illness. He still held the 'same abhorrent far right-wing racist views. It is those views, not mental illness which caused him to do what he did. He had a choice and made his choice and he should pay for his choice with a conviction for an offence of which he is guilty — the murder of his three unfortunate victims.'

While Mr Sweeney remained calm and measured, his opponent's style was more lively. Mr Wolkind said he accepted that if Copeland was just a political extremist faking his symptoms of mental illness, the jury would be justified in returning what would be a very popular verdict of murder. But he argued that Copeland was not a bad man acting evilly. He was psychotically driven to plant the bombs, and the jury should not be swayed by thoughts that a manslaughter verdict might be misunderstood by the bombs' survivors and relatives and friends of the dead and injured. Mr Wolkind again attacked Dr. Philip Joseph, the psychiatrist who had appeared for the prosecution. He was a man of charm, said the lawyer, 'but as a witness in this case he was neither reliable or fair'. He was 'isolated, maverick and wrong'. Mr Wolkind added an appeal to the jury: 'Please do not approach this case as if Mr Sweeney is presenting it for the angels and I am presenting the case for the devil'.

DAY 18 - Thursday 29 June

As the jury filed into court to hear the judge's summing up, it was impossible to read their faces. If anything, they seemed relaxed, knowing that this was not an ordinary murder trial. The defendant would not walk free if they found him not guilty. Whatever they decided, Copeland would be locked away for many years.

However, the judge, Michael Hyam, said nothing to the

jury about possible sentences. He started by setting out the law, saying that in such cases, it was up to the defence lawyers to prove their case on the balance of probabilities that Copeland's responsibility for his actions was substantially diminished because of his abnormality of mind. In other words, was he able to know the difference between right and wrong, and was he able to exercise will-power and exercise free choice? All the psychiatrists who had given evidence were agreed that Copeland was suffering from an abnormality of mind, but there was 'fierce conflict' and 'headlong disagreement' between them over the key issue — had that disease of mind or personality disorder substantially impaired his actions? If Copeland had been substantially impaired, the verdict should be manslaughter. If he was not, then it was murder.

Telling the jury to take a commonsense approach, the judge then summed up the evidence that had been given over the previous weeks. As he drew to a close at 2.45pm, he asked the prosecution and defence lawyers if there was anything he had missed out. Mr Wolkind replied that there was and asked if he could be heard without the jury. After the jury members had left, Mr Wolkind gave a long list of points favourable to the defence which had not been covered. He did not go as far as saying that he thought the summing up had been unfair, but the judge accepted that he should make the jury aware of some of these points. The exchange, and the summoning back of the jury to hear the additional summing up, left only three quarters of an hour for further jury deliberation that day. When the twelve returned to court at 4.30pm to be sent home for the day, they looked even more relaxed, some of them exchanging smiles.

DAY 19 - Friday 30 June

Anti Nazi League demonstrators had been outside the Old Bailey the night before when jurors left the building and they were there again in the morning, so, shortly after 10.00 am, the jury came into court to be told by the judge to ignore anything they may have seen or heard outside. Inside the building, those who had suffered from Copeland's 'handywork' were back in force to witness the final judgement. The trial had allowed them to understand more about the man who had caused them so much suffering. Their feelings ranged from those wanting him dead to those who felt sorry for him. One gay man badly injured in the Soho bomb perhaps summed up the views: 'We're all liberally minded and I know I shouldn't feel this, but I want revenge.' It was mid-afternoon when that moment arrived for him and all the others involved in the dreadful events.

The court was packed and surprisingly hushed when the jury returned. Bomb survivors and relatives of the dead and injured sat tensely on the benches behind the dock. To one side were two men in wheelchairs who'd lost legs in the Admiral Duncan explosion. In the dock, flanked by guards, Copeland stood staring ahead as the jury foreman was asked for the verdict on the charge of murder. His reply of 'guilty' was immediately followed by a huge roar of approval from those behind the dock and that was followed by loud clapping. On Copeland's face there was a twitch or a flicker of what could have been a smile. Whatever it was, it was impossible to tell whether it was in reaction to the verdict or to the applause from behind.

Before the judge sentenced the murderer, there were formalities to attend to and a statement on his current mental position. The prosecution asked for the forfeiture of 223 different items found in Copeland's room in Farnborough. The judge agreed and then he heard from the defence. Mr Wolkind said Copeland had been in Broadmoor for six months and an application by doctors for him to stay there undergoing treatment had been approved by the Home Secretary, Jack Straw.

Then the Recorder of London, Michael Hyam, looked at Copeland and said: 'Anyone who has heard the facts of this case will be appalled and horrified at the atrocity of your crimes. The evidence shows you were motivated to do what you did by virulent hatred and pitiless contempt for other people. On your own admission, you set out to kill, maim and cause terror in the community, and that is what you did. As a result of your wicked intentions you have left three families bereaved and many people so severely injured by the explosions you caused that they are reminded every day, and perhaps many times every day, that you alone are accountable for ruining their lives. Nothing can excuse or justify the evil you have done and certainly not the abhorrent views you embraced. It is only too apparent that you have no feeling for those whose lives you have affected. The public must be protected from you and must be assured that if you are ever released it will not be for a very long time.'

He gave him six life sentences, three for causing explosions and three for the murders. As Copeland turned to be led away, his eyes met those of some of the survivors and relatives of the dead. They responded with raised fists and shouts of 'you bastard', 'rot in hell', and 'Nazi scum'. As the judge left the court, there was more clapping and cheering, accompanied by hugs and tears.

Justice had been done, but there was also disappointment over what had not been said by the judge. In court were several of the police officers who had worked so tirelessly on the case, among them the head of the Anti Terrorist Branch, Deputy Assistant Commissioner Alan Fry, and Detective Inspector Maureen Boyle, who had been in charge of the investigation. The officers had been expecting some praise for all their hard work in catching Copeland within thirteen days of his first bomb, but it never came. Not a single word of congratulation was offered to the Metropolitan Police by the judge. This is unlikely to have been an oversight by the Recorder of London as he is vastly experienced and his sentencing speech had been prepared beforehand. But he had heard all the evidence and witnesses, including those who pointed out that if Copeland had worn a disguise and had not wandered round Brixton for an hour before planting his first bomb, then he would never have been identified from the CCTV. Perhaps the judge realised, like many others, how much luck had been involved in capturing this young man who had created so much terror.

Conclusion

'I am almost certain that if he hadn't joined the BNP and NSM,
he would be an ordinary bloke working on the Jubilee Line.'
A BNP member

'These groups are just as much at fault as Copeland is,
and the government should do something about that.
It's not just Copeland that's guilty. It's the system that's at fault.'
Phil Maddock, father of Andrea Dykes
who died in the Soho bombing.

DAVID COPELAND EMBARKED ON HIS BOMBING CAMPAIGN fuelled
by a desire to be famous and cause chaos and mayhem. He
was suffering from a personality disorder that seems to have
partly stemmed from an unhappy childhood, where he was
lonely, small, bullied and an underachiever. Following

concern about his late puberty, his worries about his genitalia and his belief that others doubted his sexuality continued to preoccupy him into adulthood. The middle of three boys, he had neither the strength and confidence of Jon, his elder brother, nor the academic ability of Paul, three years younger than him. Anger, resentment and jealousy warped his outlook on life. When his mother left home and his father, who was finding him increasingly difficult to deal with, encouraged him to leave as well, Copeland must have felt rejected and unloved. He switched his resentment to the society around him, which he grew to despise.

However, Copeland is not alone in experiencing an unhappy childhood, nor for that matter is he the only person to suffer from personality disorders and other psychiatric problems, but few perpetrate the violence he did. The fuse that ignited and directed the anger within Copeland was his involvement in the far right, initially with the BNP and later with the NSM. In between he had adopted the teachings of Christian Identity theology and made contact with several other racist groups and publications. Together, these racist and violent ideas channelled his aggression, eventually culminating in his bombing campaign. Without the crude and often violent propaganda emanating from these groups, it could be argued that Copeland was unlikely to have carried out this campaign. Perhaps he would have chosen some other atrocity or act of violence. It is impossible to know. But what is abundantly clear, is that by reading tales of race war in *The Turner Diaries*, believing in the racist nonsense of the BNP, and adopting the religious fundamentalism that viewed white people as God's chosen race while condemning others as 'mud people', Copeland would not have selected the exact targets he did. While some of these experiences would have served only to add justification to an already warped mind, it is clear that together they played an instrumental part in producing a bomber. While he had been captivated by the 1996

Centennial Park bombing at the Atlanta Olympics, it was only after he became involved in the BNP that he seriously started to try to build his own bomb.

'I am almost certain that if he hadn't joined the BNP and the NSM he would be an ordinary bloke working on the Jubilee Line,' says Arthur, the BNP infiltrator who knew Copeland. 'I think there must have been something about him that was prepared to do what he did, but I think that without that political education he would not have done it. Any racism you come into the BNP with — any homophobia or anti-Semitism — is refined in that environment. There you find people and publications that talk about race war as a credible strategy.'

Copeland's family certainly believe that his going to London and falling in with the BNP led him on to bomb and kill. 'David wasn't, in my eyes, particularly racist,' said his father, Stephen Copeland. 'I believe he is immature. He hasn't really grown up. He's still a boy, even though he's 23. I just believe he was easily influenced by people who saw they could indoctrinate him with their views. He's just gone down the wrong road, I'm afraid and no one, including myself, has noticed that. But apparently people with schizophrenic-type illnesses do have different personalities and can appear quite normal to his family, friends and whoever, but then, at other times, he's that other person. David has been badly misled and ideas have been put in his head which have snowballed and led him to have the kind of thoughts that make someone plant bombs.'

Copeland, like many others who join groups such as the BNP, was driven by a quest for power. For a young man who was largely ignored at school, who grew up without his brothers' confidence and abilities, and who felt rejected by his parents, Copeland had low self-esteem and was desperately unhappy. The desire to exert power over others drew him towards the racist BNP. There, and in the company of others like him, he finally felt superiority over people of different ethnic backgrounds. By incorporating Christian Identity into his thinking, he became one of God's chosen people. Suddenly, it gave him a purpose to live and, if need be, die for. He even saw his bombing campaign as a means of empowerment, the ability to bring havoc to other people's lives. By relishing the suffering this caused to others, he was not only making them pay for his own unhappiness, but making them share in it as well.

Copeland, the bomber, was a product of racist ideology and literature. Like an increasing number of violent racists around the world, he was inspired by events in the USA, where the availability of guns and explosives make far-right terrorism a seemingly regular occurrence.

*   *   *

The police were quick to categorise Copeland as a loner, working alone and for motives unknown. Perhaps they sincerely believed this, but more likely, it was said to calm public fears and to counter possible criticism that he should have been apprehended sooner.

In fact, Copeland was not unknown to the authorities. He was a member of the Nazi NSM and had previously been in the racist BNP, the biggest of Britain's far-right groups, attending several meetings over a six-month period. He was also well known to police in his hometown for having a violent streak, one of his three previous convictions being for assault, and another for causing damage. Immediately prior to the bombings he had been involved in angry exchanges with the police over his stolen bicycle.

Nor did Copeland make any secret of his racist or homophobic views, even to people he met for the first time, such as Anthony Sales, the previous occupant of the first floor bedroom at 25 Sunnybank Road in Farnborough. Although more guarded about his neo-Nazi religious beliefs, he expounded them to other racists he thought sympathetic.

Even something of his mental state was known. He had been to his family doctor after leaving London and his job on the Jubilee Line because of stress and panic attacks, a possible prelude to schizophrenia.

However, it was not until police released images from the Brixton CCTV that Copeland's name was brought to police attention. The CCTV proved to be the lucky break police needed. Without it, Copeland would undoubtably have carried out more bombings. And it was luck. With a little more foresight, Copeland could have avoided being caught at the scene.

He had shown the sense to take several precautions during the course of his bombing campaign to avoid detection. He always paid cash and used false names when purchasing equipment and staying in London hotels. To prevent leaving fingerprints he had constructed his bombs wearing gloves and had worn them when planting the first device. As a simple disguise for his bombing missions, he bought and wore a light-beige baseball cap instead of the dark one he was known by others to wear.

But basic mistakes led to his downfall. Crucially, he failed to wear a proper disguise at Brixton. If he had done so, it is unlikely that he would have been recognised so quickly. He failed to reconnoitre Brixton beforehand, and was unaware of how many CCTV cameras were in operation. By not undertaking a dummy run Copeland was ignorant of journey times, thus resulting in him wandering the streets of Brixton for over an hour, making it much more likely that he would be seen carrying the sports bag containing the device. Recovering the bag was another stroke of luck for the police. No one could have anticipated that anyone would be foolish enough to lift the device out and then run off with the bag.

Bad planning by Copeland also affected the Brick Lane bomb. By not doing his homework he failed to realise the market was held on Sunday rather than Saturday. By dumping the bomb in a side street rather than de-activating it and returning the following day, he increased the chances of it being noticed. While the bomb did eventually explode, police were given a good description of the device by the man who attempted to take it to the police station. Many of these simple mistakes were avoided for the Soho bomb. He had made at least two prior visits to the area to identify a target, and after planting the device in the middle of the Admiral Duncan, he had stayed there until almost the last minute, never taking his eyes off the bag.

Although Copeland was arrested soon after that, he had achieved a large part of his aims. He had created chaos, havoc, destruction and death. True, the backlash by blacks and Asians had not occurred, but he hoped to have shown the way for other racists to continue the violent struggle he had started. By killing three people in the gay bar he told police that he felt an overwhelming sense of relief, even to the point where he considered himself free.

Scotland Yard has argued that even without his basic mistakes, Copeland would have been caught eventually. It has been officially said that Copeland did not appear on any index of known extreme right wingers, but claims have persisted that his name was on a list of five hundred far-right activists. Although said to be low down on this alleged list, it is claimed that a process of elimination would have led the investigators to him. But even if his name did appear on such a list, only a handful of racist and Nazi activists are known to have been questioned over the bombings. To reach someone near the bottom of a list of five hundred names would have taken several weeks, if not months, because of all the basic but necessary detective work involved in checking out alibis, mounting surveillance operations and so on. Copeland would have had more than enough time to plant several more bombs, as he had planned to do.

The obvious relief and jubilation at the Scotland Yard news conference after his capture was tempered by one significant omission. During virtually every Scotland Yard news conference following recent arrests or trials of Irish Republican terrorists, praise has been heaped on the intelligence agencies, MI5 and Special Branch, for their key help in the investigation. In the hunt for the nailbomber, the police again turned to these agencies to provide intelligence. Penetrating and monitoring the racist right was, after all, supposed to be part of their remit. It was obvious from the news conference that Scotland Yard was far from impressed at the assistance they received. In a carefully worded statement, Assistant Commissioner Veness thanked the emergency services, various Scotland Yard departments and other police forces, including the National Crime Squad and Hampshire police, all of which, he said, had helped the Anti-Terrorist Branch. There had even been a special thank you to the media for the coverage it had given to the CCTV appeal. Missing most notably from the list of those deserving congratulation was any mention of MI5 and Special Branch. The omission was deliberate. The investigation had suffered from what one senior detective described to us later as an intelligence void.

The Security Service, MI5, and its 'eyes and ears' and operational arm, Special Branch, have an interest in any terrorist posing a threat to the state, but their efforts are concentrated on known groups, such as the Irish terrorist organisations and those from the Middle East. In the early 1990s the BNP was monitored because there was concern about its growing political strength, particularly in London. At the same time, C18 came under scrutiny largely because of its links with the extreme loyalist group the Ulster Defence Association (UDA). In January 1993, a combined force of over six hundred C18, UDA and football hooligans from all over the country attacked a London march commemorating the Bloody Sunday deaths in Derry in 1972. Four hundred people were detained by police. In the following year, a number of people were arrested for gun-running to the UDA.

According to one police source, Special Branch was

channelling information from an estimated fifteen informants in the extreme right to MI5. By the mid-1990s, however, this interest, particularly in the BNP, waned. The numbers of MI5 officers working exclusively on the right-wing desk at the Security Service dropped to one full-time person and one part-time, although, in addition, there were analysts and operational teams who would occasionally cover this ground. Although many of the Special Branch informants stayed in place, MI5 officers on the right-wing desk spent their time monitoring, collating and filing reports rather than being pro-active. While MI5 interest in C18 rose in the late 1990s, allowing increased resources for monitoring the far right, other groups were ignored.

Special Branch itself has officers attached to every police force in the country, although some have very few. In addition to national duties, these officers also have to deal with the priorities dictated by local activities and their respective Chief Constables. In the south-west, for example, Special Branch officers may spend considerable time monitoring and investigating animal rights groups, while those in the West Midlands spend more time focusing on the extreme right. In some parts of the country, the racists are hardly monitored at all, while in other regions, coverage is extensive.

Even when groups are monitored, information is not necessarily acted upon. In the summer of 1998 Special Branch and the military police conducted an inquiry into Nazi activity in the parachute regiment, which contravened Army regulations. Despite finding a dozen soldiers actively linked to fascist organisations, nothing was done until their presence was exposed in *Searchlight* almost nine months later, and even then there was intense reluctance to act. And it was not as though there were not grounds to act. In one case a paratrooper, who had previously been disciplined for a racist attack against a black soldier and later arrested with C18 activists following a street brawl with a witness in a murder case, was then pictured leading an eighty-strong C18 attack on a demonstration in central London. In another case, a soldier who had supplied C18 with ammunition and confidential information about Republican suspects in Northern Ireland was caught allowing another C18 activist to use his army travel pass. In both cases, action could have been taken but was not.

Even when Special Branch units have taken an active interest in the extreme right, their London headquarters often frustrates their efforts. A common gripe by Special Branch officers outside London is that, although they file reports to London, they get little in return either in terms of background briefings or specific information they have requested.

While senior Anti-Terrorist Branch officers feel MI5 and Special Branch let them down during the hunt for the nailbomber, the intelligence agencies dismiss the Anti-Terrorist Branch as a 'glorified forensic team'. Frustration is expressed that the Anti-Terrorist Branch did not get more out of Copeland about his connections with extremist groups and his motivations. There was also anger at attempts by the police following his arrest to portray him as a loner.

Since Copeland's arrest and as knowledge of his racist links emerged, Special Branch interest in the BNP and other far-right groups has increased. However, the extent of their knowledge leaves many unimpressed, particularly some officers in charge of London's borough-based community safety units, set up to deal with racial and domestic crime. Some of these officers, keen to be pro-active and get on top of racist problems in their areas, receive little or no help or guidance from London Special Branch. On one occasion Special Branch was contacted by one officer from north London who was working on a case involving a local resident who had received racist hate-mail purporting to be from a group calling itself the Surrey Border Front. Although that group has been active in Surrey and Sussex for several years, Special Branch told the officer that they had 'never heard of it'.

Another problem identified during the bombing campaign was the sheer number of police organisations supposedly covering the far right. Sometimes work is duplicated, while in other instances there is absolutely no coverage at all. Surprisingly, in addition to MI5, Special Branch and the Anti-Terrorist Branch, there are at least four other police organisations with an interest in right-wing violence, and in the immediate aftermath of the bombings yet another was established.

The largest of these other organisations is the National Criminal Intelligence Service (NCIS), with its headquarters in Vauxhall within walking distance of MI6, the Secret Service that monitors intelligence abroad. The NCIS is formed largely of police officers on attachment from their regular forces, but there are also representatives from Customs and MI5. Set up in the early 1990s, its remit is to fight organised and international crime, liaising between the competing law enforcement agencies, trying to ensure, for example, that police in the National Crime Squad and Customs officers are not targeting the same big-time drug smugglers. It also has a large football hooligan unit, which played a part in combating the links between the extreme right and the UDA, developed out of the attack on the Bloody Sunday march in 1993. In 1995, the NCIS lobbied the Home Office for permission to form a group, similar to its football unit, to monitor the far right. Despite the request being refused, NCIS continues to monitor the extreme right, particularly C18, through the football hooligan scene.

Another group, which often sees itself as a rival to NCIS, is the National Public Order Intelligence Unit (NPOIU), which not only has a football hooligan intelligence unit but also gathers intelligence on the racist right. Formed in 1998, the NPOIU grew out of the Animal Rights National Index, which was set up to counter activity by animal liberationist groups across the country in the early 1990s. The NPOIU is run by the Association of Chief Police Officers (ACPO) and its remit is to gather intelligence on groups or individuals deemed by the authorities to pose any threat to public order. It looks not only across the entire political spectrum from extreme left to extreme right, but also at the likes of environmental demonstrators and football hooligans. It is based at Scotland Yard, along the same lines as the NCIS, with officers attached to it from regional forces, and it also has a strong Special Branch presence. It keeps files on known individual extremists, liaising with police and advising them of potential trouble. It acts as a clearing house for public order information, so, for example, intelligence from Yorkshire of an impending demonstration in Birmingham, would be sent to the NPOIU before dissemination to the relevant bodies. As with Special Branch, however, NPOIU knowledge of some groups seems to be deficient, as their main priority seems to be simply related to public order activities.

During the bombing campaign, the NPOIU issued requests for information. One such request was for information on the White Wolves. After receiving the claims of responsibility from that group, the NPOIU circulated appeals for any information on this group to police forces around the country.

Yet another organisation with an interest in right-wing terrorism is the Terrorism and Allied Matters (TAM) Committee of the ACPO. Its annual report says it provides 'a forum enabling liaison between the Home Office, Government Agencies and Chief Officers of Police on issues relating to terrorism and allied matters.' It also advises and informs chief officers 'of all significant developments in the field of terrorism and allied matters', helping to 'develop a co-ordinated and agreed response'. It was this organisation that produced briefings for Chief Constables across the country, including one, issued days before the Soho blast, advising police forces to increase security at markets and other public places frequented by large concentrations of black and Asian people. Such a prediction did not require much intelligence, but it also proved to be wrong. There was a failure to realise that the bomber was not predictable and that homosexuals could have been next on his list. When questioned about the role of TAM during the investigation, the ACPO claimed that it had played no part whatsoever, saying that the Anti-Terrorist Branch had been in charge and we should speak to them.

TAM's annual report also refers to other organisations that appear to have interests in combating terrorism, but exactly what their terms of reference are has proved difficult to determine. TAM says, for example, that it fully supports the 'Advisory Group', one of whose members is TAM's chairman. This body 'continues to offer to all Chief Constables practical operational advice commensurate with the threat. During the year, the Committee has progressed implementation of the National Terrorist Crime Prevention Unit. The purpose of the Unit is to reduce the risk to life and property from acts of terrorism by developing the multi-agency partnership theme. The Unit commenced operationally on 5 January 1998 under the executive authority of this Committee and has close links with the Crime Prevention Agency and the Home Office Crime Prevention College.'

The seventh known group is Scotland Yard's Racial and Violent Crime Squad (CO24), set up in the aftermath of the Stephen Lawrence affair. It is led by John Grieve, the former commander of the Anti-Terrorist Branch. It had only limited input in the nailbombing investigation and did not play any role in the raids on right-wing activists either before or after the bombings. Although Special Branch continues to be responsible for monitoring extremist groups, CO24 co-ordinates intelligence on hate mail and other racist incidents, using a computer system called Delton, that has some access to SB (Special Branch) databases. Before its creation, reports or investigations into racial attacks or the sending of hate mail in the London area were not recorded centrally at Scotland Yard. Now, in theory, CO24 is supposed to receive such reports but rather than overload the original investigating officer with yet more paperwork, the analysts rely on the forensic science service or fingerprint branch, which will have dealt with the case for the original investigating officer. Special Branch and other interested agencies can then access the material when necessary. But breakdowns in communication can still occur.

CO24 liaises with representatives from the community through the Racial and Violent Crimes Advisory Group set up months before the nailbombings. Some of the group's members were furious that they had not been told by CO24 of the circumstances surrounding the arrest of James Shaw on the same day as the Brick Lane bombing (outlined in chapter six). The parallels with Copeland were obvious. Both men were driven by the same hatred emanating from right-wing literature. The only differences were their ages and the fact that Shaw's bombs were not as powerful as Copeland's. Details emerged only after Shaw's trial at the Old Bailey in November 1999.

The eighth and last known police group was set up only days after Copeland's arrest, in apparent recognition that there had been an intelligence void during the investigation. It was decided that there should be some co-ordination of the work of all the other law enforcement or intelligence agencies involved in countering terrorism, who all too often seemed to be in competition with one another. Perhaps to avoid accusations of further empire building, the Metropolitan Police announcement of the formation of a new Task Group, under the auspices of the Anti-Terrorist Branch, was without fanfare. A short news release, which went unreported in the national press, said the group would build upon previous policing initiatives:

'The Task Group will target extremists (groups and individuals) who commit or incite violent crime and those who advocate and claim such attacks. It will also focus on those who seek to intimidate innocent victims by criminal threats. It will be available on request to support forces throughout England and Wales.' Deputy Assistant Commissioner Alan Fry, billed as the National Co-ordinator for Terrorist Investigations, was then quoted as the officer overseeing the Task Group: 'The primary objective of the Task Group is to prevent, deter, disrupt and detect the criminal activities of violent extremists. We will also seek to reassure the public as a whole and those who feel at risk. The recent nail-bomb attacks in London have highlighted the need for continuing vigilance across the UK as crime by violent extremists can appear in diverse and unpredictable ways.'

Aside from the intelligence void during the bombings investigation, another reason for forming the new Task Group was the level of information generated through the release of the CCTV footage. A vast amount of material, from all over the country, had flooded in to the Anti-Terrorist Branch from the public and other police agencies. Much of it was not directly related to the bombings, but was nevertheless recognised as being valuable. Operation Overture was set up to look at all the data, some of it identifying right-wing extremists previously unknown to the authorities.

Information that came from Copeland himself was used when the new Task Group carried out early morning raids on eleven individuals in London, East Anglia and the Home Counties. Most of their names had been found in Copeland's room and most were connected to the National Socialist Movement, including the then NSM leader Tony Williams and Kirk Barker, the Hampshire Nazi who had met Copeland six months before the bombings. Also raided were two BNP officials, Newham organiser Ken Francis and London regional organiser Tony Lecomber, the man convicted of a bombing charge in the mid-1980s. Documents were seized at some of the addresses, but no one else was charged in connection with the nail-bomb attacks.

It was clear from the outset that this new group was firmly under the control of Alan Fry's Anti-Terrorist Branch. To what extent it will take over some of the responsibilities of the other police groups or intelligence agencies, or whether it will be regarded by them as simply more competition, adding to an already confusing picture, remains to be seen. Scotland Yard and the police in general are renowned for their 'turf wars' and the danger is that time spent on fighting those battles reduces the already limited effort and stretched resources being deployed against the real enemy.

And there is certainly plenty to do. Figures released by Scotland Yard early in 2000 show a staggering increase in the number of racial attacks and incidents in London reported to the police following the nailbombings and the publication of the McPherson Report on the murder of Stephen Lawrence. Comparing the period April–December 1998 with the same nine-month period in 1999, the number of racial incidents increased by 175% and the number of racially motivated crimes by 188%. However, it must be stressed that this rise is in no small part a reflection of a new willingness by the police to deal with racist incidents and increased reporting by its victims, rather than a doubling of racist crimes. The detection rate for racial crime rose by 198%.

The infighting and unclear boundaries between different police units that appear to have hampered this investigation and the fight against racist activity in general, has led some to call for a total reorganisation of Scotland Yard, making it concentrate on being a police force for the capital while shedding some of its specialist functions. The NCIS and the National Crime Squad, formed out of the old regional crime squads, were again lobbying for more responsibilities, arguing that a national police body should do national police work. An NCIS officer was quoted in London's *Evening Standard*: 'If things are being co-ordinated at the Yard, you are unlikely to get as much co-operation from county forces as you could do if it was truly national. The Yard has a long history of being arrogant and superior — looking down on the county forces.'

The various laws available to police for dealing with racists are also being overhauled, with one of the aims of the Government's Crime and Disorder Act of 1998 being to tackle racial violence and harassment. Moves are also under way to deal with racism on the Internet and to detain people like Copeland who are deemed to have severe personality disorders, even when they have committed no crime.

Lawyers who framed the new Crime and Disorder Act in 1998 added the concept of racial aggravation to a series of offences already covered by existing legislation. This means that where an offender has been racially motivated, the magistrate or judge can view this as an aggravating factor deserving an increased sentence. The new law also states that a crime may have been committed even where a victim has not been identified. Home Office guidelines say: 'Where there is evidence of a racial motivation for the offence, it is not necessary to identify the "victim" of the offence. This means, for example, that where the offender sprays graffiti at a bus stop, and where the text clearly indicates that the offence is racially motivated, it would be likely that such evidence would constitute racially aggravated criminal damage.'

Some of the maximum sentences under the new law represent significant increases when racial aggravation is established — for example, the maximum sentence for 'ordinary' common assault is six months imprisonment and/or a fine of up to £5,000, but if the assault is deemed racially aggravated, the penalty can be up to two years in prison and/or an unlimited fine. Exactly the same penalties apply for threatening behaviour and harassment, and where the harassment involves the victim fearing violence, the maximum penalties are five years imprisonment for the ordinary crime and seven years where there is a racial element. The new laws and penalties have been in force for so short a time that it is not yet possible to determine their effectiveness.

However, anti-racist campaigners say new laws are all well and good but existing laws need to be implemented fully. While welcoming the increased sentences for racially aggravated crimes, they maintain sufficient laws existed before but were not properly used. In 1997 one man was sent to prison for organising the production of *Barbecue in Rostock*, an outrageously inflammatory CD produced by the C18 band No Remorse. Campaigners argued that under the Public Order Act (1986), the songwriters, performers, manufacturers and distributors of this CD could have also been prosecuted. In one swoop, the authorities could have removed the entire leadership of C18, its magazine editors and mail order outlets. Either the CPS or the police decided not to pursue the matter further.

Time and again the Crown Prosecution Service has seemed reluctant to take legal action against organised racists. This seems to stem from belief that juries do not want to convict, as one person's racist is another's hero, or from a fear that racists will be turned into political figures. This is a view dismissed by campaigners. 'The best deterrent against organised racists is the fear of being imprisoned,' says *Searchlight* publisher Gerry Gable. 'Not prosecuting them only encourages them to continue their activities.'

Certainly, those closest to the three people who died in the Soho bomb are united in calling for some kind of action taken against the racist and homophobic groups behind Copeland. 'He claims he was a loner and he worked alone, but he was also part of these groups,' said Colin Moore, brother of Nik Moore. 'They gave him literature and things that gave him more and more hatred for certain groups and people. There must be some way that the law can vet some of this material that goes out. Everybody's got their right to their opinions, but when it gets to the extent of violence and horrible, horrific things that happen with nail bombs etc, there's got to be a way that it should be vetted by the government. If any good is to come from this, the government has got to do something to protect innocent people so the lives of Nick, John and Andrea weren't in vain.'

John Light's partner, Gary Partridge, said: 'I believe something should be done when it comes to the point of groups organising people into harming others for no-good reason. If anything, this has taught me to stand up for individuals, whether they be black, Asian, gay or Jewish. Nobody has a right to harm anybody purely on their race, colour or sexual orientation. I'd like to see the government look into controlling the distribution of literature, and in particular if anything could be done with the Internet. I also think it's down to each and every one of us to stand up and say what we believe, that we won't tolerate prejudice any more.'

'In any civilised society, there must be some way the politicians or people in authority can take action against those spouting such venom,' according to Phil Maddock, father of Andrea Dykes. 'It just isn't right that they can go out and publicly threaten other groups because they don't fit in. We have a democratic system and free speech and it doesn't really matter whether you're Conservative, Labour, Liberal, Communist. I haven't got a problem with that, but I do have when these right-wing Fascists go out, actually saying to people 'stamp on a queer' or 'kill a black' or whatever. It's abhorrent and shouldn't be allowed. Copeland was part of that and it obviously bent his mind. These groups are just as much at fault as Copeland is, and the government should do something about that. It's not just Copeland that's guilty. It's the system that's at fault.'

Anti-racists argue that incitement laws should be used in the same way as drugs laws, in that where someone is found in possession of, say, a very small amount of cannabis, there is rarely a prosecution, but if several kilos are involved, the person is clearly a dealer and subjected to the full force of the law. Similarly, if someone is caught with only one leaflet calling for racial action, there is no incitement, but if there are hundreds of the same leaflets, then the person is a distributor, aiming to incite others.

Campaigners want to change the mindset of the police and CPS who repeatedly seem to ignore the effects of racist literature. In the three months following the election of Derek Beackon, the BNP's first and only local councillor in Millwall, east London, racist attacks rose by 300%. Racist activity and literature leads to more racism. Most racist attacks and incidents are not only perpetrated by members of racist organisations, but all too often their literature inspires violence in others. Stephen Lawrence was killed in an area noted for racist activity. Time and again police seem not to understand this cause and effect.

Further complications in taking legal action over racist material derive from the fact that much of the literature and videos produced since the early 1990s has come from the USA. So where does any incitement to violence take place? Is it in the UK or the USA? And then, if distribution takes place in the UK through far-right publications, proving incitement can be difficult because the recipient reading such material is probably already a hard-line racist and is therefore not being incited. In recent years police have had to be convinced that anti-Semitic literature reaches an audience beyond Jewish people for any possible prosecution under incitement charges. Jewish people cannot be incited to act against themselves.

As for sending hate-mail, police say that perpetrators are often disturbed people or young teenagers, with neither group likely to carry out their threats. It is more difficult to catch those behind the more organised hate-mail campaigns. Those who received the threatening White Wolves letters sent before and during the nailbombings handed them to police who sent them on for forensic examination. It was hoped that the sender/s would have left traces of DNA by licking the stamps or the envelope flaps, but apparently aware of this, the senders used water rather than saliva.

Policing the Internet is also very difficult. Copeland learned how to make his bombs from *The Terrorist's Handbook*, to be found on several websites, and some of the literature found in his room came from US groups such as Aryan Nations and Christian Identity, which have Internet sites, as does the BNP. An NCIS report in 1999 says that Internet 'hate sites' have grown sixteen-fold over three years, from about 50 in 1995 to about 800 in 1998. 'Most of these websites operate from the USA and espouse racism, neo-Nazism, terrorism and so on,' says the report. 'The use of the Internet has specific advantages: it has global reach; is low cost; content can be easily targeted to particular audiences at particular times; propaganda can be disseminated without censorship; and can reach people who would not otherwise come into contact with such groups.'

That is not to say it is impossible to act against the most extreme sites. The Government is backing plans by the industry-financed Internet Watch Foundation to target Internet sites in the UK that carry criminally racist material. The organisation's chairman believes the same 1986 Public Order Act relating to the publication of race-hate material could be used to outlaw offensive sites here or to compel the main servers to block access to racists. But he concedes that the definition of what is criminally racist is complex and with so much material easily accessible on US sites, where the principle of free speech is enshrined in the constitution, little or no legal action can be taken against them. The reality is that people like Copeland will be able to continue to access racist material on the Internet and learn how to make many different types of bombs.

The Government is also planning to introduce controversial changes to mental health legislation to allow the detention of dangerous psychopaths, even if they have committed no offence. The proposals are aimed at those 'where, as a consequence of their personality disorder, there is a serious risk that an individual may kill or maim or sexually assault another person'. Such a categorisation seems to fit Copeland exactly. It is now clear that he was suffering from a severe personality disorder and probably schizophrenia when he launched his bombing campaign. So under the new proposals, would he have been detained had he been caught committing an anti-social offence just prior to the bombing?

The Home Office consultation paper on the proposals states that people would have to demonstrate at least six out of ten characteristics in order to be detained. However, Copeland, prior to the nailbombings, met only four of these criteria — criteria which could easily fit tens of thousands of people in society. He was unmarried, he had been a juvenile delinquent, he had distributed racist literature and he had abused drugs. Of the other characteristics, Copeland had no extensive criminal history, had not used a weapon, had no history of violent behaviour, no psychiatric admissions, no previous sexual offences, no serious injuries to his victims, and no failures after previously being given a conditional discharge by the courts. Even if the existing proposals had been in place, Copeland would have slipped through the net, despite the fact that he attended a local health clinic complaining of stress and panic attacks.

Although he was an active racist for three years, Copeland escaped attention by the authorities and did not have a record for any racist crime. He was that most dangerous of people — a psychopathic loner.

As a loner, Copeland drifted in and out of the far-right movements, adopting some of the ideology from each group and strengthening some of his beliefs, such as homophobia. He picked up religious fanaticism and delusion from the extremist Christian Identity movement, Nazism from a variety of anti-Semitic, racist groups, and ideas of leaderless resistance from *The Turner Diaries*.

The USA has seen the emergence of several such people since the alarms were first raised about right-wing militias in the early 1990s — a good example being Eric Rudolph, suspected of the Atlanta Olympics bombing that so inspired Copeland. A report in the *Washington Post* in July 1998 outlined the problem. Under the headline: 'A Most Dangerous Profile: The Loner', the paper claimed Rudolph was representative of a new and dangerous sort of home-grown terrorist: 'A still-classified Justice Department report describes the type as "individuals who are inspired by, but not affiliated with, terrorist groups, thus making them harder to identify and stop." This newly developed profile — inspired by convicted Oklahoma City bomber Timothy McVeigh — is the product of a federal law enforcement apparatus increasingly concerned about how to combat domestic terrorism that officials now believe is most likely to be carried out by loners like Rudolph. "We are seeing three, four, five new cases every year of people who have links to white supremacist groups, who talk the race-hating, anti-government rhetoric, and who ended up plotting or committing violent acts," said Robert M Blitzer, head of the FBI's domestic counter-terrorism section. "These are usually rootless guys with a high level of frustration in their lives who go out on their own. They have access to firearms and explosives and are prepared to use them. For us, it is a real challenge to stay ahead of them."'

The newspaper article continued: 'These solitary actors, though few in number, are now considered the most dangerous domestic terrorists, according to FBI and Justice Department officials, who continue to struggle with a key question: Are they lone wolves who need no outside guidance or the instruments of someone else's political agenda? "There is a definite increase in acts of violence committed either by a single individual or very small coteries of people who operate without any central direction," said Michael Barkun, a political scientist at Syracuse University and expert on domestic radicals. "This is becoming a major problem for law enforcement because unless the authorities are very watchful or very lucky, these people go unnoticed until they have done something."'

While the FBI claim to have recognised this new threat, pouring millions of dollars into researching and tackling right-wing militias and loners, their British counterparts have not. Groups are still assessed by the potential threat the leadership pose rather than the type of individual attracted to them. In addition, there is still confusion about the overlapping responsibilities of the different police agencies with responsibility for dealing with right-wing extremists. Perhaps now, after Copeland, things will change, but there is little sign of it at present.

One officer who worked on the investigation summed up the problems: 'The barriers between the different police units were down, such was the pressure we were under to catch the nailbomber. But all that intelligence came to nothing. We only caught him because of the CCTV.'

New technology being introduced will help to tackle less serious attacks or incidents. A new computer system due to cover London by the beginning of 2001 will mean that all racial incidents in London will be automatically recorded on a central database, providing the ability to correlate them with known racists in a particular area. It would not, however, help in catching another David Copeland. None of his three minor convictions involved racism or a major act of violence, and they were committed in Hampshire where he was living at the time. Even if his name was known to Special Branch or MI5 as a member of a racist or extreme right-wing organisation, or as a recipient of its literature, he would, once again, be very low down any list of possible suspects. Police would continue to rely on a lucky break or a mistake on the part of the bomber, just as Copeland made a fatal error in allowing himself to be filmed at Brixton for a full hour before the explosion.

Paul Mifsud, Copeland's workmate for five months and the person closest to him during the bombing campaigns and the preceding months, is equally bleak about how alienated angry young men should be handled: 'The only thing is to give them time to talk through their problems. I gave David time, but I never had a clue about what he was doing, so you could say it didn't do any good, but at least I tried to do a positive thing. I feel responsibility in a way because I was so close to him, but he was a loner. If only I had known. I will never get rid of that feeling. I didn't have a clue.'

*   *   *

Copeland was a young man obsessed with violence and suffering and the far right gave him direction and a cause. But loners such as him represent the most difficult type of people to tackle or to track down. In an age of modern communication, however, where images and texts can be transferred around the world in seconds, events in one part of the world can so easily inspire people in other continents. With the rise of nationalism and racism throughout Europe since the collapse of communism, the danger is that right-wing ideas and parties will become ever more attractive to unhappy and frustrated people like Copeland. With the explosion of Internet usage, bomb designs and tactics are becoming available in the UK on a scale not witnessed before. Slowly but surely, events and activities in the USA will increasingly dictate elements of the right-wing agenda in the UK.

Copeland set out to be the first high-profile racist bomber in the UK. While he failed to ignite the race war he thought would follow, he may, in time, prove an inspiration for others. He is unlikely to be the last racist terrorist that we see in the UK.